BEST SEAT IN THE HOUSE

BEST SEAT
IN THE HOUSE

Miles Harrison

Foreword by Gavin Hastings

AURUM PRESS

First published in Great Britain 1997
by Aurum Press Ltd, 25 Bedford Avenue, London WC1B 3AT

A catalogue record for this book is available from the British Library.

ISBN 1 85410 534 5

Design by Don Macpherson
Typeset in Sabon
Printed and bound by Creative Print and Design (Wales), Ebbw Vale

CONTENTS

ACKNOWLEDGEMENTS

This book is dedicated to my wife Helen, who has provided so much support and understanding, my parents, Clive and Ann, and Helen's parents, Neville and Margaret. I love them all dearly.

I would also like to thank those at Sky Sports who provided the production and organisational skills throughout a long and hard season which culminated in the biggest project of them all, the Lions tour to South Africa. In particular, thanks go to producer Piers Croton, my researcher Adrian Hill and my commentary partner, Stuart Barnes. Stuart and I approach life from very different angles, but I value both our working relationship and his close friendship. I must also thank Gavin Hastings for his contribution to the book. The Lions captain in 1993, Gavin was a member of the Sky Sports team in South Africa. He is one of my all-time rugby favourites and I can assure you he is as nice a sportsman as you could wish to meet.

Thanks also go to Bill McCreadie and Anica Alvarez of Aurum Press for having the desire to take on this project, and for all their hard work.

Two other people deserve special mention: Martin Knight, for providing the photographs, and Gwen Johnson, who organised our travel and accommodation in South Africa.

Finally, I save the biggest thank you of all to the players and management team of the 1997 British and Irish Lions. Their exploits gave me a wonderful broadcasting experience and memories that I will treasure for ever.

R.E.S.P.E.C.T

The success of the 1997 British and Irish Lions has ensured that this most famous of all touring sides will continue to captivate crowds throughout the world. That its future was in doubt only a few months ago because of fixture congestion in the professional era has now been confined to history. Anyone who was lucky enough to have been in South Africa for the Test matches will have been privileged to have witnessed such a historic series victory, and the celebrations which followed the successes in Cape Town and Durban were immense.

The huge travelling support which came down from the four home nations was intent on being heard as well as being seen and they played their part in no small measure. It is difficult to imagine a more perfect place to tour than South Africa with their vast stadia and tremendous playing conditions. This was rugby as good as it gets, and for the players involved it must have been a wonderful journey to have been on. The togetherness and team spirit in the whole squad appeared to be brilliant and the quality of the management ensured that nothing was left to chance. This was the ultimate triumph, with rugby men left to do their job. No false accusations were being thrown, there was no need to protect their position, there was no pussy-footing around. Here we saw experienced coaches and experienced man-managers working in unison for the benefit of the people who ultimately matter: the players. It was the players who had the confidence and the belief in themselves to carry out the tasks which were set by the management – and how well they did.

I have never seen a side more committed to the tackle, and defensively the Lions were brilliant. They withstood almost everything that South Africa could throw at them and they refused to stand down time and time again. The pride in those famous red jerseys was apparent from the opening game in Port Elizabeth, and six weeks later it was the same story, as the Lions paraded around Ellis Park with their trophy for the series victory. They had grown up in rugby terms with an edge to their play, but also as men with a confidence in their stride. Eleven victories in thirteen matches ensured that this 'Class of '97' could dine at the same table as the big boys. Rugby does that to you and it brings out the best in the men who are given a sense of direction and a will to succeed. They added courage and commitment and belief and desire and they knuckled down and got on with the job that they had been selected to do. They returned home as heroes and got what they deserved – respect.

I travelled out to join Miles and the rest of the Sky Sports team and had the pleasure of being with them for all three Test matches. Having been on camera four years ago, it was very revealing to be in front of it on this occasion. Furthermore, the opportunity to be in the post-match interview room is afforded only to a lucky few. It was a privilege to witness the joy of victory on the faces of these heroic Lions, to see what it meant to them and how much they had given to the cause. And it was the players who were lucky enough to have been on the pitch in the Tests who instantly recognised the contribution made by the others who had played some great rugby in the mid-week games. There were no weak links on this Lions tour and everyone had played their part to the full.

The management looked after their charges with a fatherly touch, but they also revealed their emotions on Test match days in front of the Sky cameras. It is not often you see Jim Telfer beaming, but when he does you know that his men have lived up to his expectations. He had been waiting patiently for almost thirty years to win a Test series with the Lions and had been like a man possessed in his pursuit of excellence and ultimate triumph. No one deserved the victory more than he did. For Fran Cotton and Ian McGeechan, this was the second time they were experiencing such emotions in South Africa and they certainly looked as though they were enjoying themselves. They had caught the Springboks napping and all through the tour they had out-thought and out- manoeuvred the opposition. Martin Johnson was literally out on his feet, but like Willie John McBride, he will have plenty of time to relive his experiences on less pressured occasions, and no one will ever be able to take away what he and his team-mates have achieved.

The Lions series victory has been a tremendous shot in the arm for Northen Hemisphere rugby and particularly for the four home nations. What is important now is that those professional players take back their experiences from the tour and encourage others to follow their lead. The Five Nations Championship is still unique in world rugby and despite all the claims about the Tri-Nations series, it still doesn't stand comparison with our tournament. History and tradition are important, but equally so is the way that we continue to promote and market the game to players, spectators and sponsors alike. The way that these British and Irish Lions played in South Africa was a revelation and triumph for all concerned. My lasting hope is for all four nations to develop a style of play that is exciting to watch and exciting to take part in. Without question, rugby is one of the greatest team sports and what was witnessed in South Africa made me feel proud to have been a part of the Lions on two previous occasions. I knew what the players had gone through and I knew how they felt about being part of this famous touring side. And I also give them something they had earned for themselves by their endeavours on the pitch – respect.

Gavin Hastings
Edinburgh, 1997

IF A JOB'S WORTH DOING . . .

'Talking to the players, they still see it as the absolute pinnacle
of their career.' – Fran Cotton after his appointment as the
manager of the 1997 Lions.

Had you told me when I was knee high to Jacques Fouroux that one day I would go on a British and Irish Lions tour then, despite my tender years, I probably would have questioned your sanity. This is not to say that I doubted my rugby ability, it is just that I never had any!

I do remember making a magnificent tackle during a school match. To this day, it remains the high spot of my rugby career. The opposition's tiny scrum-half broke away from the back of the scrum and was in danger of racing down the blindside. But, he had not bargained for the response of a tall, lanky flanker who scythed him down. Amazed to have made such a contribution, I refused to let go, and my conquest and I both slid through the mud, over the touch line, to finish right at the feet of my headmaster. He looked lovingly down at the scene of carnage and congratulated me by slapping my back like a winning racehorse being unsaddled in the paddock. He showed the warmth of a man who had only just arrived on the ground and was not fully aware of my total ineptitude for the previous seventy-five minutes. He was also blissfully in the dark over my season's record, as this was the first and last effective tackle of that year.

Indeed, all through my rugby education at school and college I was to remain more familiar with the cutting of oranges than the splitting of defences. In a seven-a-side tournament at university, my gallant captain managed to beat almost every member of the other team before committing their last man. Always aware of the glamour opportunity, I had stayed in support and, realising that another side step was almost a physical impossibility for our exhausted skipper, I called for the ball. It was delivered with perfection and, with the line no more than fifteen metres away, I proceeded to do an impression of a butler running downstairs vainly trying to hold on to his Lordship's best crockery. Needless to say, the cups and saucers were smashed, the ball knocked on and the try of the season lay in little pieces on the floor.

It was at that point I decided to accept with good grace that many more would be in front of me in the queue for an international jersey – not for me the feeling of falling over the line accompanied by a Twickenham roar. I knew, however, that the second-best option would be to watch from the finest seat in the house. I am sure that all sports commentators have this as their basic motivation. To have such a superb window on sporting occasions remains one of the greatest possible privileges.

The moral, though, is to remember your own inadequacies on the field of play. This should always serve as a constant reminder of just how difficult it is to get to the top of the mountain. Of all those sporting heroes in the playground, only very few make it to the summit. Keep this in mind and knee-jerk criticisms are kept to a minimum. No professional sportsperson goes out to deliberately under-perform. Rest assured, if they did, their team-mates would soon rectify the problem.

The pursuit of excellence is, on one level, an individual mission, but rugby, by its very nature, is a team game. The skills of fourteen others are required for the personal ambition to be realised. Anybody who has played a team sport is well aware of instances where the chemistry has not quite reacted to produce a team greater than the sum of its parts. If things go wrong at home, then at least the player can walk away from the problems, but an overseas tour can put unbelievable strain on the team ethic. Living in the pockets of others with similar ambitions and desires is stimulating but also has the potential to be oppressive. The challenge is to make it work and ensure that the tour is successful, because a winning team is, more often than not, a happy one.

Of course, the great sides find a spirit which helps overcome the majority of problems posed both on and off the field of play. They find a unity of purpose which conquers all. If there is a weak area, it is identified and attacked so that it is no longer of concern. To do this there must be an overriding feeling that everybody is in it together. No person has special status and each individual contribution is vital to the team effort. Most importantly, great teams realise that above all the tour is there to be enjoyed. There is no point being away from home for such a long period unless you are revelling in the experience. This is where rugby traditionally has a head start over other sports. The basic approach to the game is to win but is also to enjoy the company of others. The 1997 Lions would have to marry the need to be victorious in rugby's professional era, with an equal desire to have a damn good time and to forge some lifelong friendships.

Thrown together from the four home nations and perceived as being a long way behind the Southern Hemisphere in terms of modern rugby development, the Lions could not afford to hang around waiting for things to fall into place. The management team had been selected with experience in mind. There was the best domestic coach, Ian McGeechan, who had held the position on the two previous Lions tours, the leading 'forward'-thinking coach in Jim Telfer and a manager, Fran Cotton, who would wear his heart on his sleeve and always have the players' best interests in mind. In turn, they gathered around them what seemed to be a cast of thousands to act as specialist advisors. They laid their cards on the table – this was going to be a professional tour in every sense of the word. Consequently, the knives were being sharpened, with many critics anticipating a less than glorious future. But no matter how good the non-playing team is, it needs the right men on the pitch to deliver the results. The squad members were hand-picked for not only their ability to play but for potential hardness in their mental attitude. This tour would test the mind and body like never before. The management could not afford to make any dud selections, because every player would have to contribute to the cause. The playing vision had to be built around an open and fluid game and the players would have to adapt to this style which would test South Africa. To be successful they would need to reach new heights of playing ability. If they achieved all of this, then they would earn the right to go down in rugby history as one of the great teams. Most of all, they had to believe it was possible.

What follows here is one version of the story of a squad who set out with high hopes to live out their dreams, as seen through the eyes of a television commentator who lived out the next best thing to his!

PRE-NATAL

'Six Five Nations matches, four Super Twelve games and the World Cup
final all away from home' – Coach Ian McGeechan on the gruelling
schedule that lay ahead

There was no doubt as to the significance of this tour. As early as
1996, when the epic Test series against the New Zealanders took
place, the whole of South Africa was talking about the arrival of the
Lions. Sky Sports had travelled to South Africa to cover the conclusion
of the inaugural Tri-Nations tournament and the start of the three-
match series between the world champions and the All Blacks. The Tri-
Nations, despite South Africa's underachievement, had been a roaring
success and the excitement surrounding the build-up to the arrival of
Sean Fitzpatrick's team was almost uncontrollable. But, from
Bloemfontein in the heart of the Free State, to the more progressive
Cape, there was a feeling that the arrival of the 1997 Lions would
overshadow all that had gone before.

The love of a Lions visit – and love is the correct word, for South
African rugby fans are blinded by their devotion to the sport – stems
from a history of emotional clashes between the two sides. Moreover,
absence makes the heart grow fonder, and just two visits by the Lions in
the past twenty-three years were enough to make the anticipation
positively lustful.

Those fortunate enough to take part in the epic 1974 Lions tour of
South Africa I'm sure knew at the time that a rare piece of history was
being made. A whole rugby generation and their offspring were intoxi-
cated by the achievements of a truly great team. I'm English, but I was
Welshman Phil Bennett in a Lions red jersey in the playground.
Traditionally, the Lions cross all borders between the home unions, as
domestic rivalry is cast aside for the sake of a common cause. The
exploits of Irish captain Willie John McBride and his men have gone
down in rugby folklore. Quite incredibly, they went through the whole
tour unbeaten. The only drawn match was the final game, as South
Africa lost a Test series at home for the first time this century. Even that

draw in the final Test was a controversial result, and many still believe that Fergus Slattery scored a perfectly legal try in the dying minutes. The referee was unsighted and failed to give the try. The Lions had to settle with a three–nil winning margin in the Test series.

Six years later, the Lions returned to South Africa. Once again they made the trip in a volatile political climate, with many believing that they should not have gone for reasons totally unconnected with rugby. Bill Beaumont of England captained the squad, but this time South Africa took control of the Test series. The Lions' only Test victory came in Pretoria in the final match, when the overall outcome had already been decided. Previously, the Springboks had won three Tests and, although the Lions had won all the other matches on the trip, including victories over the joint Currie Cup holders Northern Transvaal and Western Province, the tour was considered to be a failure.

If recent history has taught us anything, then it is that teams are judged on the basis that only the big matches ultimately count. The problem for the 1997 Lions was that, with the advent of professionalism and the success of the Super Twelve event in the Southern Hemisphere, the South African provincial sides were going to be stronger, faster and fitter than ever before. There were thirteen matches on the tour programme and, in the words of coach Ian McGeechan, 'The schedule comprised six Five Nations matches, four Super Twelve games and the World Cup final all away from home.'

The glitzy media launch for the Lions took place at the South African High Commission, London in late January. The sight of four of the top players in British rugby posing for press photographs with a cuddly toy in Trafalgar Square was enough to make even the busy commuters turn their heads. Mark Regan of England, Jeremy Davidson of Ireland, Scotland's Rob Wainwright and Neil Jenkins of Wales looked a little uneasy as the 'snappers' shouted their orders to get the pictures they wanted. The lion, looking like a reject from the Generation Game conveyor belt, watched with a slightly amazed expression. The players, while honoured to have been invited, were probably concerned as to just how advisable it was to be photographed wearing Lions colours long before the squad had been announced. Was this tempting fate?

What really made an impact, though, were not the players who were present but what they were wearing. For the first time in their history, the Lions had secured a tour sponsor. Scottish Provident had provided the necessary financial backing and their company name was splashed across the front of the jersey. The financial commitment to the tour was quite staggering, even at this stage. It was announced that the Lions had at least three-quarters of a million pounds behind them and, also for the first time, the players were to receive a tour salary. At the news conference, tour manager Fran Cotton made it clear that all players would receive the same basic pay; bonuses were to be awarded based on the number of Test matches won. The whole squad and not just the Test players would benefit from this incentive, but the cruelty of the professional game was that an injury would hurt the pocket as well as the body and players leaving the tour because of injury faced a proportionate loss of income. For example, if a player went home after three of the seven weeks, he would only share in three-sevenths of the bonus pot. It would make the reaction to serious injury all the more severe.

In an interview for Sky Sports, Cotton stressed that there would be no distinction made between the first and second teams. 'There will be no dirt-trackers on this tour,' Cotton exclaimed. It would be an 'all for one and one for all' philosophy. It was easy to see the motivation behind such a comment. A glance at the tour itinerary showed no weak fixtures. The days of a mid-week team had gone for ever. In contrast, the days of the bigger squad had most certainly arrived. New Zealand had set the tone in South Africa in 1996 when the All Blacks had taken thirty-six men on tour. The Lions management had similar thoughts, fully aware that the players were going to be subjected to intense physical pressure. Cotton made it clear that various positions prone to injury had to be covered in depth and it was more important to have the troops ready, acclimatised and prepared for action than to have to send out an emergency call for reinforcements.

Cotton cuts an imposing figure and is a man who knows his own mind. In his playing days during the 1970s and early 1980s, his granite-like presence was one of the cornerstones of English rugby. Vitally, he had toured with the Lions in 1974, 1977 and 1980. After the boots had been hung up, Cotton had reached for other items in the wardrobe. Big Fran has been as successful in business as he was on the field. Along with fellow Sale and England star, Steve Smith, he has built up the Cotton Traders empire into one of the most powerful players in the sports and leisurewear market. He was clearly enjoying the role of Lions manager and handled the interviews and news conference with square-jawed authority.

It appeared that all the major media organisations were represented at the launch. There were camera crews from satellite, terrestrial and cable networks. There were radio microphones, journalists' Dictaphones and, of course, everybody had mobile phones! (This is why I believe that the collective noun for a group of journalists at a news conference should be a 'squabble'.) And, of course, the public relations consultants wanted to make sure that the sponsors' name was either in your shot or on the tip of your tongue. All this attention four months before the action began!

The people for whom I feel most sorry are the interviewees. They have to answer the same questions time and time again. But Fran Cotton and Ian McGeechan both know the media game and play it with skill. They answer a straight question with a straight answer. (It does help and politicians should take note!) It is a wonder just how it all works, but nonetheless, somehow everybody is satisfied, although some are inevitably more satisfied than others.

The media event was held on the Tuesday after the first round of Five Nations Championship matches. Wales had beaten Scotland at Murrayfield with an amazing second-half burst of points scoring: three tries in five minutes, inspired by the cherub from Trebanos, Arwel Thomas. Ireland had failed to score a try against France in Dublin and had been well beaten in the end. But at least they had not been put to the sword and, under the guidance of their new coaching advisor Brian Ashton, they looked as if they were about to turn the corner, albeit with the handbrake still on.

The weekend had certainly provided the Lions management with some interesting food for selection thought. I had been in Edinburgh, and on the Saturday night, as we tucked into haggis on the Royal Mile, we reflected that leek soup would perhaps have been a better choice as starter. The Welsh centres Scott Gibbs and Allan Bateman had played themselves right into Lions contention and another star reclaimed from rugby league, Scott Quinnell, had shown that he was on the way back to his union best. Aside from Thomas, these three players had been the stars of the show. Robert Howley played his part too and, even this early, seemed destined to wear the Lions number nine Test jersey. On the wing, Ieuan Evans showed that he still had what it takes at the very highest level.

Later in the week, at the Lions launch, it was clear talking to the victorious Neil Jenkins and Scotland's losing captain Rob Wainwright, that both desperately wanted to prove their form during the tough Five Nations campaign in order to achieve a higher honour. They wanted to retain the Lions jerseys loaned to them that day. Jenkins was aware that, with an away win secured, the Welsh public would start to expect such riches as a Triple Crown or a Grand Slam. Their bread of heaven, though, was to lie in crumbs just two weeks later, when Ireland sliced through their defences in Cardiff. Wainwright had his mind firmly fixed on the Calcutta Cup match at Twickenham, a game that would represent a great chance to rescue his team's season. But Scotland were blown away by English power in the second half and Wainwright's chances of leading the Lions receded. Both Jenkins and Wainwright knew that their form in the Championship would essentially determine if they were going to have their baggage checked in at Heathrow in May. The Five Nations, however special, comes around every year. Lions tours do not.

As February drew on, the selection debate was brought to the fore on the Monday after England's fine victory in Dublin and Wales' gutsy performance in Paris. The Five Nations Championship had only passed the half-way point, but the Lions tour was about to swing into action. Monday, 17 February was the day when Fran Cotton and Ian McGeechan revealed their initial hand. Sixty-two players were chosen for the stand-by list, with the intention to slim down the squad to thirty-five at the start of April. Twenty-seven from England, thirteen from Ireland and Wales and just nine from Scotland made up the chosen many. There were, however, some notable absentees.

Despite England's excellent performance against Ireland, some key figures were missing from the Lions list. Captain Phil de Glanville and his three-quarter line international colleagues, Jon Sleightholme and Tony Underwood, were overlooked. The former England captain, Will Carling, had already ruled himself out of the tour. Carling was looking forward to a summer off and reiterated the comments he had made at the end of the last Lions tour to New Zealand, in 1993. At that point, Carling had registered the view that, for him, the Lions were to be no more. His form in the autumn of 1996 had demanded a continued inclusion in the England team, despite the loss of the captaincy, and he had taken this new lease of life into the New Year during the victories over Scotland and Ireland. On that basis alone, it was inevitable that there would be a clamour to include him in the Lions party. Some were even suggesting that the captaincy should be given to England's most successful skipper of all time. One or two reports went even further. They claimed that Fran Cotton believed Carling would only agree to go to South Africa if he was the captain. Following some public relations posturing from the Carling camp and some straight talking from Cotton, it became apparent that the name W. D. C. Carling would never again be printed onto a Lions team sheet. The whole debate became academic, however, when Carling announced his retirement from inter-national rugby at the end of the season.

The controversy surrounding the rejection of the current England captain took the spotlight away from the Carling issue. Phil de Glanville had been under a lot of pressure ever since his appointment to lead his country back in the autumn. His form was widely accepted to be some way short of the high standards he had achieved earlier in 1996. It now seemed ironic that De Glanville, having spent so much time sitting on the England bench when many thought he should have been on the field from the first kick-off, was now struggling to justify his place in the starting fifteen. I must admit it was hard not to feel desperately sorry for De Glanville on the day of that first Lions selection. Here was a man who had taken a bagful of criticism following his appointment as captain and then, just hours after celebrating a record England win in the Five Nations match against Ireland, he was confronted with negative questioning: 'Why does Jack Rowell rate you Phil, but Fran Cotton doesn't?' The answer, in my opinion, is that De Glanville lacks pace at international level and, because of this, I had to agree with his exclusion.

Cotton stressed that the position of centre was not an area causing great concern to the management, as he thought there was an abundance of talent in that department. Few could disagree, but the selection of the uncapped Leicester centre, Will Greenwood, was a slap in the face for De Glanville. Subsequently, the England captain hinted at a possible rift with Cotton, pointing to a few choice words exchanged when De Glanville was representing the interests of the players in negotiations with the Rugby Football Union during the turbulent pre-Christmas period. At this time, the players had become increasingly frustrated with the lack of progress being made by the governing bodies concerning the future of the sport. Cotton was one of those who wanted to maintain long-held traditions, arguing for the interests of the grass-roots clubs as well as those at the top of the tree. The senior clubs, however, with much money already invested, wanted to speed up the rugby revolution. The players were caught in the crossfire, and what they saw at this point was intransigence and resistance to change. They recognised that their loyalty was now divided between country and club. After midnight oil supplies had been drained, it eventually became apparent that the sides were not so far apart after all, and the wheels of change slowly started to roll again.

The decision to exclude De Glanville was taken prior to the match in Dublin, a day when England scored six tries on their way to a total of forty-six points. De Glanville played his part, but so did wingers Jon Sleightholme and Tony Underwood, as both scored two tries. Personally, I found the omission of Sleightholme to be the most surprising. I am not saying that I would have taken the Bath winger to South Africa, but to leave him out of the sixty-two seemed wrong considering his try-scoring record at the time. When I spoke to Sleightholme shortly after the victory, he was bubbling with confidence and a sense of achievement. Who could blame him? His finish for England's first try was classy, and ever since his début in Paris at the start of 1996, Sleightholme had proved himself to be a player for the big occasion. Just before the camera started rolling for the interview, I put it to him that it was going to be some night in Ireland's capital and that his intake of the dark stuff might exceed the average. Sleightholme smiled and, with banana in hand, the true professional insisted that his first task was to replace the liquids lost during the match with energy drinks. How times have changed!

Following the squad announcement, Cotton said, 'Those players omitted at this stage should not feel despondent.' It was now up to the likes of De Glanville, Sleightholme and Underwood to prove their worth to the Lions. But, of course, the tests provided by France at Twickenham and Wales in Cardiff would pose the England wingers more defensive problems than had been the case against Scotland and Ireland – and it was their defensive abilities that caused the doubts over their Lions involvement.

The other notable absentees from the squad were the Welsh pair, fly-half Arwel Thomas and second-row Gareth Llewellyn. Thomas had provided Wales with some thrilling moments at Murrayfield and his exclusion could only have been based on his lack of physical presence as opposed to any lack of footballing ability. The Lions clearly wanted big men for a big job. The thought of the eleven-stone Thomas (and that's when he's just eaten his main meal of the day) being confronted by the South African back-row was all too easily brought to mind. My commentary colleague at Sky Sports, the former Lions, England and Bath number ten, Stuart Barnes, expressed his disapproval at the overlooking of Thomas. Just outside the dressing rooms in Edinburgh, Stuart had given the mercurial Welshman a hearty slap on the back after his magical performance. They chatted as Thomas waited to be inter-viewed by all and sundry. There was an approving look in Stuart's eyes, which recognised the potential genius in the little strip of a man. Just like all the great playmakers, Thomas can unlock a defence. Scotland's Gregor Townsend is perhaps the only other British outside-half who possesses the same combination to the safe; others might have the right tools, but they only finish the job just before the alarm bell sounds. By this time, Thomas and Townsend would be in the getaway car. It was therefore disappointing not to see Thomas involved at this early stage of Lions development.

On the other hand, Gareth Llewellyn was not achieving his best form, either for his club, Harlequins, or his country. The most-capped Welsh lock of all time had never played for the Lions in a Test match and now it seemed that he never would. Llewellyn, like De Glanville, said after the announcement that he now expected not to make the trip. They both felt that the size of the squad was such that Cotton, McGeechan and assistant coach Jim Telfer's main aim would be to pare down the existing list and not to increase it.

De Glanville's exclusion meant that one international captain was ruled out of the Lions leadership race, but the overall outcome was still no clearer. Rob Wainwright was in charge of Scotland, Jonathan Humphreys his Welsh counterpart and Jim Staples the captain of Ireland. Full-back Staples was standing in for the injured hooker Keith Wood, whose impressive season had been interrupted by another shoulder injury. Staples had made it clear that he was keeping the seat warm for Wood, but already there were inevitable question marks over Wood's long-term fitness. Early indications were that he would not be back on the playing field until April. It was unlikely, therefore, that on this occasion the Lions captaincy would belong to Ireland. As both Humphreys and Wainwright were struggling to achieve top form, it became apparent that the Lions would have to look away from the established leaders for their captain.

Ieuan Evans, Gregor Townsend, Jason Leonard and Martin Johnson all had legitimate claims. They possessed differing qualities as players and as leaders, but, most importantly, they were all likely to demand inclusion in the Test team. The Lions could not afford to have a captain who was not a first-choice player. This mistake had been made before, notably in 1983, when Ireland's Ciaran Fitzgerald, a Triple Crown winner at home, failed to lead with conviction in New Zealand. His position was constantly undermined by the fact that he was not worth his Test place.

At this stage of the 1997 selection, one concept gathering momentum was that of a Lions team with no captain; if there was no outstanding candidate, then the best policy could be to pick the side for the Test matches and then the captain. A match-by-match choice of leader seemed an appealing idea. After all, so many traditions had already been broken in the modern game that this news would hardly come as a great shock to traditionalists – barely causing a fizz in their gin and tonics.

March came in like a lamb rather than a lion and England were hunting the Grand Slam. Victories over Scotland and Ireland had improved the spirit in the camp, and there was a feeling in the run-up to the French game at Twickenham that the England players left out of the original selection were about to show the Lions management that they had got it all wrong. For an hour against France, England could do no wrong. But only for an hour. They built up a healthy lead only to see the French come back with such style that even the most ardent of English supporters would raise a glass of appreciation at the final whistle. England had contributed to their own downfall, yes, but France were superb and deserved their kiss of life having scrambled to the lifeboat.

England's demise in that game had revealed a potential problem for the Lions. When things turned against the most powerful team in British rugby, they looked rudderless. Tactically, England had got it wrong both on and off the field. A lack of clear direction on the pitch and a failure to use substitutions to replace tired legs all conspired to leave England off the pace both mentally and physically. Wrong decisions were being taken at half-back; Andy Gomarsall of Wasps was to receive the bulk of the criticism and lost his place for the final match against Wales in Cardiff. It was felt that, at twenty-two, he had time on his side. Also implicated was fly-half Paul Grayson, who worryingly lost his way as the game went on. But he was luckier and held onto his England place.

As I left Twickenham that night, once again my thoughts turned to the issue of the Lions captaincy. Fran Cotton had been talking openly in the press about the runners and riders and the field was narrowing. It was now coming down to three individuals: England's Martin Johnson and Jason Leonard, plus Ieuan Evans of Wales. Gregor Townsend was drifting out of the picture, as his form throughout the Five Nations had been very disappointing. Townsend's unique style of play was suddenly proving to be a liability for club and country. He was playing like a man with too much on his mind and the extra burden of captaincy was not what he needed. Even his place in the eventual Lions Test team was now under threat, and that had been unthinkable earlier in the season.

Martin Johnson is a quiet, unassuming man who rarely smiles in public. Cotton said that he did not mind this, although there were clear reservations elsewhere as to Johnson's ability to deal with the demands imposed by the modern media. Johnson is, however, a giant on the field and his presence in the line-out had become vital to the English pack. Barring injury, he would be certain of his Test place, and although Johnson was never going to be a Willie John McBride in the way he developed relationships with those on the periphery, he would get the respect of all those around him in the dressing room and lead by example. My impression was that Cotton had begun to favour the option of choosing the Leicester Tiger – a would-be Lion.

There remained one further doubt, however, regarding the choice of Martin Johnson as the Lions captain. His lack of discipline on the field had let himself and his team-mates down on two occasions still fresh in the memory. At Twickenham before Christmas, foul play by Johnson had prevented a perfectly good try from being scored. Jeremy Guscott was not amused. On the final weekend of the Five Nations Championship in Cardiff, Johnson did it again. The England full-back, Tim Stimpson, who had probably played himself into the tour party with his finest international game to date, raced up to the touch line with no Welshman in sight. However, Stimpson found his celebrations cut short as the touch judge had seen a Johnson short arm in action. At the news conference after the match, the England coach Jack Rowell expressed his displeasure with his second-row. Stimpson must also have been fuming. Johnson had to learn to keep a lid on his temper.

That match in Cardiff produced mixed news for the Lions management. Early in the first half, Welsh full-back Neil Jenkins broke an arm. This promised to have a devastating effect on the balance and composition of the Lions squad. Although Tim Stimpson had played well in Cardiff, Neil Jenkins, the most reliable goalkicker in British rugby, was understandably being lined up as the Test full-back in South Africa. This is not Jenkins' favoured role, as he would much rather play at fly-half; and, indeed, on one notable occasion in the Five Nations Championship, he was caught out of position when French winger Laurent LeFlemand exposed the full-back and scored a try during the Welsh defeat in Paris. The Lions management knew however that with Jenkins in the team, there would be a good chance of slotting the majority of the penalties conceded in what would be an abrasive series, and they would be able to pick a playmaker at stand-off and not someone who also had to kick the goals. But it soon became apparent that Jenkins was to have a metal plate inserted into the arm and his availability for the Lions tour was under severe threat.

The great vote for number ten was about to begin, and by this I do not mean the announcement of the impending General Election. The coveted jersey worn with such distinction by Phil Bennett back in 1974, when the Lions brought about a virtual landslide of victories, was up for grabs. There was a gathering lobby for an old campaigner by the name of Jonathan Davies. Now thirty-four, Davies was to play his final match for Wales against England in Cardiff. He played behind a well-beaten pack, but made telling contributions in defence, dramatically stopping Jon Sleightholme just a metre short of the Welsh line and then, most memorably, catching the England super-sub, Jeremy Guscott. Davies galloped after Guscott like a young foal and simply rolled back the years as he brought Guscott down with a tap tackle. Guscott fell like a steeple-chaser at the final hurdle – and Davies had made a strong, if belated, case for inclusion in the Lions squad.

The whole match was played in something of a time warp. Rob Andrew's return to the international stage surprised no-one more than the Director of Rugby at the Newcastle Falcons. Jack Rowell, who had ignored substitutions a fortnight earlier at Twickenham, brought Andrew onto the field for a final five minutes of sentimental glory alongside his old friend Will Carling, who was also probably playing his final game in an England jersey.

The performances of the day, though, came from two men of Bath. Jeremy Guscott proved that he should not have been left on the England bench for a season of international stagnation. In Cardiff, Guscott danced his way through the Welsh defence and into the Lions party. At the post-match news conference, Jack Rowell said that he would have Guscott in his Lions team and that Fran Cotton and Ian McGeechan had a different set of objectives, as they were picking a team for the moment and not for the future. Curious then that Will Carling, a man who had hinted at his international retirement all season, had played in all of England's internationals in the winter of 1996–1997!

Guscott's club colleague, Mike Catt, was the other man to stand out in the emotion at the Arms Park. At seven o'clock on the morning after the international, the bulldozers were due to move in to begin the demolition of the old stadium to create a ground fit for the 1999 World Cup final. After his wretched performance against Argentina just before Christmas, Catt must have thought his international career was as good as buried underneath the rubble. On that day, Catt shook his head in disbelief as he slipped down the greasy pole of international rugby aspiration. But, in Cardiff, he ran the game with high-class kicking and some beautifully judged passing to release the England backs. The question: would it be enough to make the Lions selectors forget what had gone before? Or did they feel that Jonathan Davies had seven or eight big games left in the tank before his retirement? Or would they look elsewhere? All would be revealed at the start of April.

Wednesday, 2 April was the day when the hopefuls were put out of their misery, one way or another. The planning for the tour had been taking place for nearly a year, with fact-finding missions to South Africa and no expense being spared. The players would stay in the finest hotels, with the best back-up service imaginable. It was now just a matter as to who would be on the plane.

The squad announcement was to take place on live television. The Chairman of the Four Home Unions Committee, Ray Williams, along with Fran Cotton and Ian McGeechan, gathered at Sky Television's headquarters in west London. Also invited to attend for the morning programme, which was to be beamed live to South Africa, were Robert Howley of Wales, England's Jason Leonard and Keith Wood of Ireland. Obviously, none of these players knew for certain that they would be in the squad, although they must have been confident. I was due to host the news conference at Sky and, as I pulled into the company car park, I saw Robert Howley getting out of his car. Howley's smile was as bright as the sunshine that morning, and there was no doubt in my mind that his journey along the M4 had not been in vain.

Clearly, the makers of the programme had been told in advance of the composition of the squad. It takes time to construct a television show and the department in charge of the on-screen graphics, not to mention the producer, needed the information to assemble a broadcast which would make a visual impact. As Ray Williams announced each member of the party, a large photograph of that individual was to appear over Williams' shoulder. It was an effective television tool, especially as seen on the giant screen being used for the benefit of the other media present at Sky that day. One or two individuals outside the Lions management team had been privy to the top secret information, but this had been kept to an absolute minimum and a respectful silence had been observed.

Jason Leonard was very wary of taking part in the live programme. It seemed that the most-capped English prop of all time was a little superstitious or, at least, did not want to tempt fate. He insisted that he did not want to appear on the programme, as he was not one hundred per cent sure of his selection. It was, of course, unthinkable that a man with such experience with both the Lions and his country would be left behind and, remember, at one point Leonard was being considered as a possible leader of the Lions. The producer making the cajoling telephone calls was, shall we say, certain that he was not backing the wrong horse by encouraging Leonard into the studio, but Jason remained the immovable object, almost as if he was propping up the England scrum. Eventually, after much persuasion and a breakfast-time phone call on the morning of the show, Leonard agreed to attend, and his worst fears were not realised. As we had all expected, the Harlequins captain was going to spend his early summer in South Africa.

The press corps gathered for the news conference about forty minutes before the scheduled start of the programme at half past eleven. The format of the morning was, in theory, fairly simple. I would welcome the audience before the commencement of the live show and we would then cross to the studio as they went through the last-minute preparations for the programme. Then it would be time to settle back and enjoy the excitement of the names being revealed and of seeing the reactions of some key individuals. In the opening address, I made the point that we would also go live to Welford Road in Leicester. This was to be the venue for the Courage league game that night between Leicester and Wasps. It was fortunate for us that events had fallen this way, as all the outside broadcast equipment was already in place and six Leicester Tigers were invited along to be part of the morning programme. Our other piece of technological wizardry was a decidedly more ambitious project: we planned to hook up to South Africa and talk to the former Springbok fly-half, now broadcast journalist, Naas Botha. Frantic checks had been made to Leicester to make sure that the players there could speak to the studio in London, but a short satellite link to the East Midlands is a little more reliable than one with the Highveld. Thankfully, though, Johannesburg could hear us and it was all systems go.

It seemed that every rugby journalist was present at the event, plus every television and radio station. A glance around the room confirmed that all notebooks were at the ready as the scribes waited to see if their morning paper predictions were about to come true. The man who was closest to getting all thirty-five names on the squad sheet was Peter Jackson of the *Daily Mail*. I have great admiration for such investigative work because this kind of inside knowledge can only result from the cultivating of friendships and contacts over many years. Jackson scored thirty-four out of thirty-five; the only name he did not get right was that of Simon Geoghegan, the Irish winger, and he would have made the trip had it not been for a career-threatening foot injury.

It is a tradition of the Lions that the Chairman of the Four Home Unions Committee reads out the full list of names. Ray Williams had rehearsed his role and he performed with great aplomb, providing just the right amount of drama and pace. It was a tense moment and it must have been a fantastic experience for those fortunate enough to be included in the party.

This is how the squad read...

Full-backs: Neil Jenkins (Pontypridd and Wales); Tim Stimpson (Newcastle and England).
Wings: Nick Beal (Northampton and England); John Bentley (Newcastle and England); Ieuan Evans (Llanelli and Wales); Tony Underwood (Newcastle and England).
Centres: Allan Bateman (Richmond and Wales); Scott Gibbs (Swansea and Wales); Will Greenwood (Leicester); Jeremy Guscott (Bath and England); Alan Tait (Newcastle and Scotland).
Stand-off Halves: Paul Grayson (Northampton and England); Gregor Townsend (Northampton and Scotland).
Scrum-halves: Matt Dawson (Northampton and England); Austin Healey (Leicester and England); Robert Howley (Cardiff and Wales).
Props: Peter Clohessy (Queensland and Ireland); Jason Leonard (Harlequins and England); Graham Rowntree (Leicester and England); Tom Smith (Watsonians and Scotland); David Young (Cardiff and Wales).
Hookers: Mark Regan (Bristol and England); Barry Williams (Neath and Wales); Keith Wood (Harlequins and Ireland).
Locks: Jeremy Davidson (London Irish and Ireland); Martin Johnson (Leicester and England); Simon Shaw (Bristol and

England); Doddie Weir (Newcastle and Scotland).
Back-row: Neil Back (Leicester and England); Lawrence Dallaglio
(Wasps and England); Richard Hill (Saracens and England); Eric
Miller (Leicester and Ireland); Scott Quinnell (Richmond and
Wales); Tim Rodber (Northampton/Army and England); Rob
Wainwright (Watsonians/Army and Scotland).

The captaincy went to Martin Johnson of Leicester, one of six players
from that club, which equalled the record established by London Welsh
in 1971. The Exiles had actually added to this total when a replacement
was sent out, making it seven in all during the trip to New Zealand. For
historians, it was also interesting to note that all the other Englishmen
to have led the Lions played at lock. In 1924, it was Ronnie Cove-Smith,
in 1930 Doug Prentice, who like Johnson was also a man of Leicester,
and then, of course, there was Bill Beaumont, who took the Lions to
South Africa in 1980. Johnson fully deserved his chance to take on the
highest honour in the domestic game. His initial reaction hinted at the
enormity of the task in front of him and his team. He acknowledged that
the tour was going to be more physical than the Five Nations and that
his squad would have to be prepared for the intimidation tactics used by
the South Africans, but he also predicted that it would not be a dirty
tour. We all hoped that he would be proved right.

    One of the major reasons behind the choice of Johnson was his
physical presence. At 6ft 7in and 18st, Johnson would make quite an
impact when he visited the opposition before the game. In Cotton's
own words, 'The sight of Johnson knocking on the dressing room door
in the minutes before a Test will concentrate the Springboks' minds
wonderfully.'

    I remember interviewing a young Johnson in my days at BBC
Radio Sport. It was the eve of the Five Nations match between England
and France in 1993 and England had lost the services of one of their
most loyal and valuable servants, the Preston Grasshoppers second-row,
Wade Dooley. Dooley's thigh injury had meant a late call and a
motorway dash for a lock from Leicester by the name of Johnson. He
had been preparing to play for the England A team against France. The
news had come through during the late afternoon; and after a call from
my producer to the England team's hotel, the phone was passed from
manager Geoff Cooke to the man of the moment. In the short interview
that followed, it was clear that Johnson was a quiet, taciturn man, but
one who made his point effectively and concisely. Above all, Johnson
was clearly not fazed by what was just around the corner – a new cap
in what was being billed as the key match in that year's Championship.
On the day, inevitably Johnson performed as if to the manner born and

he was desperately unlucky not to continue his international career two weeks later in Cardiff. England won against France and lost to Wales. The penny was destined to drop in the minds of the selectors, and Johnson's permanent inclusion in the England side was a natural progression.

A few months later, Johnson flew out to New Zealand to join the Lions party, again as a replacement for Wade Dooley. After a horrendously disjointed plane journey, Johnson eventually landed in Christchurch. He was spared the ordeal of being thrown straight into the first Test, just days after his arrival, but the Lions manager, Geoff Cooke, later admitted that he was perhaps wrong not to push his man straight into the first team, just as had been the case earlier in the Five Nations. Johnson proved to be a fine Lion and played out of his Tiger skin in the second and third Tests. His place in the international big top was assured.

One year on, Johnson experienced some of the more testing aspects of rugby life in South Africa on tour with England. Johnson's lights were turned out without the need of a dimmer switch when he was punched. It was a lesson learned in the hard school of international rugby and, since then, he has rarely come off second best. Johnson had won the vote for Lions captaincy because he could look after himself and his colleagues and set the best possible example as a first-class player who is totally sure of his own ability.

The breakdown of the squad was eighteen from England, eight from Wales, five from Scotland and four men of Ireland. The oldest man chosen was Ieuan Evans, who would be going on his third Lions tour, as would Jeremy Guscott, overlooked by England until his fine display in Cardiff as a replacement. The youngest man to be given the opportunity to tour was Eric Miller, the twenty-one-year-old from Leicester, whose form in his four internationals had been of such high quality that his selection was very much a foregone conclusion.

The full-backs Jenkins and Stimpson were probably most people's choices. Jenkins still had to prove his fitness following his broken arm, but his points-scoring record for Wales – five hundred and thirty-four in fifty internationals, and all at the relatively tender age of twenty-five years – represented an incredible return and made him a prime candidate for Test match status. Stimpson's forceful running and his ability to hit the line at pace, augured well for the hard grounds of South Africa. His strong physique would make him a potentially powerful weapon in the Lions armoury. Although at the highest level Stimpson was still unproven and he had a lot to learn, he would now at least get that chance.

The Newcastle theme continued on the wings, where club colleagues John Bentley and Tony Underwood joined Stimpson in the party. Bentley, one of six returnees from rugby league in the Lions squad, had played twice for England back in 1988 before leaving union to join the then sole professional code. Bentley is as strong as they come and his time at Leeds and Halifax had improved his power. Earlier in the season, I had seen him take apart his old rival Martin Offiah in the big league two clash between Newcastle and Bedford. He hadn't done enough to earn an England re-call, but he had caught the eye of Cotton and McGeechan.

The selection of his wing-mate at Kingston Park was equally controversial. Tony Underwood had only regained his England place because of the concussion suffered by Bath's Adedayo Adebayo in a game against Harlequins before Christmas. Underwood had bounced back after a serious knee injury and the scarring experience of facing New Zealand's Jonah Lomu in the World Cup semi-final in Cape Town. Two years on, it appeared that his Lions chances had gone when he was left out of the original selection, but he had come through to take the place vacated by the injured Simon Geoghegan.

The other wingers were the unrivalled Ieuan Evans, who seemingly gets better and better, and a man who was arguably England's man of the match in his only international appearance to date, Nick Beal. On that day in December, Beal played at full-back against Argentina and showed how versatile a rugby player he had become. His jack-of-all-trades reputation had been brought to the attention of a wider public at the inaugural World Cup sevens, when England won at Murrayfield in 1993. The speedy Northampton back was an ideal squad choice. There was no place then for Adebayo or his Bath team-mate Jon Sleightholme, and I thought that another unlucky player was Scotland's Kenny Logan, who was settling in well at his new club, Wasps, and would not have let the touring team down.

The issue at centre had been more clear cut, with the Welshmen Allan Bateman and Scott Gibbs having been two of the stars of the international season. Bateman, who had impressed in his early rugby union days with both Maesteg and Neath, had left to join rugby league, like John Bentley, in 1988. Warrington had benefited from his talents and it must have been with some pleasure that Wales welcomed Bateman back. He had not disappointed. He quickly found his feet at his new club, Richmond, and had returned after a cartilage operation to turn in a marvellous display for Wales against France in Paris. Scott Gibbs' time in rugby league had been a little shorter, but during those three years between 1993 and 1996, he had piled on the muscle and added immense strength to his already powerful game. Gibbs had been preferred to Will

Carling in the final two Tests of the 1993 Lions tour to New Zealand, and now he was all set to continue in a Lions jersey.

The main threat to an all-Welsh combination in the centre would come from two Englishmen. Jeremy Guscott simply had to be on the tour. Any other decision would have been a travesty. Will Greenwood also thoroughly deserved his selection. He was the only uncapped member of the squad and, during his first season at Leicester, had proved that he had the potential to become one of the best centres in the Northern Hemisphere. After having led the A team with distinction, he was already being mentioned as a future England captain.

The fifth member of the centre brigade could also, like Nick Beal, have been seen as the squad's utility back. Alan Tait must have thought his chance of playing for the Lions had gone after he had made the decision to go to rugby league (having been capped by Scotland for the first time in 1987). Tait won sixteen caps for Great Britain, mainly at full-back, and returned to play union with Newcastle concentrating on the role of centre. At thirty-two, he had made a good impression for Scotland against Ireland and France in the Five Nations Championship and scored three tries in the process, two of them in Paris. Tait had won the day over Jonathan Davies of Wales and England's Mike Catt – two players who also had strong claims for inclusion in the squad.

The crucial area of outside-half was to be filled by two men from the same club, both with vastly different reputations. Paul Grayson of England had been a model of kicking consistency ever since he won his first cap against Western Samoa at Twickenham in the back end of 1995. I first met Grayson some years ago when I went to Waterloo to make a radio feature for the BBC's *Sport on Five* programme. This was just as he was signing for Northampton and at that stage he was being talked about as one of the best kicking fly-halves in the English game. At the time, Rob Andrew was the England number ten, so it was inevitable that comparisons would be drawn, especially as Grayson was also slotting the kicks from all over the field. As the interview progressed, it became apparent that Grayson had a steely determination to make it to the top. Sitting in his parents' living room, there was a look of intent in his eyes that one day he would fulfil all his early promise. Ever since his elevation to the national team, however, there has been a doubt over whether he can expand his game to show a wider vision. It was because of this that he lost his England place in the autumn of 1996; but then, having won back the number ten shirt from Mike Catt, Grayson started to show that he could play a more expansive game when required. In the spring of 1997, he proved that he could provide a good mix of risk taking and conservatism, a blend which every international fly-half needs to find. Although that final twenty minutes against France had brought the doubts back. However, injury robbed Grayson of what seemed to be a vital final chance to impress the Lions selectors against Wales, and Mike Catt came in and played his best game for England in that position. In the end, Ian McGeechan stuck by his own club man and, ironically, due to a lack of goalkickers in the squad, it was probably Grayson's good old trusty boot which meant that he got the nod.

Trust is not a word that you could have applied to the play of Gregor Townsend over the previous nine months. Townsend is a world-class player and, during his international career of twenty-five caps for Scotland, has provided some memorable moments. Few will ever forget the famous inside 'toonie' flip pass from the young star which set the old warrior Gavin Hastings steaming away from the French cover to give Scotland their first win in Paris for twenty-six years. There was also that blistering run out from defence against England in the Calcutta Cup match at Murrayfield in 1996. Mind you, that would be hard to forget, as it was the only interesting event in the whole eighty minutes! But the season of 1996–1997 was proving to be a trial of strength of character for Townsend. He was appointed caretaker Scotland captain in the autumn of 1996 in the absence of the injured Rob Wainwright. Admittedly, this coincided with a losing period, but, even on Wainwright's return, Scotland fared little better, and much of the blame was directed at Townsend. Nonetheless, there remained the constant thought that Townsend was the man to cause maximum damage to South Africa, and McGeechan was probably using all of his management skills to bolster the confidence of a young man with his thumb resting firmly on the cork to the Lions' champagne.

The Northampton connection continued at scrum-half, where Matt Dawson, England's number nine of a season ago, was selected as one of the three choices. A serious knee injury had cost Dawson much of his season, but McGeechan clearly regarded his pupil as a little closer to the front of the class than Kyran Bracken, Andy Gomarsall, Bryan Redpath, Gary Armstrong and, in my opinion, one of the club players of the season, Andy Nicol of Bath. As you can see, this was not an area lacking in talent, a point made even more forcibly when you consider the skills of the other two scrum-halves who were named.

Robert Howley of Cardiff and Wales was in pole position for the Test match place and his potential battle against Joost van der Westhuizen of South Africa would be one of the highlights of the series. I hoped and prayed that injury would not deny us this rugby treat. Howley's aggressive, muscular play from the base of the Welsh scrum singled him out as a world star, but breathing down his neck and eager for his place would be Austin Healey. Healey, now of England and the most self-assured man that you could ever expect to meet, had gone through a massive season. In his first year at Leicester, he had helped to take the club all the way to the Heineken European Cup final and broken into the England side. Healey was now starting to achieve some of the great things that had been predicted for him, and his decision to move from winger to scrum-half was paying dividends.

Two seasons ago I went to Edge Hall Road, the home of Orrell Rugby Club with the intention of seeing the first team training later that evening, as they were to appear in a live broadcast on the following Saturday. These sessions are invaluable, not only to the players but to commentators as well! When the grounds get muddy and the shirt numbers are obscured, or your commentary position is such that you can only just see around two long pieces of metal piping and a cameraman's backside, those crucial moments spent checking the way players run or how they part their hair are absolutely vital. On this particular occasion, I had arrived at about five o'clock for a half-past-seven training session. The local fish and chip shop, which I have to say produces some of the best haddock and chips in the Northwest, was sadly shut, so I went to the club on the off chance that one or two players would be around for a chat. This was before the professional days, so I drove into the car park more in hope than anything else. There was no sign of anybody. Just as I was about to leave, I heard the sound of some hard work being done in the weights room. I opened the door and there was Austin Healey. Half an hour later, he was on the pitch practising his box kicking and passing off the ground. He was in the process of trying to convert himself back into his schoolboy position of scrum-half, having spent the majority of his time with Birkenhead Park, Waterloo and then Orrell as a winger with the headline writer's dream of a name. Later that evening, I continued my research in the bar, with the former England winger, now selector, Mike Slemen. Slemen is a softly spoken man to whom you should always listen, and he assured me that one day Austin Healey would leave the others sniffing the exhaust fumes as he sped away into the England team.

Velocity was surely not the main concern when the Lions management team sat down to discuss the alternatives at prop forward, but having said that, mobility is a major consideration for all players in the quick, modern game. The preference for Peter Clohessy hinted at other motives, however, suggesting that the selectors believed a hard competitive edge up front was paramount. During his turbulent career, Clohessy has twice been banned for the illegal use of the boot. The latest occasion was in Paris in 1996, when he stamped on Olivier Roumat's head in full view of the television cameras. Since that low point, Clohessy had made his way to Australia, and his performances for Queensland in the Super Twelve series had helped him back into the public eye for the right reasons. His scrummaging was strong and his experience against some top South African provincial sides would be invaluable.

There could have been very little debate over the inclusion of England's most-capped prop forward, Jason Leonard, or his international partner, Graham Rowntree. It was also generally accepted that David 'Dai' Young of Wales had to be given a chance to re-live the experience of 1989, when he was a Lion in Australia and played in all three Tests. In the meantime, rugby league had given Young a profitable career with Leeds and Salford.

The group of five props was completed by Tom Smith of Watsonians. Here was a man who certainly did fit into the mobile category. This ability to get around the field and his general ball carrying skills had helped propel Smith into the spotlight and a début for Scotland against England in 1997. I watched Scotland train before that match on a chilly January morning at Bracknell Rugby Club. It was one of those days when the weather dictated that notes were compiled from behind the glass of the clubhouse window. Eventually, it was necessary to venture outside, though, because I was keen to get a good look at Smith, as all I had seen so far was video footage from the Australian tour games in Scotland in the autumn. First impressions were that Smith looked small for a prop, but, after further investigation, it became apparent that he weighed in at 16st 7lbs of prime Scottish beef, and that's on a par with Clohessy, Leonard and Rowntree.

The position of hooker seemed to have been fairly clear cut, with most people successfully predicting that Keith Wood and Mark Regan would occupy two of the places. Ireland's Wood still had to prove that his shoulder injury was not an obstacle to him making the trip. All-round fitness is key to his wholehearted dynamic approach. The question marks also remained over his throwing-in and, if this were to become a problem for the Lions, then Regan, who had been much criticised in his earlier appearances for England, would be an accurate and reliable thrower to his jumpers.

The third choice of hooker came as something of a surprise. Barry Williams of Neath had made just one appearance for his country and was little known outside the Welsh game. But he was said to be in the Wood mould and, if he was considered to be better than Phil Greening of Gloucester, England's reserve hooker, then I for one was keen to see him in action. Williams also had the reputation of being a happy-go-lucky character who would be a good tourist. He could prove to be the joker in the pack, in more ways than one.

The second-row was another area of the team where the fog had lifted during the previous few months of international competition.

Captain Martin Johnson was destined to be joined by his England colleague Simon Shaw of Bristol. Shaw, a giant of a man standing at 6ft 9in and weighing in at 20st, had hardly put a big foot wrong in his opening six matches for his country. His career had been threatened recently by two serious injuries, but this had only served to inspire him to achieve his goal of playing at international level.

There was a strong feeling that a third England lock forward would go on the tour. Gareth Archer, who had been a team-mate of Shaw's at Bristol, but who had moved to take up a lucrative offer from Newcastle, was being backed by those who thought that his aggressive style of play would help the cause in some fiery moments in South Africa. Archer must have been close to selection; but, in the end, the man alongside him in the Newcastle engine room, Doddie Weir, was picked to add the experience gained from forty-five appearances for Scotland and for his proven ability to perform against top-quality opposition. Weir had been Scotland's best forward in the 1995 World Cup in South Africa and, more recently, had continued to play well in a disappointing Scotland team. The same could be said of the youngest lock chosen, twenty-two year old Jeremy Davidson of Ireland. He had quite literally stood head and shoulders above some of his colleagues during the Five Nations Championship and the feeling was that, alongside players of a higher standard, Davidson would prosper and really start to come of age.

Our journey through the thirty-five names takes us finally to the back-row and perhaps the most interesting selection of them all. Ever since his arrival on the rugby scene, Neil Back of Leicester has always been one of the most talked about talents in the game. He is one of those sportsmen who inspires debate and polarises opinion. His inclusion in the starting line-up can dictate the way the whole team is going to play. Football had Glenn Hoddle, and now has Paul Gascoigne, with the accommodation of both players determining the way in which a team fashions its approach to a game. Of course, in rugby, the issue of size is of equal consideration to style and this has been the area where Neil Back has been criticised through no fault of his own. At 5ft 9in, Back is small for a modern day forward. Early indications from the Lions management were that the emphasis was going to be placed on a strong physical presence in the back-row to counter a powerful South African assault, and this would count against his inclusion. But Back, omitted from the original squad of sixty-two, could offer much to a team playing on the hard and fast grounds of South Africa. In the end, style had won the day over size and Back, so often dismayed by his lack of England recognition, had earned the right to be judged on tour in the best company. Following the squad announcement, his reaction to the questioning about his Lions inclusion was diplomatic in the extreme. A player who had been outspoken following previous rejections by England was not going to get off on the wrong foot with the Lions. It was good to see a man who had worked so hard get his reward.

The man who had been wearing the England number seven jersey with such distinction during the Five Nations Championship, Richard Hill, was going to start in front of Back in the pecking order for the Test place. Hill combines size with style and had been the greatest success story for England in a winter when Jack Rowell had been looking at options with the 1999 World Cup very much in mind. Hill had come through and given Rowell what he had been thirsting for, an openside flanker with pace, power and guile. Hill, who has represented England at all levels up from the age group of sixteen, had also given his club, Saracens, a great sense of pride, becoming their first Lion.

Lawrence Dallaglio continued the England theme in the back-row and, like Hill, would be first in line for a place in the Test side following a magnificent season for both his country and his club. In his second year as the Wasps skipper, Dallaglio had overcome the disappointment of failing to gain the England captaincy but proved that his leadership qualities were beyond question. I went to a Wasps training session just a short time after England had named Phil de Glanville as their new captain. Prior to the announcement, a fair portion of the hot money had been placed on Dallaglio, so it was thought necessary to send a camera to Wasps that night to obtain the view of the man who had just missed out on the top job. Dallaglio had obviously taken the news of being overlooked in his stride and showed maturity well beyond his years and level of experience. He bristled a little when I suggested that, because of the age gap between himself and De Glanville, his time would probably come. In my mind, he clearly thought that he was ready then for the challenge of national leadership, but at no time did he hint that his loyalty would not be placed right behind the new skipper. Dallaglio had resolved to prove to his employers at Wasps that, although England might have made the wrong decision, his club had certainly not. Moreover, once he was moved by England back to his more natural position of blindside flanker, he blossomed; and what followed was a lesson in professionalism, as he steered Wasps to a first league title in seven years.

Another club captain was the fourth English member of the Lions back-row union. Northampton's Tim Rodber was going back to South Africa with a score to settle following his sending off on the England tour of 1994. During the first Test match Rodber had been nothing short of amazing. Few would dispute that it was one of the finest-ever displays by an England player, but his tour lay in tatters just three days later when he was sent off for retaliation in the battle of Boet Erasmus against Eastern Province in Port Elizabeth. Since that point, Rodber has struggled to command an England place and has not been helped by being moved around the back-row to allow other selections to be made. But now Rodber had found a settled berth in the England team, in his favourite position, number eight, and the army man would surely prove to be an able lieutenant to his club boss, Lions coach Ian McGeechan.

This left three non-Englishmen to fill the other places in the back-row and it was a story of one Irishman, a Welshman and a Scotsman. The Irishman was the find of the season, Eric Miller of Leicester. Miller, an all-round sportsman who has also played Gaelic football and soccer to a high standard, had filled the ample boots of Dean Richards at his club. He had played so well that Leicester had not missed 'Deano', their talisman. In the Pilkington Cup victory over Bath at the Recreation Ground in February, Miller had put in one of the finest club performances of recent times, and it was only concussion early on during Ireland's heavy defeat to England in Dublin a week later that provided a comma in Miller's impressive tale. At twenty-one, Miller was the youngest man chosen for the squad and he would undoubtedly be pushing Rodber and Scott Quinnell all the way for the number eight spot in the Tests.

Quinnell, rather romantically, was following in his father Derek's footsteps. Derek Quinnell had been a Lion on three tours in the 1970s and 1980s. After a twenty-seven-month spell in rugby league, Quinnell the younger was now with Richmond earning big money and putting in some high-class performances. For Wales, though, he had not fully recaptured his form of old and was at times prone to losing the ball in the tackle, a surprise considering the importance placed on upper body strength at Central Park, the home of Wigan R.L. There were, however, enough signs that Quinnell was worth the faith being placed in him and, because of his proven ability, many felt sure that playing with and against others at the very top of the sport would bring the best out of him, especially as an aggressive runner with ball in hand.

The one remaining place in the back-row was filled by the Scotland captain Rob Wainwright. Here was a man who would arguably have led the Lions had the tour taken place a year earlier but, following serious groin and Achilles tendon problems, Wainwright had been in genuine danger of not making the tour at all. His early season form had done little to suggest that he was an automatic choice, and it was only after a lot of hard graft during the Five Nations that Wainwright had been included.

That was the squad then but in the back of every player's mind must have been the thought of possible injury and the denial of the opportunity to live out the schoolboy fantasy of a Lions trip. There were still many hard games left in the domestic season.

It was starting to be an extremely busy time for all involved in the sport. I knew from a Sky Sports perspective that a schedule of four live matches in a little over a week was going to be hard work! But this was nothing to the stresses being put on the minds and bodies of the players caught up in the most thrilling and dramatic end to any domestic season. For the first time, teams were not playing just to win the championship and to avoid the prospect of automatic relegation, but for the chance to get a money-spinning top-four place to qualify for the lucrative European Cup. There was also the need to stay in the top division where the big investments could be made. Consequently, it seemed that all twelve teams in division one, plus the top four clubs in division two, had something to play for in the run-in at the end of the season. In Lions terms this was potentially catastrophic.

It did not take long for these fears to be realised. In the Courage league two clash between Bedford and Newcastle, Lions winger Tony Underwood was stopped in his tracks by his Bedford counterpart, Paul Hewitt, and forced to leave the field. At the time, it seemed like a perfectly legal challenge and, on closer inspection of the video evidence, I still stand by this view. There were members in the Newcastle camp who thought that Hewitt should have been made accountable for his actions, but in my opinion, although it was a robust tackle, Hewitt had not gone dangerously high on his opponent. The upshot, though, was worrying, because later that evening Tony Underwood was diagnosed as having a fractured jaw. It seemed so cruel that a man who had battled back following that confidence-battering encounter with Jonah Lomu in the last World Cup had now seen his chance of going back to South Africa put in jeopardy by this unfortunate collision.

The season was taking its toll and Underwood was just one of a number of Lions feeling the effects. In the week before the Pilkington Cup final between Leicester and Sale, I went to the East Midlands to conduct some interviews. Martin Johnson revealed that he was already over the forty-game mark and this compared unfavourably with the thirty top matches that he had played during the previous season. Yet, stoically, Johnson added, 'You've always got another big game in you.' And, as he towered over me, I did not disagree. But now Johnson would have to find at least another six high-quality performances. I hoped that he had enough gas left in the tank.

A TOUR IS BORN

'We have a million rugby players in this country – we will not run short!' –
SARFU President, Luis Luyt, reflecting on his country's confidence before
the tour began.

The clock was now ticking before the team's departure on Saturday,
17 May, and in a way, the first week of the tour had already begun.
Shortly after the Cup final, and just a week before departure, the Lions
went to Weybridge to gather their thoughts and gel together as a squad.
Not only did they go through the ritual of posing for a team photograph; here was where the process of actually becoming a team started.
Indoors and out, the bonding process began in earnest. In seminars they
talked like keen university freshers eager to stick to their homework
timetables; then they moved outside and competed over land and water,
as if they were paratroopers on their first survival course. Fran Cotton
even got a dunk in the river for his troubles. The players' world seemed
a happy place – now they had to take that spirit of Surrey on the long
journey to South Africa.

The squad came from all corners of the British Isles and Ireland,
but one man had a little further to travel. Peter Clohessy had been
playing with Queensland as part of their squad for the Super Twelve
series in the Southern Hemisphere. He was now thirty-one and, having
just missed out on selection for the Lions trip to New Zealand in 1993,
must have been delighted with his inclusion four years on. This time,
though, a long-standing injury caused him to pull out of the 1997 squad.
No sooner had Clohessy walked off the plane from Australia than he
developed a back muscle strain in the very first Lions training session.
The long-haul flight from the other side of the world probably did not
help the condition, especially as Clohessy had a history of back
problems, having slipped a disc earlier in his career.

In these situations, however, one man's bad luck is another's
fortune and Paul Wallace of Saracens, who had been preparing to travel
with Ireland on their development tour of New Zealand and Western
Samoa, changed his plans and joined the Lions camp. It was Irishman

for Irishman and the inevitable accusations of a political appointment
were bandied around. But the Lions had proved with their original
selection that country of origin counted for little and that choices had
been made on merit alone. Wallace had accumulated twelve caps for his
country since his début against Japan in the 1995 World Cup. Now he
would return to South Africa after his opening season of league rugby in
England. His brother Richard, a winger, also plays at Saracens and
would perhaps pass on some Lions advice, as he had been called out as
a replacement on the last tour in 1993.

I knew from a personal perspective that there were not enough hours in
the day. My preparations for the tour had begun months in advance. In
conjunction with the Sky Sports rugby union researcher, Adrian Hill, I
had started to compile three separate notebooks – one dedicated to the
Lions, another to South African teams and a third to general notes about
the tour. The coverage of the Super Twelve competition had greatly
increased our level of knowledge concerning some of the South African
provincial teams. The Natal Sharks, the Gauteng (formerly Transvaal)
Lions, the Free State Cheetahs and the Northern Transvaal Blue Bulls
were no longer strange animals to a British audience. But the tour was
more far reaching than that, as, in addition to the Test matches, other
games were to be played against an Eastern Province Invitation Fifteen,
the Border Buffaloes, Western Province, Mpumalanga Pumas, Northern
Free State and the Emerging Springboks. The work to seek out the information and assimilate it into pertinent points for commentary purposes
was well underway.

    Lions tour records and histories formed the bulk of the preparation,
along with individual profiles of all members of the squad, plus details of
the venues and of notable South African performances against the Lions.
The amount of detail was reaching mind-boggling proportions, and this
was all before we had left London and tapped into the resources of the
South African Rugby Football Union and other contacts in the provinces.
It was time to keep a cool head and remember that only a small
percentage of this research would eventually go on to air. Of course, the
problem is that before the matches you do not know which parts will be
of use and which sheets of paper will end up in the broadcasting dustbin.
I concluded that, if I wanted to stay sane, it was well worth taking my
thoughts off the tour for a couple of days before leaving and trying to
make a few runs in one of the rare cricket matches that I would be able
to play in during the summer. (Having said that, those who play cricket
with me would probably advise me to take some homework to the match
because of the time I would be likely to spend in the pavilion.)

    May is not only the time of year when the cricket season wakes up from its winter slumber, it is also when the domestic rugby season is finally put to bed and rugby's official functions honouring those who have achieved great things take place. Add to this the various pre-tour Lions gatherings and in the next few days my glass rarely would be empty. Sky Sports had their own Lions launch party in the City of London. A number of top players from Lions days gone by turned up to lend their support. The former Lions and Scotland back, Andy Irvine, had travelled down from north of the Border and felt sure that the Lions of 1997 would not let anybody down. Irvine was convinced that the Lions would win at least one Test and, although he felt that there could be reverses in the matches leading up to the Test series, he was sure that when the going got tough the Lions would get going. Joel Stransky, fresh from his Cup final win with Leicester, was also present at the party. Stransky was less confident for the Lions, however, and thought that his nation would clearly have the upper hand in the series. During the evening, Stransky was asked to kick a ball over a specially erected set of goal posts inside the impressive hall in Bishopsgate. Behind the mock posts was a Sky logo, and the aim was to clear the crossbar and hit the cardboard logo to win a prize. Stransky stepped up and nonchalantly landed the ball on the target. Moments before his kick, for fun we had shown him and the rest of the audience a decidedly more important attempt at goal in the 1995 World Cup final. His winning drop goal sent a nation into rugby heaven and Stransky revealed to me that, as soon as he had kicked the ball on that famous day, he had known that it was sailing through the posts. Lions supporters hoped that his prediction for the outcome of the forthcoming tour would not be so accurate.

The following night the social whirl continued with the annual RFU awards dinner at the Hilton hotel on Park Lane. Some of the Lions party were present and Martin Johnson was named as the English player of the year. When questioned on stage about the Lions' chances and his prediction for the outcome of the series, Johnson wryly said that he would quite happily settle for an overall victory of one–nil, with the other Test matches being drawn. Two more young English Lions stepped up for awards. Richard Hill won the accolade for best England début during the international season and Austin Healey won try of the season for his blistering run which began from inside Leicester's half of the field in the European Cup match against Llanelli back in November. It was a magnificent score and the general feeling in the audience was 'more of the same, please' over the next few weeks. Healey, always the comedian, joked that he was delighted to be wearing his Lions blazer, although he claimed that it did not fit. On a more serious note, however, he indicated a burning ambition to win the scrum-half spot for the Test matches and added that he would be more than happy to continue to take orders from his Leicester captain in the red jersey of the Lions.

Earlier that day, just forty-eight hours before the Lions were due to fly to Durban, injury-doubts Neil Jenkins, Keith Wood and Tony Underwood all reported fit after their recent problems. The squad were leaving a week before the first game so that they could acclimatise to the conditions and, according to assistant coach Jim Telfer, they all needed to adjust to the differences in culture and the South African way of life. Telfer had been there and done it all before. His wily presence was certain to prove vital to the squad.

It was becoming apparent that the Lions would find South Africa a little more in tune with the euphoric events of the 1995 rugby year than the rather unsettled period in 1996. During the World Cup, the South African nation had united behind their rugby heroes and President Nelson Mandela had been at the head of the queue when it came to heaping praise on the coach Kitch Christie and his captain François Pienaar. There was no more graphic illustration of the special relationship formed between the new government and the Springbok team than when Mandela wore the famous green jersey to present the trophy to his country's victorious skipper. But the bond between the South African rugby world and their leader was put under great strain just a year later. After André Markgraaf had taken over as coach, the President became increasingly reluctant to attend matches and official rugby functions. When Markgraaf resigned early in 1997 after a secret tape recording was made public in which the coach allegedly made racist remarks, the tension seemed to ease. The appointment of the new coach, Carel du Plessis, and the new black manager, Arthob Petersen, brought a feeling of a fresh start. In the week before the Lions left, President Mandela said, 'In 1996, the sport struck trouble on and off the field, but now we look forward to rugby continuing to play an important role in the new South Africa.' The Minister for Sport, Steve Tshwete, added that in 1974 and 1980 no black South Africans had wanted to see the Lions come to the country but once they had arrived then the whole of the black population had got behind the British team. Thankfully, much had now changed and this time South Africans were looking forward to being able to support their own nation, although there was still a great deal of scepticism in the black community. There was a growing need to see more visible signs of player integration at the highest level of rugby, and the politicians knew it.

There was politics of a different sort back at home, which was threatening to disturb the Lions preparations. Fran Cotton had added to his job portfolio by becoming the president of the newly created Rugby Football Union Reform Group. In short, this Group had called for the resignation of the RFU secretary, Tony Hallett, and was critical of the way the authorities had handled the new television deal struck with BSkyB. The decision by the RFU to nominate Bob Rogers of Sussex to oppose Cliff Brittle as the chairman of the new management board had also upset the Reform Group, and it was shaping up to be another summer of discontent. Cotton refuted any suggestion that this off-the-field involvement would hinder his task with the Lions. He was asking for one hundred per cent focus from the players and stated that he would match their commitment.

There remained, however, the prospect of unrest in the English committee rooms, and the administrators in South Africa knew that their mettle would be tested should any on-field violence start to grab the headlines. When questioned at the news conference just prior to departure, Cotton did not want to make too much of the issue, but he did allude to the area of discipline and a code of conduct for his players. In drawing comparisons with the famous 1974 touring team, Cotton merely wanted to highlight the good team spirit building in his modern-day side. In 1974, the famous 'ninety-nine' call had gone down in rugby folklore. The story goes that Willie John McBride's team knew as soon as any player signalled danger by yelling out that number, then his colleagues would be on hand to sort out the trouble. But the game had moved on since then and Cotton freely acknowledged that with the increased use of television replays from every possible angle, flying fists and stray boots would not go unnoticed. He expected his players to show a professionally restrained approach to any potential flashpoints. The only ninety-nine call that the 1997 Lions would hear would come from an ice-cream vendor on Durban's beach.

The topic of potential violence had been picked up in South Africa, with the Springbok coach, Carel du Plessis, finding it hard to understand just how the forthcoming series could possibly tip over the edge. Du Plessis was of the opinion that the modern-day rugby player simply did not have the time to get involved in off the ball incidents. The game was now too quick to permit the antics of 1974. Then, players could almost afford to be off the pace as long as they were helping the side's cause by settling a score, even at the expense of contributing to one! This cannot be allowed nowadays, because any one of the fifteen players caught up in an off the ball incident and not involved in playing the game is a major liability to his team. Du Plessis went even further by claiming that he could not remember the last time a South African team had been involved in a major brawl. I knew what he meant, but this said, the rugby world still recalled the 1995 World Cup when the host nation played Canada in Port Elizabeth and three players were sent off. Moreover, on the same ground just a year before, England had come off second-best in the battle of Boet Erasmus. Tim Rodber got his marching orders for retaliation and Jonathan Callard received twenty stitches.

Before the tour began, it was clear that neither side wanted a war of words. Nevertheless, it was also true that it was not going to be a tour for a shrinking violet. Despite any code of conduct laid down, Martin Johnson's team were unlikely to shirk the challenge if it were to present itself. The role of the officials was going to be vital. Consequently, the Lions arranged a meeting with Freek Burger, SARFU's refereeing development officer and the former international referee, Steve Strydom. The idea was to draw the battle lines and to establish the relevant interpretation of the laws, especially the ruck and maul.

When the Lions arrived in South Africa, they were greeted by the outspoken President of SARFU, Louis Luyt. Encouragingly, Luyt said that he wanted the Lions to join the Tri-Nations tournament in the Southern Hemisphere as a fourth team, and to play home Test matches at the end of a tour of Britain and Ireland by South Africa, Australia or New Zealand. These were interesting thoughts, and if they were to come to fruition, it needed a fine performance from the Lions over the coming weeks to prove that they were not only part of rugby history but were also key to the sport's future.

The enormity of what just lay around the corner had really started to hit home. In South Africa they could not wait to see how the Lions matched up to the great sides of years gone by. Furthermore, they wanted to assess the present state of British rugby in the professional age. To be part of bringing the coverage of this major rugby event to a domestic audience was going to be a quite a privilege. Needless to say, the cricket match on Sunday, 18 May duly gave me even more time to reflect on the trip ahead. We won the toss and I lost the rather one-sided contest with the opposition's opening bowler. Faced with an afternoon of contemplation, I speculated, not about the English summer that I was about to leave behind, but the South African winter that I was to enter on the next day.

Flight SA239 was due to leave Heathrow at half past seven on the Monday evening and, after a circuitous route from my home in Berkhamsted, Hertfordshire because of a nasty accident on the M25, I eventually managed to arrive in good time, thanks to some fine navigation from my local taxi firm. I checked in for what I felt sure would be the trip of a lifetime. There was going to be no getting away from the tour now – we would live and breathe the Lions for the next seven weeks. Once airborne I glanced inside the in-flight magazines and they revealed article after article on the tour. The crew also distributed the South African newspapers and I had to rub my eyes and look again when I saw the headline, 'Natal mauled by the Lions'. There was, however, no cause for any alarm. No, we had not missed the start of the tour. The article referred to the Super Twelve game between the Sharks and the Gauteng Lions and it further illustrated the strength and depth in the South African game. Natal were set for a semi-final place and were about to qualify from the league stage of the competition. But Gauteng, who had not qualified, gained some consolation by giving the Sharks a real mauling.

The flight was comfortable enough and after a brief stop in Johannesburg we flew on to Durban, where the Lions had been in residence since early on Sunday morning. The world's most talkative pilot illuminated this short second journey on the Tuesday. He freely mixed his metaphors and in the same sentence amusingly described his Boeing 747 as the Ferrari of the fleet, which sat right at the top of the food chain! Our chattering captain also had time to wish any Lions supporters on the plane a pleasant stay in his country but, like so many others, felt confident that his nation were on the verge of a home-series win.

The fervency that surrounded the build-up to the tour cannot be adequately explained in the time I have here. It is a cliché but also true to say that South Africans are mad about their sport and especially their rugby. From the moment we stepped off the plane in Durban airport, we were bombarded with references to the Lions. Having checked in at the hotel, which was beautifully situated on the seafront, we decided to have lunch and, inevitably, walked straight into another conversation about the Lions. The owner of the fish restaurant called Langoustines was not only enjoying his magnificent view back to the city of Durban, he was also looking forward to hosting the Lions squad on the Thursday evening before they departed to Port Elizabeth to play their first match against Eastern Province. Interestingly, he was a little more pessimistic about South Africa's chances than our chattering pilot had been. He claimed that there was an air of uncertainty in South African rugby following the change of coach. His food had been good and he had given us food for thought.

The last twelve months had been an unsettling period for South Africa which had seen coaching upheavals and a non-stop journey around the world to play high-intensity rugby. It was not only the British players who had been feeling the pace. The South African injury list already included winger Jacques Olivier, second-rows Mark Andrews and Kobus Wiese, plus the majestic full-back, André Joubert. Joubert had just returned to action at the weekend coming on as a replacement for Natal in that defeat to Gauteng. His ability to enter the back line with searing pace and seemingly minimum effort would be pivotal to a

successful series for the home team. Olivier was already out of the series
having suffered a serious knee injury, but Andrews was hopeful of being
fit, although he would need a shoulder operation, and Wiese was about
to try and prove his fitness against the Lions on Saturday.

I picked up a newspaper, turned to the back page and saw that the
Eastern Province selectors had named their squad for the tour opener
and included alongside Wiese was the Springbok back, Hennie Le Roux.
He also had doubts over his physical state and both would use this
match against the Lions to encourage the national selectors to pick them
for the squad for the international season that lay ahead. The Lions
always knew they were not going to get it easy in Port Elizabeth, but the
chance for Eastern Province to choose on an invitational basis meant
that the kick-off to the tour looked even more difficult than first
thought. In addition to the two capped players for South Africa, two
overseas stars were part of the Eastern Province squad. Australian international Sam Scott-Young and New Zealander Matthew Webber had
just signed one-year contracts with the Province and were looking to
impress on début. Some thought that ambush tactics had been used, but
the Lions were not whingeing. They were aware that tough matches
would come thick and fast and there was no reason to expect an easy
start. All the players wanted to do was get on with the job of playing.

In some respects, the first week in South Africa must have been
frustrating for the Lions and they must have felt as if they were spending
a lot of time kicking their heels. But just as the time spent in each other's
company at Weybridge had been an essential part of building a team
spirit, this week would help to overcome the 'newness' of being on tour.
Although they were obviously anxious to get to the matches, the team
bonding exercises were as important as the training that McGeechan and
Telfer were putting them through. There were still many unknowns for
the squad. For a start, room arrangements had to be sorted out. Fran
Cotton explained that his captain Martin Johnson had the right to a
room by himself and had taken up that option, although he was free to
change his mind at any point. The other players had been split up in what
appeared to be a very sensible manner. Aside from Johnson, there were
seventeen Englishmen on the tour and when the rooms were allocated
they had all been kept apart. So it was Englishmen with an Irishman,
Scotsman or a Welshman and if that wasn't designed to break down the
jingoistic barriers then nothing was. Early impressions were that the
atmosphere in the party seemed a healthy one. Cotton confirmed this and
was delighted with the team spirit. Ian McGeechan singled out John
Bentley as a driving force behind the humour. Bentley, a tough no-
nonsense Yorkshireman, had been named as the chairman of the tour

entertainment committee and was clearly delighted to have been given the chance to act as team motivator. The tall Scot, Doddie Weir, was his deputy. It was their job to keep the off-field activities bouncing along.

Less likely to put smiles on the faces of the players were the hard training sessions that they were put through on arrival in South Africa. On the first Monday of the tour, those who were unfamiliar with the methods of Jim Telfer soon became accustomed to his style. Telfer, the son of a shepherd on the Scottish Borders, first coached on a Lions tour in New Zealand in 1983 and, having been involved in two Grand Slams, has impeccable playing and coaching credentials with Scotland. He moves in a positive way, striding with purpose around the training paddock and slapping on the sun cream with equal vigour. Even the ultra-violet rays probably think twice about burning Telfer's neck.

Durban is a steamy city even at the time of year when South Africans claim that it's winter. Twenty-seven degrees Celsius seems pretty warm to those less accustomed to such a climate, and the players certainly felt the heat during those early training sessions. Drinks were called for after just fifteen minutes of running in the sun. But Ian McGeechan was delighted with the conditions and said that it was ideal for the squad to work in the hardest possible environment. The first two Test matches were going to be at sea-level, so the altitude problem, despite being encountered in some of the early provincial games, would not affect the Test series until the final match in Johannesburg. A little like New Zealand a year before, the Lions knew that they could not afford to go to the high ground of Ellis Park needing to win. South Africa would play every Test match in Johannesburg if they had the chance.

It was Wednesday, 21 May and our thoughts were turning to the possible line-up for the first match of the tour. The Lions were due to name the team later on that morning. Looking a little further ahead was the sports photographer Dave Rogers, who was conducting a survey of all the media asking everybody to predict the side that would be chosen for the first Test match in Cape Town. This was, of course, complete with a little wager; even so, I had to rather coyly scribble down my prediction on a piece of scrap paper. Fran Cotton was just metres away and this hurried the process somewhat. Just for the record this is what I thought at the time – Jenkins, Evans, Bateman, Gibbs, Guscott, Townsend, Howley, Leonard, Regan, Young, Johnson, Shaw, Dallaglio, Hill and Quinnell.

I wondered about the merits of playing Guscott on the wing and realised that this was not the best use of his immense talent. But Allan Bateman had been one of the most impressive players in the Five

Nations Championship and if he could reproduce that form for the Lions, then he would almost demand inclusion alongside his fellow countryman, Scott Gibbs. At least playing one of the three centres on the wing would get them all on the pitch.

Guscott remained a class act, however, and for one moment during that training session he dazzled as brightly as the Durban sunshine. A routine had been devised, with the former Director of Coaching at Natal and now Technical Coaching Assistant for the Lions, Andy Keast, overseeing this section of practice. Keast, now in charge at Harlequins, could provide some useful inside information. In this routine, the idea was for some of the players to work in small teams of three or four and try to outwit the opposition over a short distance by using effective support play and neat passing. There was very little room to move, but when Guscott got the ball he showed an alternative route to the pretend try line. The man who has graced the international field for the best part of a decade motioned to pass once, then twice, and with all around him screaming for the ball, Guscott ignored the options and went on his merry way. After two beautifully executed dummies he had taken out all the potential tacklers, and with an air of arrogance, as the man is entitled to have, he put the ball down as if to say, 'That's how to do it.'

The Lions had a gruelling two hours that morning in the heat at King's Park before they got back on their coach and took the short drive up the coast to their hotel. The Beverley Hills at Umhlanga Rocks is luxurious in the extreme. The waves crash into the beach and the garden and terrace look out to the lively sea – complete with the standard complement of Natal sharks. The Lions management had organised a media day at the hotel to coincide with the team announcement. The squad was in a relaxed mood and mingled with the journalists in a convivial atmosphere. The Lions also put on a braaivleis, 'braai' for short, which is a South African barbecue, and on offer were some typically Durban foods. The influence in this part of the country is predominantly Indian, with spicy meats the order of the day. Large quantities were consumed, but the England flanker Richard Hill assured us that, for him, the sweets and cakes were out of bounds. Hill was not only itching for a slab of cheesecake, but was eagerly awaiting the start of the action which, for the whole of the squad, could not now come quick enough.

Hill got his wish to be part of the opening encounter. The team was read out by Fran Cotton and confirmed the inclinations which had been formed towards the end of the training session. The side to play the Eastern Province Invitation Fifteen was – Jenkins, Bentley, Guscott, Gibbs, Beal, Townsend, Howley, Smith, Wood, Leonard (captain), Weir, Shaw, Dallaglio, Hill and Rodber.

Ian McGeechan had put a few cards straight on the table. There was a clear indication of future plans with the selection of the Townsend and Howley half-back combination. They had been working well in training and the feeling was that Gregor Townsend was starting to win back his confidence. There was another revealing choice with the incorporation of the entire England back-row. Tim Rodber was set to return to the scene of his sending-off in the England match against Eastern Province in 1994. Rodber had not spoken to the management about the possible effect of that experience and we were told that they had not brought up the subject either. His place remained in doubt, however, because he had not trained in the morning and, like full-back Tim Stimpson, was suffering from a stomach upset. Paul Grayson had not been considered because of a reduced training involvement during the first week. He was still feeling a twinge from a long-standing thigh muscle strain.

The other man in the party who was not fully fit was the skipper Martin Johnson. Johnson was actually part of the selection committee and, after consultation with Messrs Cotton, McGeechan and Telfer, he had decided not to involve himself in the first match. He, above all other players on the tour, had taken a battering during the long season back home. The Lions masseur, Richard Wegrzyk, said that Johnson had been working with him and, although there was nothing serious, it was generally agreed that more rest time would be a good idea. Wegrzyk also told me that his treatment room in the hotel was rapidly turning into a common room. The players had the option of a massage, acupuncture or even social work from a man who had won great respect during six years with the England team; and anywhere up to seven or eight players were regularly gathering to discuss possible ailments and to put the world to rights.

The man who had the honour of leading the Lions as they opened this historic tour was Jason Leonard of Harlequins. Leonard, capped fifty-five times by England, had led his country out on two occasions: first, when he was awarded his fiftieth cap, as is the tradition, and second, when he was officially captain against Argentina. On that day, England had been booed from the field, but when questioned about his feelings during that unwelcome response from the crowd, Leonard joked that at the time he was more concerned that hooker Mark Regan was trying to claim his try, Leonard's first in an England jersey. Leonard also speculated as to what he would do with the team's lion mascot when running out onto the pitch. The captain is normally expected to carry out the lion and place it beside the flag on the half-way line. The sight of the tough England prop running onto the field with this cuddly toy promised to be the most amusing moment of what was going to be an anxious day. The Lions needed to start their tour with a win and the whole of the Eastern Province was determined that they would not. It was time to go to Port Elizabeth and get the answer.

The horrendously early check-in time of five-thirty in the morning did nothing to help my general well-being, but my mood was distinctly cheered by reading more about England's victory in the one-day cricket international in Leeds. I read all the reports in the morning newspapers with much satisfaction even though I had seen the action live via the SuperSport channel on the previous day. As I had watched the fine performances of the Surrey pair, Graham Thorpe and Adam Hollioake, it dawned on me that what we were just about to do was to instantaneously transmit the coverage of the whole Lions tour to a British and Irish television audience. No matter how involved I become with the media, I never cease to be amazed by the technology of it all.

I could feel the nerves starting to take shape as well. The day before a major broadcast I get a little bit fractious, just ask my wife, Helen. I suppose that the mood swing is dictated by the anxiety of cocking it up – calling the wrong name of the try scorer, failing to let your voice catch the excitement of the event or maybe some awful technical failure which renders the whole broadcast meaningless. I'd like to think that these things happen very rarely, but it's the fear of them coming around the corner and hitting you head on which keeps the adrenaline flowing. But if that's how I felt, then just imagine what was going through the minds of the players. They were reasonably tense and tight earlier in the week but as the match grew ever closer they were probably going through all kinds of emotional contortions.

The first thing we did when we arrived at Port Elizabeth was to go to the ground. The stadium is now called Telkom Park, because of sponsorship, but to any rugby follower it will always be known as Boet Erasmus, the scene of many a rugby battle. Three years ago, England had come up against a fierce Eastern Province team and the result was ugly. A year after that, South Africa met Canada in the World Cup on the same ground and three men were sent off after a brawl. Further back in time, the Lions also had a violent encounter on this infamous turf, having decided to fight fire with fire on the day they met Eastern Province in 1974. Many believe the tour was won there and then, as the Lions let it be known that they meant business and that they refused to be dominated. The ground certainly had a history but the hope was that this game would be remembered for all the right reasons.

The Lions had generally enjoyed success at Boet Erasmus, having won there on seven previous occasions. They were starting the tour as clear favourites to make it eight. The news from the Lions camp was bad, though, and after the withdrawal of Tim Rodber with that stomach upset, both Scott Gibbs and John Bentley pulled out on the Friday morning before the game. Gibbs had a thigh problem and Bentley a bruised toe. Their places went to Will Greenwood, who, remember, was still to play for his country, and Ieuan Evans, the proud owner of a record number of Welsh caps, tries and appearances as captain. His experience on this tour was crucial.

The final lick of paint was being applied to the posts, and the grass, which already looked perfect, was being mowed for the umpteenth time. The ground is open at both ends and along one side has a mass of bench seating. That was where the singing would start if Eastern Province began to get the upper hand. The locals were keen for a change in fortune for their team and, with some new investment having been made in both the stadium and players, there was definitely a feeling of optimism just twenty-four hours before kick-off. We then investigated the interview position and in doing so went to the tunnel area. The walk from the dressing room to the pitch was down an appreciable slope and even at a leisurely stroll it seemed as if the ground was falling away. The effect was to throw you right forward as you left the underneath of the stand and entered into the arena. At that point, the roar of the crowd would hit the players. For so many of the Lions it was going to be a new experience and one which would test their character.

As we recorded a piece for the tour preview programme being put together in London, a familiar figure walked down the steps of the stand. The new Springbok coach, Carel du Plessis, had arrived to oversee a coaching clinic. He had also come to see the Lions play the next day and felt that many of the touring Test team were going to be on display. Du Plessis suggested that the Lions had a potential weakness at full-back. This was where he wanted to see them put under pressure. On the South African front, Du Plessis, a former winger himself, expressed disappointment that Jacques Olivier was going to miss the series through injury but added that this gave James Small a great chance to return to international competition. The rebel winger, who had done so much to keep Jonah Lomu under control in the World Cup, had taken a liking for the Cape Town nightlife. His modelling photographs had kept him in the spotlight for reasons other than rugby, but it now seemed that he was being offered a way back from the wilderness.

The Lions were putting together their final preparations in Durban. They would set off for Port Elizabeth later on Friday afternoon. There was work to be done all round, especially for a certain commentator who now had to make sure that he was familiar with the physical appearance of the Eastern Province side. I met the captain, Jaco Kirsten, and he kindly invited me to go along to a local steakhouse where the team were meeting up that evening. I spent twenty or so minutes with the players who must have thought they were in some kind of identity parade. As they tucked into their rump steaks, I scrutinised their distinguishing features – I have never seen a set of men look so self-conscious. Then it was off to the ground again for an eve-of-match reception hosted by the Eastern Province Rugby Union. Then I can assure you it was straight to bed, because five-thirty in the morning was starting to seem a long time ago. Tomorrow was going to be as big a day as they come.

Port Elizabeth is a perfectly pleasant place, but, as it is the third-largest port in South Africa, signs of industry mainly dominate the view of the bay. It is also known as the windy city and when the gusts get up the surfing is meant to be good just off the four main beaches. But although we woke up to another magnificent day on the Saturday with the early morning temperatures feeling decidedly too warm for a game of rugby, such pleasures as messing about on the water were strictly out of bounds. It was time for one more final read of the commentary notes and to get ready for the short journey to the ground to watch a match which could shape the rest of the Lions tour.

Interestingly, Jim Telfer was quoted earlier in the week as saying that the result didn't necessarily matter. He felt that at this early stage of a tour it was more about performance than anything else. This was undoubtedly a fair comment, but Telfer also knew that for his team to beat the second-best side in the world they would have to beat the majority of the provincial teams. There were no straightforward games on the tour, and even though this one fell towards the easier end of the spectrum, tours are also about momentum. In order to get up a head of steam, the Lions had to win if they were going to return home with a record to be proud of.

The Lions received some bad press on the morning of the match. The local newspaper, the Eastern Province *Herald*, headlined one of many stories previewing the match with the words 'Tight-lipped Brits have no time for fans at PE Airport'. Apparently a small crowd of about fifty people had gathered at the airport on the Friday evening to greet the Lions. Many were looking to get the autographs of their heroes but the article claimed that the Lions had walked through the airport foyer, 'without so much as a smile or a friendly hello'. The Lions were clearly focused on the job in hand, but, even if this story had been embroidered with a local 'spin', it was still disappointing to read such a story. The public relations role is just as much part of the modern game as it was to the successful tours of days gone by. Players are professionals – and this does not just mean playing rugby. Look at the recent transformation in the New Zealand squad's relationship with the media and therefore public. If players are accessible, then more people are going to want to play or watch the sport. It could only be hoped that the South African press would not be given any more opportunities to criticise the tourists on this front.

On arrival at the ground at about midday for the quarter past three kick-off, the anticipation in the air was almost tangible. It is the norm in South Africa for build-up matches to take place prior to the main event and this obviously encourages a rugby-mad public to arrive at the stadium in good time. On this occasion, a healthy crowd watched the British Police take on their South African counterparts. I can vouch for the fact that these policemen took no prisoners in what was a fiercely competitive game. In the end, South Africa were easy winners and we hoped that was not a bad omen for the rest of the day.

The first thing I like to do on arriving at a ground is to check out the commentary position. This is important, because if there are any alterations to be made, then this is the time to do it – not fifteen minutes before kick-off. There is always a feeling of trepidation when mounting the steps to find the seat where you will park yourself for the match. What will the view be like? Will there be enough room on the work surface to put all your notes? Is the monitor in the correct position? And where will I put my biscuits? These and a hundred other such questions all spring to mind. Our production team had journeyed out to South Africa long before the tour began to check all these matters for the Test venues; but clearly it would not have been practical to visit the other outlying grounds, and we were in the hands of the host broadcaster, M-Net, to provide the facilities. Their help had been superb, though, and so far no fears had been realised. They had given us the best seat in the house, with a stunning view across the ground from our high position on the half-way line.

There were, however, some frantic efforts taking place to establish sound contact with our studios in London. Our sound engineer, Brian Mullholland, and production manager, Martin Knight, were working up quite a sweat as they hurriedly switched around wires and made electronic connections that lesser mortals would not have deemed possible. I tend to find that on these occasions the technicians quite rightly only care for their expensive gadgetry and the commentators are left to their own devices. Television commentary is a highly technical business. The engineers have to ensure that there can be anything up to ten different sound sources simultaneously in the headphones. During the match I listen in to the director, the on-site producer, the London-based producer, the programme sound from London (i.e. the voices of the presenter and guests), my own voice coming back, Stuart's voice, the effects of the crowd, the referee's microphone, the programme assistant counting down to commercial breaks and Uncle Tom Cobbleigh, who always has his say. (You can see why I get an early night on the eve of a match!) The collection of leads in the commentary box looked like a massive bowl of spaghetti, which didn't do much for the butterflies in my stomach, but after an hour or so contact was made and the whole Sky team breathed a huge sigh of relief.

Kick-off was now fast approaching and it was time to go down to the pitch and record a link with London. The noise in the stadium was increasing all the time as more and more people flocked through the gates – but the volume was about to reach new heights: the Scottish Pipe Band were preparing to come out and offer some homely pre-match entertainment for those who had made the early trip to follow the whole of the tour. There were a number of Lions red jerseys in the crowd and it was good to see. But we knew that if we wanted London to be able to hear our words, then we would have to get the short chat between myself and Stuart Barnes over with as soon as possible. I like pipe music, but I could think of better moments for the band to strike up. Quickly we did the piece and beat the band. As we left the pitch, it was time to shake Fran Cotton by the hand and wish his team all the best. Cotton had been pacing the touch line like an expectant father and looked as keyed into the task as the boys in the dressing room. There was a general realisation that it was now time for the war of words to cease and the action to begin.

The Lions could not have wished for a better start, tackling with ferocity and then creating a lovely opening try for Jeremy Guscott. He finished the move with his usual grace and elegance. A ten points to three lead was gradually eroded, though, and either side of half-time the Lions seemed to lose their way. They also lost the advantage when the nimble Eastern Province winger, Deon Kayser, sped away from the cover and scored a well-worked try by leaving the Lions' full-back, Neil Jenkins, for dead. This was one of the more worrying aspects of the match from a Lions point of view. Jenkins kicked with his usual precision, although strangely he missed two attempts that he would normally have expected to land over. Having said that, both efforts hit the upright, because if Jenkins does miss, it is never by much. The question marks still remained, however, over Jenkins' positional play at full-back, as his lack of pace had been exposed. It looked as if Carel du Plessis was right.

The other area of emerging concern was at half-back. Robert Howley was having a super game. Sometimes his service lacked precision, but in the loose he was hungry and always looked to take on the opposition back-row around the fringes of the scrum. But outside

Howley, Gregor Townsend found it hard to settle. His punting was not showing signs of any great improvement after some extensive kicking sessions with specialist coach Dave Alred. Townsend, who had said that the pressures he went through during the domestic season had been self imposed, was still falling short of the standards he would have expected to achieve. The dilemma for the management, though, was that the best Lions moments came from Townsend's artistic moves in broken play. Time and time again his brush strokes were the ones that mattered. But his kicking just could not be relied upon. We had known about this diffi-culty before the tour started and it seemed set to remain one of the central issues at the heart of Lions success and failure.

The forwards dug deep to haul the Lions back in front of Eastern Province, and after the excellent Doddie Weir had pushed his way over the line, the Lions started to open up and the home side began to run out of steam. Guscott got his second try, Will Greenwood rounded off a fine display with a score of his own and Tony Underwood, who had come on as a late substitution, made quite an impact and got a try in the process of impressing. The Lions' late rally gave them what by then seemed like an easy victory – thirty-nine points to eleven – and they left the field feeling reasonably satisfied with a job well done. The crowd voted with their feet and registered their displeasure with the home side by drifting away from the stands long before the final whistle. By and large they had been denied the sound of another whistle – this time from the train perched behind the large open stand. It is tradition in Port Elizabeth for the train, the carriages of which are now used for hospitality boxes, to signal the home team's dominance with a resounding 'toot' after every try. A single sad whistle was all that it was able to muster.

After the match, Jason Leonard made the point that, despite a lengthy period of preparation, this had been the first time that the squad had played together in a match situation. There were still things to work on, but on the whole the captain for the day had been encouraged. The Eastern Province skipper, Jaco Kirsten, said that he felt his team had underestimated the Lions, but on the day's evidence, the Springboks would be able to take on and beat the Lions up front. He went even further than that and claimed that the highly successful New Zealand province, the Auckland Blues, would probably beat a Lions Test side. Fran Cotton inevitably had a different point of view and felt that, although his team had taken time to establish control of the match, at least by the end they were starting to look good. Certainly more genuine tests would come later in the tour, but the Lions had achieved what they set out to do and that was to secure a victory in their first game.

The day had been an exhausting one all round. The players had done their bit and, from a television perspective, I can assure you that a lot of nervous energy had been expended. All parties had wanted to get a game under the belt. We did, and the reaction from back home had been favourable. A win for the Lions and a successful broadcast for Sky. It was time for a little drink in celebration. We went to a local bar for a quick refresher and were greeted by Sky Sports coverage of the England versus South Africa football international at Old Trafford. The South African footballers, the Bafana Bafana, gave it their all and it was only by virtue of a controversial goal from England striker Ian Wright that the home team had managed to secure a two–one win. And if that wasn't news enough, our general well-being was improved by news from home of England's success in the second one-day cricket international against Australia. Just at that moment, the Lions squad walked in for an evening of relaxation and we were reminded of their victory earlier in the day. We could all drink to that!

CLIMBING THE MOUNTAIN

'If they continue to run like that they are definitely going to give the Springboks a lot of grief.'– Western Province number eight Andrew Aitken after the Lions had beaten his team despite having been overpowered up front.

Having won the first match, it was now much easier for the squad to think in terms of their performance. The most encouraging aspect of the display against Eastern Province was that the Lions had clearly identified a style that would give them a chance of taking the ultimate prize. The South African press had given the Lions a reasonable write-up. They generally felt that there was room for improvement but that the Lions had done enough during two explosive passages of play to be satisfied with their start. This was true, but the Lions had to improve significantly if they were going to get anywhere near the required standard to beat the stronger provinces, let alone the South African Test side.

The party left Port Elizabeth on Sunday afternoon taking the short flight to East London. The packing and unpacking of the suitcase was already starting to get me down. This was worrying because we had only been through one week of the tour and I wondered what state my mind would be in come the end of week seven. Living out of a bag is one of the most irritating experiences of the job, but I had to chastise myself every time that I felt angry about the chance to fly around the world and visit different places and stay in top hotels. The problem is that basically I am a home bird. Anyway, it was time to stop being so churlish and enjoy the trip for what it was – the experience of a lifetime.

There was a warm welcome waiting for the squad on their arrival in East London, with a local group of majorettes providing a colourful sight just off the runway. But the greeting party had their spirits a little dampened by the rain, which started just as the Lions and the media corps went down the steps of our aircraft. The torrential downpour continued all through the night and the thought was that if it kept on raining, then the weather could have a major say in the Lions next match against Border, on Wednesday, 28 May.

The heavy rain actually determined where the Lions would train on the Monday morning. They had originally planned to use the local cricket ground, Buffalo Park; but after one of the television trucks had got stuck trying to cross the ground, the Lions decided to make their way over to the Basil Kenyon Stadium, which was where Wednesday's game was due to be played. This suited the Lions; in fact, they were delighted to get the chance to sample the surroundings of the main stadium.

The Lions were travelling around on their team coach. Consequently, they were avoiding some of the local taxi drivers, who, on the whole, were an extrovert breed. On that morning in East London, I stumbled across one who was a few sandwiches short of a picnic; in fact, he was minus an apple and yoghurt as well. The simple instruction was to leave the hotel and head for the rugby ground. East London is not a big place and the 'knowledge' required by a local cabby couldn't be the most demanding of examinations. Now, had we been looking for a tiny little back street, I would not be so critical. But to fail to find the focal point of the city, the rugby ground, well, that was remarkable. To add to my woes, the driver had a penchant for bird impressions. He was a cross between Percy Edwards and Freddie 'Parrot Face' Davies. It was a great relief when we finally stumbled across the ground, more by luck than judgement. On the offer of his card in case I needed a lift back to the hotel, I smiled and said the walk would do me good.

I had gone to the ground to meet the coach of Border, Ian Snook, and was surprised to find the Lions out on the main pitch. Snook was annoyed that the turf was going to cut up and his team would have to use the rather rough practice ground behind the stadium when they trained later that afternoon. The coach's assessment of his players hinted at an easier game for the Lions than had been the case at Eastern Province. Border had lost to, and finished behind, Eastern Province in the Currie Cup in the autumn of 1996. Since that point, they had played poorly and were in the process of rebuilding their squad following the departure of some key personnel. Interestingly, Ian Snook had been a coach at Bedford in England and also Old Wesley in Ireland, where he had tried to select Eric Miller when Miller was still in his schooldays. Snook had spotted a rare talent and was pleased to learn of the Irishman's inclusion in the Lions squad. After his spell in Ireland, he travelled back to his native New Zealand and then on to South Africa. In typical Kiwi fashion, he mocked my request to find out the name of the best kicker in the Border side. He said that all us British are preoccupied with the boot and that his was a running team, as all rugby sides should be. He was realistic about their chances; however, Border were expected to lose heavily. Certainly our colleagues in the South African media felt that the Lions should win by a big score and that even a score of forty-plus would start as a minimum requirement. Snook merely wanted Border to put up a good show in the match against the Lions. He felt that such a performance might encourage the rather disillusioned local public to return to support their team.

The Lions training session had caused a few sparks to fly. Pride is at stake on tour and, although the rivalry predominantly remains friendly, things can get a little overheated in the white-hot environment of a full-contact session. This happened on that Monday morning when the two hookers, Mark Regan and Barry Williams, squared up to each other. There was a head-butt and a few choice words. It wasn't long before things calmed down, but the incident illustrated just how competitive it was becoming for places in the side which really mattered – the Test team. The newspapers seized on the story and made good capital out of it, but the flare-up simply showed the desire to beat off other contenders. Rob Wainwright, who had been one of the peacemakers, said that live scrummaging was always difficult to reproduce in training without the aid of a referee, but that the two main protagonists had soon laughed and joked about their fracas. The required 'do or die' commitment was building all the time. It was good to see that they were shaping up to be a tough team.

Shortly after training, the fifteen for the match against Border was announced at a lunch-time news conference. The management had been true to their word and tried to give everybody a chance of action in the first couple of games. There was, however, one exception: Martin Johnson. The captain was being rested for a second time, having already failed to appear in the first match. Once again, the reason given was Johnson's energetic season, which had just concluded back in England. We were also assured that he would play in the next match, against Western Province in Cape Town on the following Saturday. Nonetheless, there was a nagging doubt emerging over Johnson's fitness. It was common knowledge that he would require surgery on his return to Leicester for a long-standing groin problem. He wasn't taking a full and active part in training and it was most unusual for the captain of the squad to miss out on the opening two matches of a tour. The Lions management knew, however, that Johnson had to be fit for the Tests and were taking no risks.

The side for the match against Border read – Stimpson, Bentley, Bateman, Gibbs, Underwood, Grayson, Healey, Rowntree, Regan, Young, Weir, Davidson, Wainwright (captain), Back and Miller. This meant that, in addition to Johnson, only Alan Tait, Matt Dawson, Paul Wallace and Tim Rodber were yet to be involved. But the point was reiterated that there was every intention to make changes during the match versus Border, so all bar Johnson should have seen some action by the end of Wednesday afternoon, having come off the bench. The selection also revealed various sub-units, as had been the case in Port Elizabeth. Ian McGeechan had opted to use the Newcastle back three of Stimpson, Bentley and Underwood, plus two of the Leicester back-row in Miller and Back. But most interesting was the choice of the Welsh centre combination of Allan Bateman and Scott Gibbs. They both knew that Greenwood and Guscott had performed admirably on Saturday and that they were in for a hard battle for Test places. In fact, Gibbs heaped praise on Greenwood, who had adapted so well to the highest level. The Welshman also added that he thought Guscott was on fire in training. But the duo from the valleys welcomed the challenge and this was going to be a fascinating tussle.

No sooner had the team been announced than another change looked inevitable. There was more bad luck for Tim Rodber, who had missed out on making his first appearance against Eastern Province because of a stomach ailment and now had to go to hospital, having received a nasty cut following a collision during training. The wound required stitches and, as the team for the Border match had been picked prior to the training session, there was every chance that Rodber would miss out again.

On a personal note, it was time to unwind for a spot of lunch and to break the cycle of training sessions and 'keyboarditis'. Stuart Barnes and I went for a stroll on the seafront and watched the waves crashing in from the Indian Ocean. It was a stunning sight, with the awesome power of the breakers having almost trance-inducing qualities. You could have watched the waves for hours and, although East London is a little down at heel and has clearly fallen on some tough economic times, the place has its own beauty and it's called the sea. The centre of town offers very little in comparison. There are one or two Victorian buildings but many more ugly and dilapidated constructions. The name East London is not the only connection to the big smoke in England. The main thoroughfare is called Oxford Street, and if that made the likes of Jason Leonard feel a little more at home, then some of the more experienced scribes would have felt positively wistful as they drove down Fleet Street. But by far and away the most intriguing aspect to the city is the presence of a dodo's egg in the local museum. It is purported to be the only surviving such egg in the world.

Ability on the pool table is almost as rare a phenomenon as the dodo's egg, as far as Stuart and I are concerned. In a moment of madness, we had decided to inflict our lack of skill on each other and hit upon the idea of a tour-long competition, with the prize being a meal at a restaurant of the winner's choice. Back in Durban, I had established a two–one lead. The pool tables of Port Elizabeth had been spared the indignity of our presence, but in East London we were at it again, and Stuart, like Guscott on the training pitch, had caught fire. He went ahead by four frames to three, finding pots that neither of us thought possible. If you are sad enough to be interested in the progress of this irrelevant side show, then I will keep you up to date.

If the foolhardiness of the Sky commentary team at the pool table wasn't bad enough, then even more unbelievable was the same two men taking to their jogging gear and running the short distance from our hotel to the Border training session. Tim Rodber, who had just returned from receiving treatment for his cut, spotted us leaving the reception area. The look of amazement on his face said a thousand words. The uphill climb to the stadium took its toll and, when we arrived, we slumped at the side of the pitch and thanked the rugby gods that we talked about the game and didn't play it.

The session was built around passing movements between forwards and backs, and it became clear that Border were going to run the ball at every opportunity. The local newspaper reporter confirmed that this was the only way they knew and the coach would not let them play any other way. Even so, there were a lot of handling errors and we saw nothing to worry the Lions unduly. We left feeling that our prediction of a comfortable win for the tourists was the right one.

It is very easy to become removed from the outside world when on tour. To eat, drink and sleep rugby is inevitable, but it is also important to understand that life goes on outside the confines of the hotel. This was brought home to me later on that evening. We ate at a bar restaurant by the name of O'Hagans. There is a chain of such places all over South Africa and inevitably some are better than others. Around East London there were various advertisements proclaiming that this particular eating-house had what was 'rumoured to be one of the best views in Africa'. This rather self-conscious piece of salesmanship sparked a great deal of curiosity. Were the rumours true or was it just a cunning plan to trap a naïve tourist like me? On arrival at O'Hagans, I discovered that nobody had lied, and as we ate and looked out to the ocean, the moon illuminated a track of shimmering light all the way from the horizon to our table. South Africa and even little old East London had much to offer aside from rugby pitches.

In the morning, it was back to reality: another day and another training session. But the weather wasn't getting any better and, as the wind picked up, we read reports of sleet in Johannesburg and temperature drops all over the country. Some regions had seen the daytime temperature go down as far as just two degrees above freezing. By our standards back in the United Kingdom and Ireland this is, of course, insignificant, but South Africa was bracing itself for a cold snap and the possibility of some heavy snowfalls. Perhaps the thermals in the bottom of the suitcase would come in handy after all.

The heavy rain local to East London already meant the postponement of the curtain raiser to the Lions match, and the Lions kickers had been denied the chance to have a specialist session with Dave Alred on the main pitch because of a fear of further chopping up the ground and creating a mud bath. The rain kept falling and my heart kept sinking. It was unlikely to be the spectacle of running rugby that we had all been hoping for. To cheer ourselves up, Stuart and I retired to a local bar called Buccaneers and, like the good, old-fashioned journalists we are, resolved to remain there until the rain stopped. What a great decision this was, as courtesy of the mobile phone and the non-stop deluge, we were able to set up office and relax for the next eight hours.

Those players who missed out on the first game were having to show great patience in the build-up to the second match, which was to be played a full eleven days after their arrival in South Africa. There is only so much time that they can spend on the training field or in the gymnasium. In Durban some of the squad had gone 'boogie boarding' off the North Beach. Eric Miller described the sea as the warmest that he'd ever been in. Fortunately, none of the players had encountered any of the sharks that swim the coast in this part of the world.

But what did the players do with their spare time? East London, like Durban, offered a health and racquet club to test other sporting abilities and inevitably there were the traditional card schools and pool competitions. In fact, Paul Grayson was asked about his rivalry for the stand-off position with Gregor Townsend, and amusingly replied that he was leading at darts but was down at table tennis. Entertainment chairman John Bentley was doing his best, but the confines of touring were clear to see. The rigours of professionalism dictated that the players had to stick to the sensible: this was the modern age, and bodies and minds were being directed to the main goal of winning rugby matches. It needs a certain type of character to tolerate the discipline.

There could be no doubt that the match against Border was at the forefront of everybody's mind. Tim Rodber had decided that discretion was the better part of valour and he sat out the game, thus giving his cut more time to heal. The captaincy had been given to Rob Wainwright, a man who had led his country eleven times, but who now described this as the highest honour available in the sport. His leadership abilities were to be tested in what proved to be a trying experience for the Lions. The rain had continued to lash down overnight and when we arrived at the ground the heavens burst again. There's only so much a pitch can take and areas of standing water were starting to form. (Thankfully, there was not enough water to encourage the attendance of a local crocodile, which had escaped from 'Doc Croc's' crocodile farm. Doc Croc had been unable to keep up with his bills and had fled East London. Three of his crocs had got a little bit inquisitive as to where their master had disappeared, so they had taken it upon themselves to go in search of the Doc. Two had subsequently been caught, but one was still on the loose. The trap that had been laid had only managed to cage a local Alsatian dog that had fancied the live chicken on offer as bait.) Just as we had feared since our arrival in East London, weather conditions were going to play their part.

The incessant rain may have been good news for escaped crocodiles, but it kept a large number of fans away from the match and the attendance was short of the anticipated fifteen thousand. Nonetheless, those present got more than they had bargained for. Few could have expected such a struggle for the tourists, especially after they had made the perfect start, with John Bentley finishing off a slick handling move, making a mockery of the conditions. But if it is possible in sport, the Lions had started too well: and after that high spot, they slipped and stuttered in the mud. It took a dubious try from Mark Regan to settle the nerves.

I called it as 'no try' and stand by this, having seen the replay. Regan grounded the ball just short of the try line, but this didn't stop him giving me some terrible stick that evening. He had telephoned home and had heard that the commentators had tried to deny him his moment of glory. It was all very good natured from a man who had shown the kind of spirit in adversity which could well propel him into the Test team, but the look in Regan's eyes reminded me that what you say live on air can often hurt. This is no reason for not saying it, though, and the day I stop calling a game as I see it will be the day to stop broadcasting altogether. The commentator must never be swayed by personal influences, but I knew things could get a little rough if the tour started to go badly and the comments became predominantly negative.

Up until Regan's score, Border had battled gamely but with no cutting edge – that is until a mistake from fly-half Paul Grayson, who was having a shocking afternoon, let in the winger André Claassen. Grayson had been missing his kicks from positions where he would normally expect to score. The conditions underfoot were certainly a problem, but even so, Grayson could not find a rhythm – and in broken play he was failing to control the game in his key position. I felt sorry for a player who had not been in action for two and a half months because of injury, but we had been told he was fit and raring to go. This

Pride of Lions – the squad gather before the adventure begins.

The hard life – week one and it's already time to relax, as the Lions host a braai.

Austin Healey looks to spike the opposition.

Doing our best to hide the nerves – the author and Stuart Barnes before the opening match in Port Elizabeth.

It never rains, but it 'paws' – the Lions hit their first sticky patch in East London.

Uphill task – the Lions try and solve their scrummaging problems.

Jim Telfer, the man behind the punishing forward sessions.

A match of two halves – fly-halves: Barnes with Grayson, injured after just one week of the tour.

Room with a view – what a way to wake up!

The not so beautiful – Johnson, Cotton and McGeechan field the questions in Cape Town.

Looking cool – Matt Dawson and Jeremy Davidson relax in the shade before the match against Mpumalanga.

The effects of the ugly challenge from Marius Bosman which ended Doddie Weir's tour.

It's sickening, isn't it?! – not only can the man play rugby, Townsend plays golf like a true Scot.

On the verge of greatness – the early star of the tour, Robert Howley, has his journey ended.

A day in Soweto.

The boys from Buenos Aires: Bracken, Diprose, Redman and Catt.

The Fab Five – not quite Abbey Road.

was not the performance of a Lions-standard outside-half and deep inside Grayson must have known it.

Early in the second half, Border took the lead; and when they went in front by fourteen points to ten, a shock result was more than an outside possibility. The conditions had played their part. To their credit, the Lions had tried to play the expansive game which they knew was the ultimate route to success on the tour, but when it became apparent that they had to start to adjust to the unhelpful surroundings and play with more responsibility, they failed to solve the problem. The correct decision-making was not forthcoming.

The referee did not help their cause and some of his decisions were very hard to fathom. Ian McGeechan was mystified by the referee's willingness to allow players to dive over the top of the ball at the ruck. But the official could not be blamed for the Lions teetering on the edge of defeat. Our guest in the studio, the former Welsh fly-half Jonathan Davies, said that the Lions had been naïve and it was true. They were in a mess of their own making and needed the forwards to find a way out of the swamp. Paul Wallace made an effective contribution when he came onto the field for Dai Young, who had been pretty well anonymous. It was too early to say for sure, but Wallace looked the part. Doddie Weir had his second fine game of the tour and Eric Miller showed a maturity well beyond his youthfulness. Another telling factor was the contribution made by the ex-rugby league men. John Bentley did not just score a try, his professionalism also shone through and he was rightly awarded the title of most-valuable player by South African television. Likewise, Scott Gibbs and Allan Bateman rolled up their sleeves, but there was an alarming moment when Gibbs fell awkwardly and had to leave the field on a stretcher. The initial scene looked ominous, but only half an hour later Gibbs was walking again. (Nonetheless, the following day he was put on the first flight out of East London and went straight to Cape Town. On arrival, he had an x-ray but thankfully nothing was broken.)

If I had to single out one man for his contribution towards the end of the match, it would be the skipper for the day, Rob Wainwright. His fearless approach set the example and with great strength he struggled over the line to score the try which effectively won the match. Later that evening when we had the pleasure of dining with the Lions, Wainwright lamented the fact that the game had been played in such awful conditions. He remembered that at one point he had to turn his face out of a puddle when at the bottom of a ruck to avoid the prospect of drowning! Perhaps fourteen–eighteen had been an appropriate score line when you consider that the Lions had fought their way out of the trenches with mud on their faces. But in adversity Wainwright had triumphed and he had turned into one of the leaders on the tour. His presence along with the captain Martin Johnson, Ieuan Evans, Tim Rodber, Jason Leonard and Lawrence Dallaglio was proving to be vital. Their character would be needed because the squad could not afford any more performances like the one in East London.

Border had almost emulated one of their finest moments. They beat the Lions back in 1955 and forty-two years later they were about to write another page in the history books. Considering that coach Ian Snook had told us that all he could hope for was respectability, both he and his players must have been delighted with the result. The captain, Ruhan van Zyl, who had legs built like one of the crashing waves coming in off the Indian Ocean, did have some sobering thoughts for the Lions management. Van Zyl said that his advice to the Springbok coach Carel du Plessis would be to take the Lions on in the front five. This statement echoed the words of the Eastern Province captain Jaco Kirsten. The Lions knew that the games and packs they would face would get harder and harder. Their forwards had been stung into action in the final fifteen minutes but had not taken control before that point. It had almost proved to be too late.

One of the nicest moments of the day came in John Bentley's after-match interview with our reporter Phil Edwards. Bentley had asked whether it would be possible to mention his wife and young children at the end of the piece. 'No problem,' Phil said, because he, like us all, was deeply missing his family and loved ones. They got towards the end of the interview and in the heat of the moment Bentley was about to forget to say those crucial words. Despite the instruction to hand back to the studio, Phil kindly asked one more question about people back home who just might be watching. Bentley's eyes lit up with gratitude and he sent home an 'I love you' message, which we all identified with.

To top it all, the showers in the dressing room failed to work on this of all days. The Lions were forced to go back to the hotel for a wash. Once again, Stan Bagshaw was the man of the hour: although he made the receptionists' jaws drop by hauling sack after sack of dirty laundry off the coach. His quick thinking and warm words made all the difference. The title Baggage Master may not seem a very grand one, but Stan was responsible for some of the most important elements of the trip. His tasks included making sure of the check-in arrangements at the hotels and ensuring that six extra-long beds were supplied for some of the taller members of the squad. There had to be medical rooms set aside and the coach and assistant coach had to be next door to each other. It was all a logistical nightmare which needed to be planned like a military operation with the sole aim of creating the perfect environment. Now all we had to do was play better rugby.

The Lions just wanted to wash those nightmare conditions out of their system. It was a day to forget. Two games played and two games won, but neither in the manner which suggested there were great things to come. There had been flashes of brilliance and expertise in both matches, but the Lions had to dig deep to find the resolve to come out of problem situations. The sobering thought was that the chance to obtain a 'get out of jail free' card comes more easily against Eastern Province and Border than the likes of Natal and Gauteng.

After another long call home, it was time to leave East London. Inevitably the sun came out on the morning of our departure and the whole place lit up. Sadly we had not seen the city at its best. Southport on a wet day is how I described it to Fran Cotton and Cotton, a man of the Northwest, did not disagree. (I have nothing against Southport, in fact Helen and I have had many romantic walks on the sands there, but like most seaside places it does not put on the Sunday best when the clouds are grey and the precipitation is horizontal.)

The whole squad were looking forward to our next destination: Cape Town, one of the most beautiful cities of the world. The food and wine would reach new heights and, hopefully, so would the rugby. Western Province posed the Lions a major threat. Province had faxed over their team just before we left East London. I showed it to Ian McGeechan and his knowing smile said it all. The first major examination awaited and the coach was eager to put all the hard work to the test. As Fran Cotton said, 'We know that we've got a great bunch of lads, now we will see how good they are as rugby players.' The good news was that the players wanted to find out as well.

The flight to Cape Town was one of the most enjoyable journeys that I can remember. The skies were clear and the anticipation of the view of the approach into the city was all consuming. At the end of two hours in the air, the sights were simply wonderful. All around the rugged mountains carved an opening in the landscape almost drawing you through this trail of beauty. It is hard not to be mesmerised by the stunning splendour of the multi-coloured rock. The russet ground and green fields down below blended together to look like an elaborate tile mosaic fit enough to grace the finest country residence.

On nearing the runway, though, a devastating contrast was provided by the underprivileged townships which still sadly surround Cape Town. It makes you rue the fact that you ever fell in love with the place. Feelings of immense guilt spring from the realisation that such a vision of loveliness lives hand in hand with such despair and devastation. If I was a Capetonian I hope I would find it intolerable to the point where I would have to act and not sit passively. As an infrequent visitor, I suppose I tell myself that it's not my problem and that deep down I don't sufficiently understand the history of the Cape area or the people. It is easier to say it is not mine to meddle in. Ultimately, for the casual traveller, a trip to Cape Town is nothing more than a raunchy affair: you can get what you want in a passionate fling with a seductive city. Then, having 'loved it', you can 'leave it', safe in the knowledge that you saw the best while some others have to live and deal with the worst.

The city was bidding for the 2004 Olympic Games and in doing so was using the slogan, 'If Cape Town wins, we all win.' There is no doubt that the cardboard version of the city, which sprawls alongside the main route in from the airport to the centre, would have to go if any bid proved successful. It wouldn't do for all the VIPs to have to speed pass the 'in-dignitaries' on their way into town. The countdown to the bid decision was big news in Cape Town and it was to be hoped that if they did win, then what used to be one of sport's great unifying forces, the Olympics, might just provide some help. The commercial muscle of the modern Games could on this occasion provide something more than just another round of Coca-Cola adverts and big cheques to the already fat cats.

We were there, of course, to see another form of cat, the Lions, and they hardly roared into town following the indifferent performance against Border. This was to be a harder task altogether and that view was solid-ified on arrival at Western Province training on the Thursday afternoon. Stuart, the producer, Piers Croton, and I had been allowed into a session to spot the faces of some of the lesser-known players. We didn't struggle to identify James Small, though, and the word was that Small was fit and raring to prove to the selectors that he was the right man for one of the spots on the wing in the Test team. Small looked sharp, and along with the other Springbok international in the back-line, Justin Swart, gave the team genuine pace. Province were equally well served in the pack by international forwards Fritz van Heerden, Gary Pagel, Keith Andrews and Robbie Brink, even though this was not thought to be their strong area. After allowing us to watch the training session for about half an hour, the Province coach, Harry Viljoen, wanting to keep some moves up his sleeve, politely asked us to leave. They are a team who tradi-tionally look to entertain and, with the azure skies above and the forecast set fair for the weekend, the Lions were going to have to be at their most alert.

The Lions had announced their team just as our plane was leaving East London. The side was as follows – Stimpson, Evans, Guscott, Tait, Bentley, Townsend, Howley, Rowntree, Williams, Leonard, Johnson (captain), Shaw, Dallaglio, Hill and Rodber. At last captain Martin Johnson had been unwrapped from his protective packaging. Tim Rodber had also avoided injury for a week and the unlucky Northampton captain must have been the most relieved man in the party when the medics finally gave him the all clear. Rodber would have to put in an awesome display if he were to dislodge Quinnell and Miller from the Test reckoning.

The most striking feature to that team was the lack of a recognised goalkicker, or at least that was the case at the start of the tour. Dave Alred had been working hard with a select but not so small band of merry men eager to shoot their arrow. This group included Tim Stimpson and Gregor Townsend. The thinking for the Test team was now becoming clearer. Both front-line goalkickers, Jenkins and Grayson, had been exposed in the first two matches: Jenkins for a lack of pace at full-back and Grayson for a lack of composure at stand-off. Stimpson had hit the line well from full-back and Townsend had shown the kind of touches that others on the tour were not capable of producing. One of them had to kick and Stimpson would start on Saturday.

For the Lions read England as far as the pack was concerned. Only Welshman Barry Williams broke a line of roses planted to create a blanket of English colour. Ian McGeechan joked that Williams had already started to lose his accent. The English forwards were set to raid the sweet shop of selection and a pattern seemed to be emerging; hopefully they would win the ball and the tries would then be scored by the rest.

Friday, 30 May started well. There aren't many days in your life when the first thing you see is a shaft of early morning sunlight shining down on Table Mountain. The night had been chilly and, as is typical of South Africa, the day gradually grew warm. As the sun gets stronger, the mountain turns from subtle shades of red to the fiery hard tones of midday. When the sun starts to weaken, the light softens, and a haze shrouds the mountain in mystery before it goes to sleep in the darkness of evening. Don't let me ever moan again on this tour about living out of a suitcase!

That said, I left the lunch-time news conference wondering why I had bothered. Nothing of any note came out of the questioning. In the tension before a big match, players and management were even more guarded than is normally the case. At that point I should have returned to the hotel to continue my commentary preparation, but instead I went to a bank to change some traveller's cheques. This proved to be a big error – and with one of those twists of fate, I came face to face with a wasp. If only it had been Lawrence Dallaglio and not one of South Africa's finest hornet wasps. It had the body of a bird and a sting to match. It decided that my neck was fair game and sank its weapon as far in as it could go. I was left hopping around in a busy street causing much amusement to the shoppers of Claremont. Now, because I'm male, I immediately considered the possibility of instant death due to the bite of a wild African creature that obviously should have been extinct long ago. How this insect had travelled to the inner city of Cape Town and whether its valiant journey was worthy of respect, I did not take time to consider. My only thought was to seek medical advice at the first available opportunity. After all kinds of commotion in the hotel, convinced I was breathing my last breath, I was directed to a local doctor, who removed the offending sting and anaesthetised my entire neck – some would say all this was rather dramatic, I say too right – all for eighty rand. But the moral of the story is clear: change your money before the wasp gets you!

There was just time to compose myself after this traumatic ordeal before an interview with the South African tearaway winger, James Small. He had come to our hotel, the Vineyard, to gather for a pre-match meeting and meal with the rest of the Western Province team and he was happy to discuss the prospects for the game. Small is a bit of a bohemian and in recent years he had enjoyed Cape Town's unique nightlife to the full. He is a notoriously bad timekeeper and true to form he was running late. His general inability to play things by the book had cost him his South African Test place. The authorities have not always warmed to the ways of Small, but I instantly liked his manner. He was laid-back and charismatic, looking like something off the front of an album cover in his trendy clothes. But he was level-headed about his form and thought that he had little to prove to the selectors. The game against the Lions was being billed as a make or break match for Small, but he was just looking forward to putting on a show for the big home crowd and not for the men in power. He also thought that there was better to come from the Lions and that it was wrong to jump to any hasty conclusions this early in the tour. Fair enough. After the match against Small's team, we would all know a whole lot more about the Lions of '97. The doubts set off by the narrow mid-week victory would be compounded by a defeat to Province. The mind games could be won and lost in Cape Town.

Newlands is a peerless place to watch rugby. It is the oldest rugby field in South Africa and the memories of the past are enshrined perfectly in a modern stadium that was deemed an appropriate place to start the 1995 World Cup. The ground has an intense, claustrophobic feel and there is nowhere else in the country where the crowd get more actively involved in the game. The stands seem to walk in over the pitch and breathe history on the players down below. Cape Town also know how to throw a party and this attitude is fully apparent in their rugby.

The morning of the game was another gorgeous one, with the mountain looking as proud as ever, but it was a mountain of a different kind that the Lions were hoping would make an impact in Johnson's first opening on the tour. His presence was central to the overall master plan and he was about to play for the first time. It was a big moment for the Lions. Johnson cares passionately about his rugby but he pays little attention to the media's viewpoint. He went on the offensive in the build-up to the match against Western Province. Following another bout of questions concerning the accusations from the opposition that the Lions forwards had not started well, Johnson hit back and said the squad was out to achieve its own goals and that it didn't really matter if the South African or British press had different ideas as to how things were going. Those around the squad were certainly aware of what was being said about them because the Media Liaison Officer, Bob Burrows, was receiving faxes of articles from back home. This was the first sign of a siege mentality, and there was no doubt in my mind that if things started to go sour on the field and the articles became increasingly less complimentary, then the captain would lead the retreat away from the crossfire. Either way, this match would be closely scrutinised by all parties.

The atmosphere around the stadium had the aura of a big occasion. The colourful stalls on the side streets were doing good business selling the blue and white colours of Province and the multi-coloured scarves and flags of the rainbow nation. The calamari burgers were sizzling away on the hot plates and the Castle lager was beginning to flow. People were arriving in some rather unconventional ways, precariously hanging off the back of trailers. They had come in their thousands to see the Lions and the expectation was for a high-scoring game.

Locating the commentary box was, as ever, my first job and I was delighted to again discover a viewing point over the half-way line in pole position. It was then time to head off to the dressing-room area to check the teams and to make sure that there had not been any late changes. This is a vital task and the effort once again paid dividends: Western Province had switched around the jerseys for their numbers six and seven. Later in the match when number six Robbie Brink crossed the line for a try, I was grateful for that time spent correcting the numbers before kick off. Moreover, to be down in this inner sanctum just minutes before the start of a big game is another one of the great privileges of the job. In these moments you see the raw emotion of the final few minutes before the action begins. I passed John Bentley as he came out of the Lions' dressing room and saw the desire etched on his face.

The Bentley versus Small confrontation was going to be one of the most appetising offerings on a full menu. They didn't let us down and it was Bentley who struck first blood by scoring the Lions' opening try, just as he had done three days earlier. It was no more than the Lions deserved because they had come out all guns blazing for the third time on tour and again they had rocked back the opposition. But like before, they couldn't keep it going. Province began to work their way back into the match. Surprisingly, it was the Province forwards who started to get control. Remember, no fewer than seven of the English pack were playing for the Lions that day, but in the scrum they were pushed back by Province, with home props Gary Pagel and Keith Andrews making their mark.

The referee, Arrie Schoonwinkel, didn't help the game. He was one of the most pedantic officials that I have ever been unfortunate enough to see in such whistle-happy action. On one occasion, he called back Gregor Townsend to take a re-start for a second time because the ball for the drop kick had not landed exactly on the half-way line. Schoonwinkel translated from Afrikaans literally means 'shoe shop', and I wondered during the commentary whether our referee would be better off peddling some leather uppers as opposed to meddling with rugby matches and sticking his size twelves where they weren't wanted. But the Lions could thank the referee for one lapse. He failed to give the home team a try after the ball had been legally grounded following a charged down kick.

The Lions were also grateful to Tim Stimpson who took a giant step towards solving the biggest problem of the tour. Stimpson kicked his goals and his eighteen point haul was one of the most satisfying aspects of the day. Gregor Townsend, who had a much better all-round game at fly-half, was now free to do his own thing. It wasn't a kicking match and the policy from both sides to run the ball resulted in a thoroughly entertaining afternoon.

The Lions knew that victory was vital, but, in a repeat of the Eastern Province and Border performances, they had to drag themselves back from the cliff edge of defeat. At the moment when a loss seemed more than possible, there was a piece of skill which I will remember for a long time. Robert Howley picked up the ball and ran like a hare away from the Province cover. It was a burst of pace and a piece of vision with world class stamped all over it. For a moment, it seemed as if a young Gareth Edwards had been dragged back onto the field. Howley drew the final man before releasing his fellow countryman Ieuan Evans and Evans finished in his own inimitable way. When the try was scored I gleefully screamed, 'Everyone in Wales will bottle that moment!' At that point you could see the hope drain away from the faces of the home team.

Other tries by Alan Tait, who further increased the options at centre with an excellent performance, and John Bentley with his second, took the Lions to safety and a memorable win was recorded. The final score was Western Province twenty-one, the Lions thirty-eight. It all showed what the Lions were made of and it was a display to make the South African critics sit up and take note. But this was not to say that it was all good news. Indeed, the English roses had wilted quite alarmingly up front and had the Province coach Harry Viljoen not taken off his prop Gary Pagel with over twenty minutes still to go, then the outcome could have been so different. More fuel had been added to the fire concerning the lack of forward power in the Lions squad. The Lions were in for some more tough talking from Jim Telfer over the weeks ahead. The irony was that the scrum wasn't expected to be an area for concern. Yet another defeated South African, the Province number eight, Andrew Aitken, said it was easy to see where the Lions could be taken on and beaten. We were getting used to hearing that after-match assessment.

In other aspects, though, the Lions were learning quickly. At the post-match news conference, Ian McGeechan said they were starting to get used to playing under immense pressure and having to concentrate on their skills more than at any time previously in their rugby lives. Martin Johnson said that the game at Newlands compared favourably with the Five Nations experience. He added that domestic internationals are played at a similar pace but not with the same skill level. It was a steep learning curve for the Lions, and although they had three times fallen away in the middle of a match, each time they had come through with a win, which was giving the side confidence. Now they had done it against a more recognised outfit and, according to Robert Howley, 'Newlands was where the tour began for real.'

My one abiding memory of that day, though, was the confrontation between Small and Bentley. Bentley had got that opening score, but Small evened things up when, with an injection of blistering pace, he left Bentley behind and decided to rub it in with one or two mocking gestures. After this, Bentos, as he was now commonly known on tour, hauled his opposite number into touch with such ferocity that Small took exception to it and clearly lost his temper. Bentley, sensing he was now on top, rounded off the victory with the final try and went looking for Small to make sure that the South African knew that the last laugh belonged to the Yorkshireman. Small refused to shake Bentley's hand at the end of the game. Seconds were out and round two was eagerly awaited.

The Lions had got through another game relatively unscathed but we woke up to the depressing news on the Sunday morning that Paul Grayson, who had struggled so badly in the match against Border, was to fly home because of injury. The outside-half was understandably devastated and it was sad to see him staring at the departures board at the airport. Considering Grayson's thigh problem and how this had obviously affected his form, it was a blessing that the Lions could call on Mike Catt. It also gave the Lions more options at full-back as well as fly-half; and, in my opinion, their hand was strengthened and not weakened by the change. I had seen Catt at the Sky Sports Lions launch in the City of London shortly before flying out for the tour. He was getting ready to go to Argentina with England. I joked and said, 'I'll see you in South Africa,' because Catt must have been at the top of the stand-by list. In the meantime, Catt had played his part by putting in some reportedly excellent shows for England. He was unlucky to miss out on the Lions tour in the first place and now he had the chance to prove that he should always have been there.

We flew out of Cape Town to Johannesburg before making the short drive on to Pretoria. This would be the Lions' base for the next eleven nights. On the flight I sat next to Martin Johnson. He along with manager Fran Cotton and coach Ian McGeechan came in for a lot of stick from the players, because the leaders had been upgraded to business class, along with the Sky team – it's a tough life! Having said that, someone the size of Johnson makes even those comfortable executive seats seem far too small. The Lions captain was in fairly upbeat mood after his side's win and was pleased with the exciting spells of innovative back play and forward movement. He had also enjoyed Cape Town and had managed to find time to drive out to take in some of the scenery. He was clearly in South Africa to do a job, though, and sightseeing was not top of his list of objectives. Johnson declined the food and wine offered by the crew and made sure that he stuck religiously to the team's strict diet. The sobriety of the squad knew no bounds. When we had dined with the Lions in East London, Fran Cotton had pointed out that he had never eaten so healthily. Being around the players he had felt compelled to try and stick to the right things. But Big Fran did not turn down his in-flight meal, this would have been too much of a sacrifice. (Anyway the players at the back of the plane couldn't see him eating because of that wretched curtain that divides the passengers on an aircraft.) Nonetheless, I could not help thinking that the professional age had changed tours out of all recognition. The constant daily rounds of training, video watching and team meetings required total commitment. It was a sobering thought, perhaps quite literally, that the 'orange juice tour' had come of age.

It was important to remember, though, that the week had ended on a downer. Following our arrival in Pretoria, I walked into the hotel lift where I met Paul Grayson. He had been sorting out his laundry before facing the trip that he didn't want to make. He said that he knew the game was up after he had felt the injury during the early minutes of the match in East London. A Lion he had been, but the memories were short and the journey home would be a long and lonely one. Credit must go to Jeremy Guscott and Jason Leonard who sat with Grayson in the bar that night and no doubt tried to come up with the right words.

WEEK 3

BOSMAN'S RULING AND A LOAD OF BULLS

'The Lions must realise that the scrum is not just a way of restarting a game.' – Victorious Northern Transvaal coach John Williams on the continued need for the Lions to get the basics right

Honesty was going to be at the heart of this week. The Lions had to face up to the reasons behind their poor tactics in Border and the overpowering of their forwards in Cape Town. Tours don't allow much time to sort out these difficulties; the decisions have to be quick and therefore sometimes harsh. Injured players are expected to offer a sincere assessment of their fitness and those not showing the right kind of form must also do the decent thing and accept the situation. The climate being created by the management meant that the whole squad felt they were in it together. The fact that they were constantly being told that there were no dirt-trackers also allowed individuals to come to terms with their initial thoughts of rejection and to come out fighting to win back their place. With the mind having been set in the right mode, the body would be better prepared to cope with the physical challenge expected from the next opponents. Only the players themselves knew how deep this ran and, in quieter moments, many probably dreamt about sticking pins into an effigy of their main competitor. They would not have been human if they hadn't, but this would be a week when it would be good to have fourteen mates on the field!

Waking up to the neon lights of a TGIFriday's restaurant outside your window was not quite the same as a Table Mountain view, but we were in Pretoria now and would not return to Cape Town until the week before the first Test. The wounded Paul Grayson would not go back to Cape Town at all. He had been booked on the Virgin Atlantic flight due to arrive back in Heathrow on Tuesday, 3 June. Meanwhile, Mike Catt was coming the other way: he would arrive from Argentina via Brazil and would land in time on Wednesday to be whisked away to the game against Mpumalanga, the next on the tour.

Catt's release by England had been a foregone conclusion because of the unwritten rule that the Lions had first call. I would have given a lot of money to eavesdrop, as the conversation between Fran Cotton and the England coach, Jack Rowell, must have been an interesting one, to say the least. Cotton said that Rowell was keen to keep hold of Catt until after the second Test match against Argentina. But Cotton knew that, although this might have helped England, it would be nonsense for the Lions. He needed Catt to arrive as soon as possible and the player's blazer was already being called for from Twickenham, where it had been hanging in readiness. There were stories of a rift between Cotton and Rowell, but the Lions manager was adamant that no argument had taken place, asserting that the delay in Catt's arrival had been caused by the England coach taking time to consider his options.

There were also rumours flying around concerning the long-term fitness of another one of the Lions backs, Nick Beal, who had been suffering from tendonitis; but he was given a chance to prove that he was match fit when he was named as part of the team to play in Witbank on the Wednesday. The team read – Beal, Evans, Bateman, Greenwood, Underwood, Jenkins, Dawson, Smith, Wood, Wallace, Weir, Davidson, Wainwright, Back and Rodber (captain).

Tim Rodber became the fourth captain of the tour in only the fourth match. The policy was to tap into the high level of experience of a number of the senior professionals and to spread the honour of captaincy around to further promote the bonding in the team. Rodber had been substituted in the match against Western Province and, as legs tired, his removal from the field had allowed Scott Quinnell to come on and make an impact. Regardless, Rodber would thrive on the role of skipper and understandably he looked a proud man at the news conference to announce his appointment. He also bristled at the suggestion that sooner or later a dirt-trackers mid-week team would start to emerge. Rodber washed his mouth out at the very mention of the 'd' phrase. There was no distinction between a first and second team. This was commendable, but everybody knew that in the week before the first Test it would become apparent who was being earmarked for places in the series. The cream would eventually rise to the top and some of the combinations being chosen were starting to show the management thinking. For example, the trio – Smith, Wood and Wallace – would get a chance to stake their claim as a unit.

On the injury front, Scott Gibbs was running again following his ankle injury, but Eric Miller had damaged a nerve in one cheek. He had been advised to rest and not to take any facial contact over the next couple of days. Miller was a vital part of the squad and his versatile presence in the back-row kept all members of that particular union on their toes. He was not a player the management wanted to lose.

Training on that Monday morning had been a lively affair. This was predictable, considering the questions asked of the pack in Saturday's nail-biting win over Western Province. Jim Telfer had read the riot act and the air had been blue with vocal encouragement. There were forty-six scrums against the scrummaging machine in just forty minutes. Telfer admitted that he had never witnessed such a ferocious session. He wanted honest players who could 'look themselves in the mirror' after a work-out. He had identified a technical fault in the scrum, feeling that the second-rows were not getting down into the right driving position. Consequently, the props were finding their job to be even more difficult. If anyone knew what he was talking about it was the Scot, and he viewed that morning of hell for the players as 'money in the bank'.

The squad were being trained at altitude for the first time, which caused its own set of problems. Lungs were hurting and throats were dry, but, after a spell of agony, the players felt that they had ridden through the worst. Ian McGeechan said that there is now evidence to suggest that the body can adjust to the rigours of altitude within a couple of days, so in one fell swoop the coach had ruled out the thin air as an excuse, should his team face a reverse over the next ten day period when they were to play in Witbank, Pretoria and Johannesburg.

That scrum work-out could have had major implications for the rest of the tour but the main story of the day concerned an accusation from James Small that John Bentley had been guilty of eye gouging during the match at Newlands. Small claimed that Bentley had 'fingered him in the eye when he was defenceless'. On reading the morning newspapers, Bentley had gone up to Fran Cotton's room to put the manager straight with his side of the story. The Lions winger denied any wrongdoing and Cotton was clearly incensed by the reports. 'We are here to talk about rugby and not to massage James Small's ego,' was Cotton's response to questioning at that day's news conference. Cotton also felt that Small was trying to disguise the fact that he had a pretty average game. I watched the video of the incident closely and, although Small was clearly hurt, there was no evidence that Bentley had been the perpetrator. As Andy Irvine later said in our studio, 'Bentley is a hard man but he's no thug.' It was the first hint of a controversy on the tour: the Lions had started to make South Africa sit up and take note with that win in Cape Town and the quarrel reflected the way in which the trip was now gathering pace.

The clock was now ticking towards the big days at the end of the tour. Enticingly, the Bentley–Small confrontation was on schedule for another instalment, because Small was one of the twenty-seven players announced in the South African international squad for the match against Tonga and then the Test series against the Lions. The selectors' doubts about Small's temperament obviously had been left aside. As regards the rest of the squad, I was surprised to see no Hennie Le Roux or Kobus Wiese named by coach Carel du Plessis. In my opinion, Le Roux had tested the Lions when he represented Eastern Province in the opening match of the tour. Wiese had not played so well that day, but had been hindered by some poor throwing into the line-out. Both men possessed the necessary experience to make an impact on the big stage and the immediate reaction to their exclusion was to talk about a possible move out of South African rugby to ply their trade in England.

Moreover, the home nation, while obviously having an abundance of talent in key positions such as full-back, half-back and back-row, were short of options should injuries start to occur. There was little doubting the class of the likes of Joubert, Van der Westhuizen, Honiball, Kruger, Venter or Teichmann, but, although a Springbok squad can never be described as weak, I had seen stronger and sensed a period of transition. Looking at the Springbok squad on paper, I felt the Lions had a chance if they could continue their progression.

Travelling around the country on the Lions' tail was an experience which at times became a 'mission impossible', let me explain. Sky News had requested a copy of the Paul Grayson interview about his departure from the tour. We decided that the quickest way to send the tape back to London was as air freight from Johannesburg airport. Now, finding your way around most airports is often highly confusing, but getting around Jan Smuts airport makes exploring the Congo look easy. We circled the airport roads like a plane endlessly waiting to be called in by air traffic control. Then, having eventually got to the courier office, we were told that it wasn't possible to get the tape to London for at least two days. After a few frantic phone calls, we decided to throw in the towel. But then we were told that there was a local contact who might have been able to help us. The trouble was, this contact was not contactable!

We left the airport and got on the road to Pretoria. About thirty kilometres down the motorway the mobile phone rang and we were informed that a man called Barry would meet us back at the airport to take charge of the package. We swung the vehicle around and headed back at full tilt, only to sit and wait for him to arrive in what was now not only a remote but a deserted car park. It was like a scene from a movie. We were looking out for a white BMW and would make the drop-off at an appointed time and place. Goodness knows what the security cameras were picking up. This white 'Beamer' rolled silently into the car park. The driver circled around and then spotted our lonesome Kombi sitting furtively in wait. The door opened slowly and out stepped a shadowy figure. How would we know it was Barry? Perhaps we should have asked him to carry a copy of the *Financial Times*. After a few seconds, the handover took place and we sped away into the night. (I still think we should have added a note to Sky News saying that, after they had played the insert on their bulletin, the tape would self-destruct in five seconds.)

All this horseplay amongst the team helped pass some of the more humdrum moments but we had reached the two week barrier on the tour – the point of stark realisation that we had been away from home for a whole fortnight and still had five weeks on the road. I must admit I was feeling quite homesick at this juncture and was counting down the days to when Helen would join me. The phone calls home were getting longer and, although I was doing the job I loved, I was not with the one I loved. Hotel rooms can be luxurious but lonely places. The extremes of emotion were sometimes difficult to balance. On the one hand I was having the time of my working life, but on the other I felt that I wanted to share it with those that mattered and they were a long way away.

There is, however, always someone with a predicament to make your own situation seem trivial. Take that of the Welsh hooker Barry Williams, who had made such a good start to his tour. He must have been going through some incredible emotional highs and lows. Williams was loving every minute of the trip and why not? His unexpected selection had thrown him into the limelight and he had grasped the opportunity. His move from Neath to Richmond had been announced right at the start of the tour and he told me that this necessitated a house move from Wales to England on his return. He was also in the midst of rearranging his marriage, postponed because of the Lions tour, which would take place as soon as he got back. Williams had a lot on his plate, but his smile was as wide as the Welsh valleys. Here was a man on top of the world who decided to take his mind off all the pressures by seeing INXS in concert in Pretoria – well, each to their own! Due to his excellent efforts on the field, Williams was getting in line for a Test place. Keith Wood was ahead in the fight for the honour of wearing the number two jersey, but it was close.

Another man who was now starting to be talked about as a likely member of the initial Test side was full-back Tim Stimpson. Following his fine kicking display at Newlands, I caught up with Stimpson on the hotel terrace in Pretoria. I was interested to find out what was going through the mind of a man who was on the verge of making his dream come true. Stimpson reflected on the fact that this trip to South Africa was a world apart from a previous tour as a schoolboy. Then, the young Stimpson had been actively encouraged to spend as much time as possible going out and about to learn more of the country and the people. In 1997, Stimpson the man was focused on the professional job at hand. He was happy to attend a small number of receptions but felt it was important to keep the extracurricular activities to a manageable level. For the most part, the players had been given the opportunity to regulate their own free time. They had been treated with respect, and were expected to act responsibly in return.

What about the existence of cliques in the squad? Stimpson was definitely the man to ask about the possible presence of splinter groups because, as a trained anthropologist, he told me he was on the look out for such traits. From the outside, it seemed that very few such groups had formed. All four nations were mixing well and although there were obvious existing friendships from club level, no group seemed to be breaking away from the mass. Stimpson confirmed this impression. He enthused, 'It's a once in a lifetime opportunity to play with the lads who you really respect from the other four home unions. The chance to socialise with these guys as well is fantastic.'

The course of events for Tim Stimpson would be interesting to watch. He was teasingly close to going down in rugby history as the Lions Test full-back of 1997. His immediate aim was to try and hold his kicking form and let nothing deflect him from his goal. Only time would tell if the other aspects of his full-back play were good enough to get him there.

Our own Sky Sports team bonding had taken on a new dimension as we spent an afternoon playing golf. Now, I don't know if you've ever tried to play thirty-six holes in a day, but it is a gruelling experience. The stakes were high as well: to give the match an extra bit of spice we had decided to put some Rand on the table. This was a serious business and we made time to walk the course and take in the various hazards. The first hole was a real tester: a dog-leg bending sharp to the right. It needed a good strike and a steady nerve on the tee. But the course didn't get any easier and water was a common feature. This worries any golfer, whatever the standard, and to cap it all, the eighteenth was virtually unplayable. On this last hole you had to time your stroke to perfection, because if you failed to do so, the windmill came crashing down and threw your ball off the course. Yes, you've guessed it, crazy golf was the game and we were reduced to giggling schoolboys during an afternoon of mayhem and hilarity.

It was great fun and the pressures of work melted away. The only down-side was that as we played one of the holes on the extreme of the course, the Lions' bus pulled up at a set of robots (South African for traffic lights). We tried to cover our faces, but it was too late: at the front of the coach, the real coach, Ian McGeechan, rolled around having a good laugh at our expense.

(By the way, for those of you who have been waiting in breathless anticipation, the Harrison versus Barnes pool match had moved on, taking in Cape Town and now Pretoria. It was an extravaganza of inadequacy the likes of which the cue experts of Africa had never quite seen. Leading by nine frames to five, I was feeling pretty confident, but a Barnes clearance when I had only potted one ball trumpeted his intention not to give up without a fight. Unfortunately, a show of petulance by yours truly meant that we now had to look for a new venue: disgusted by my inability to compete in the final frame, I took a wild swing at the cue ball only to see it bounce off the table and miss the proprietor's shin by a matter of inches. We skulked out of the door fully aware that we could not show our faces in there again. The contest would have to resume in Durban.)

Wednesday, 4 June was the day for a contest of a different kind: the Lions went to play the newly named Mpumalanga Pumas, formerly South East Transvaal. It was also my birthday and, after opening the cards and reading a fax from Helen, I felt a bit soulful. My mood wasn't improved when I discovered that the hotel laundry service had managed to shrink my underpants in the tumble dryer. The commentary that day was all set to be pitched at a higher level than usual!

But I wasn't the only person with clothing on my mind. The representatives of Adidas, the sportswear manufacturer, were trying to sort out the problems with the Lions' kit. I had lost count of the times when shorts had needed to be changed or shirts had been ripped during the opening three matches. Numbers were falling off with alarming regularity and, considering the amount of money invested in kit sponsorship and the revenue which results from such a financial commitment, I was staggered by the inability of the kit to stand up to the rigours of the sport. I admit to having a vested interest here – and that was not intended as a pun. It is vital for both spectators and commentators to be able to see the numbers on the backs of players. There is also nothing more frustrating for the players or the crowd than to stop the flow of the game, not because of injury, but merely to change a jersey or a pair of shorts. I hoped that a solution or at least a needle and thread was going to be found.

After an early breakfast, it was time to set off for Witbank, the home of Mpumalanga. The road across the veld is as straight as anything the Romans had to offer and, after about sixty-five miles of driving through the barren countryside, we got to our destination. Witbank is in the heart of the mining region with over twenty collieries still in operation in the area. Arthur Scargill would be green with envy at the thought of such a thriving industry but the black gold had always been an integral part of the South African economy and there still seemed to be plenty more underground. Unlike some of the old coalfield areas in Britain, though, Witbank is not a pretty place. Quite frankly, it could do with a clean air act and the smog which hung over the town was a depressing pall made for the industrialist and not the tourist. If you are ever in the area, don't hang around. Drive on to the more pleasing scenery of the Lowveld and get to some of the great game parks, which are only a short distance away.

Smog wasn't the only smoke in the air on that day. As we arrived at the ground we could see the braais already sizzling away. Even at ten o'clock in the morning a South African can find room for a sausage or a steak. The crowd started to arrive early because it was a big day for the locals, the first time ever that they had welcomed the Lions. Of course, this kind of occasion is what touring is all about. After the splendour of Newlands on Saturday, we had moved out in the sticks. Off the pitch the initial welcome was friendly, but the locals' desire for notoriety on the field of play was all consuming. The home team had a reputation for being one of the toughest in the country. The Lions knew they were in for a physical and torrid afternoon. The posters advertising the match said it all – it was the battle of the wild cats, the Pumas against the Lions. The claws were set to come out.

The stadium was basic but comfortable and compared favourably with many grounds back home. The striking feature was a preponderance of wooden chalet-style hospitality sheds which were built on stilts and were placed haphazardly all around the ground. They looked like a cross between a Scandinavian sauna and a hut on Eastbourne beach, and were all packed with guests who were becoming increasingly under the influence of the local brew. The crowd was a lively one, perhaps too lively. I got a first-hand taste when Stuart and I were down on the pitch setting the scene from the stadium. At the time, their reaction was reasonably jocular; but a little later, some of the abuse hurled at our cameraman, Leon Hagen, was not repeatable. I was relieved that he was wearing headphones. If only they had known he was South African, they would not have thrown him into this verbal bear pit. The Lions were in for a tough afternoon unless they got on top of the opposition, and therefore the spectators, right at the start of the match.

That is exactly what the Lions did. What followed was a near-perfect display that gave us all every reason to think that this Lions squad was becoming a formidable unit. The conditions were perfect for the Lions to play the running game to which they had committed themselves, and within eighteen minutes Rob Wainwright had scored a hat-trick of tries. It was his first trio since university days and the Lions were almost out of sight. It was one of those afternoons when backs and forwards interlinked to produce a performance of stunning quality. Ten tries were scored in all, and Mpumalanga, who had beaten Wales in 1995 by forty-seven points to six, were simply blown away by a far superior team. Mpumalanga is a Zulu word which means 'the place where the sun rises', and the sun had certainly come out to shine on the Lions.

It was one of those team displays which made it very difficult to single out individuals. Nick Beal made a fine attacking contribution at full-back to keep up the pressure on Tim Stimpson and Neil Jenkins. The wingers Evans and Underwood finished moves with real class. Allan Bateman was once again magnificent and the conundrum at centre had reached unfathomable proportions. It would take a brave man to leave Bateman out of any Test side, but the same could have been said of Guscott, Tait, Gibbs and even young Greenwood, who despite one error, when he failed to get the man away on the overlap, put in another mature game. Dawson and Jenkins, looking happier at fly-half, proved that there was back-up at half-back. But most satisfying for the management was the performance of the pack and in particular the scrummage. Telfer's hell on earth session had paid off and the props, Tom Smith and Paul Wallace, not only more than held their own in the scrum, but also offered more around the pitch than any other props had done so far on the tour. In the great scheme of things, these were key contributions.

The rest of the pack all played their part, but if forced to pick a man of the match, then I concur with South African television and go for flanker Neil Back. After the match, he chatted briefly with me and Stuart, and Stuart jibed that during the commentary he had given Back the fanfare only for the Leicester man to immediately miss a tackle. Back responded by pointing out that this was the only tackle that he had missed all day. He was right and he was also correct to assert that his infamous lack of size was best approached as a positive factor on this tour. Back said that he was able to get under the advancing man and tackle from a low position. Few would disagree, having seen him drive back the big Mpumalanga captain Tobie Oosthuizen. On that evidence, Back had given the team another option at openside flanker. He had revelled in the firm ground and told us that he was relieved to have had the chance in the sunshine following the awful conditions in East London.

The key question was what had that performance, a sixty-four points to fourteen win, told us about the overall picture? At the after-match news conference, Will Greenwood had whispered, 'You know they weren't very good, don't you?' It was an honest comment and immediately put the victory into perspective. Mpumalanga were not in the top bracket of South African teams. But Greenwood admitted that to score ten tries in such style against any team on tour was heartening, and the upshot of it all was a number of new selection posers for the management. All of a sudden the Lions had choices to make.

At the start of the tour few had thought that there was genuine competition for places, but after the fourth game this had changed. I believed Howley and Townsend were destined to start the first Test match as the half-backs. In addition, I couldn't see anybody taking the jerseys away from Lawrence Dallaglio, Jeremy Guscott, Ieuan Evans and of course, if fit, the captain, Martin Johnson. But the areas of full-back, the other wing, the other centre, the other lock, both props, hooker, openside flanker and number eight, were much less clear-cut. The two vital ingredients for any successful tour – a close knit squad and rivalry for positions – were now both in the mixing bowl. You could see the edge of competition written in the players' expressions. They knew that the field was widening. As we drove back from Witbank on that cool crisp evening, the stars shone brightly in the clear sky above. Although that was a sight of some beauty, I was more uplifted by the sparkling performances of some other stars who had been in action earlier in the day. The Lions squad was unquestionably moving in the right direction.

There was, however, a massive down-side to what had been an otherwise positive day. We had been warned of the uncompromising style of some of the Mpumalanga players and in particular their two locks, Elandré van den Bergh and Marius Bosman. Both had a reputation of being hard to the point of recklessness. Van den Bergh had been involved in the aforementioned battle of Boet Erasmus and it was unlikely that he was on Jonathan Callard's Christmas card list. Callard had required multiple stitching following an incident in that match in Port Elizabeth in 1994. Bosman also had a history of losing his cool on the pitch, and during the match in Witbank both men were lucky to stay on the field considering some of their acts with the boot. On this day, it was Bosman's stray foot which caused the major problem as, with inexcusable cruelty, he perpetrated an act of violence which television replays did little to improve. Doddie Weir was standing on the edge of a ruck when Bosman took it upon himself to walk over to the Scot and kick out viciously at his knee. Weir hopped away in pain, as if he had been caught in a mantrap, and soon dropped to the floor. The other Lions players watched in disbelief. Staggeringly, it all happened in front of the referee, Carl Spannenburg, who felt that a caution was sufficient punishment. This had to be woefully inadequate for what was a wanton act of barbarism which had no place on a rugby field.

Weir suffered severe knee ligament damage courtesy of Bosman's unwanted attention and was forced out of the tour. When Weir lay on the floor injured, the Lions management reacted furiously and during the commentary the message came up from the bench that Ian McGeechan wanted to cite Bosman for his actions. In our after-match interview,

McGeechan reiterated this intention, but later, in the news conference, he retracted it. He did so, though, only because, as the referee had taken action during the match by awarding a penalty, this option was not available to the touring team. But his anger had not been diminished and Fran Cotton made it clear that the Lions would report the incident to SARFU. He made the point that everybody in rugby shares the responsibility for seeing that players are disciplined for such acts.

I found the defence of Bosman by the home team's management at the news conference as nothing short of incredible. It was their initial opinion that both major incidents, the one involving Bosman on Weir and another when Van den Bergh was accused of stamping, were unintentional. This was straight out of fantasy land. Admittedly, Bosman may not have meant to hurt Weir to the extent he did, but he must have been aware that the consequences could have been catastrophic. The Mpumalanga management did promise, however, to study the video evidence. Surely, in the light of such irrefutable proof they would act in the best interests of the game. Talking to Fran Cotton after the news conference it was clear that he would not let the matter rest and the injury to Weir had ruined an otherwise super day for the Lions.

On a personal level, the commentary on that game had got me thinking about where I should stand editorially during the tour. The Lions had played to such a high standard and with such flair that I admit to getting wrapped up in their performances. I thought Robert Howley's break to set Ieuan Evans free at Newlands was the highlight of the tour to date and thought I would find it very difficult to get more excited than I had done at that moment. But in Witbank, when Allan Bateman brought in Evans off the right wing to put Tony Underwood on his way to score in the left hand corner, it was such a heavenly move I did get a bit carried away, screaming, 'You beauty!' when Underwood put the ball down.

The whole incident brought to my attention a professional dilemma which was starting to emerge. I was British and I was broadcasting to a British and Irish audience, so surely I was entitled to let it go a little. But it is always a dangerous game, and not one that I feel comfortable playing. All too soon, the commentator can sacrifice journalistic principles and clearly side with one team. To go that far would be wrong.

I reminded myself of some of the famous partisan commentaries of the past. We all remember Brian Johnston rejoicing in England's regaining of the Ashes at the Oval. Nobody would claim that Kenneth Wolstenholme was anything but pro-England in the 1966 World Cup final. Ron Pickering ran every step and leapt every jump for Mary Peters in Munich, and more recently, Barry Davies memorably asked the question, 'Where was the German defence?' only to come up with his own response, 'But frankly, who cares?' when Great Britain won the hockey gold medal in Seoul. Those great broadcasters could not all be wrong.

I concluded that I had to reflect what was going through the minds of our audience and that my obvious enthusiasm over Lions tries and concern over opposition scores and dirty play was entirely acceptable on a tour like this one. What I had to avoid was a flag-waving partisan style of commentary which would ignore the abilities of the other team and create a 'them and us' situation. I had to refrain from saying 'we' and had to reserve the right to be critical as well as complimentary. I know it sounds trite, but even if South Africa went on to win the series, I would still go home happy if the rugby played had been of such high quality that the sport had been the ultimate winner. As a rule, one of the main objectives of a commentator is to iron out any personal prejudice and be the impartial observer. I resolved to trust my patriotic and journalistic instincts and hope for the best.

The day after the night before revealed further anger in the Lions' camp over rugby's version of the Bosman case. Fran Cotton said that the Lions would not be taking any further action just yet, but they had made it abundantly clear to the local union in Mpumalanga that they wanted to see the union respond within seven days. If they failed to do so, the Lions would reconsider their position.

The Lions wanted to see steps taken against both the loose cannons in the Mpumalanga second-row, Bosman and Van den Bergh, and the legal implications were far reaching. Rugby is now having to come to terms with the fact that no longer can such incidents be swept under the carpet. Livelihoods are at stake and careers are on the line. Furthermore, to set standards that can be judged favourably by the outside world, rugby has to accept that, as a professional sport, it has an obligation to not only the players and officials inside the game, but also to those who pay money to watch or are considering taking up the sport. Sport can no longer be played in isolation. Part of the beauty of rugby is its aggression, but it must be positive and clean. Nobody would want to take the physical aspect away from the game, but certain acts are intolerable and the authorities at whatever level must be seen to be firm in their response. I feel very strongly about this, and if rugby is to keep out of the courts, it must not shirk the responsibility. If it does, few could argue if outside legal influences become a regular feature of the modern game.

Certainly in the current age of television coverage very little is missed by the cameras. Many believe this is harmful, but I feel that such scrutiny is a good thing. Fran Cotton agrees. 'Quite rightly, these incidents get extensive coverage,' he said. It was a sickening sight for the

Lions management to re-examine the Weir injury taking place, but it had to be done in order to cement their opinion. They wanted justice to be done.

Doddie Weir cut a forlorn figure sitting by the pool at the hotel. He knew that his tour was over and a scan later that Thursday afternoon revealed that the ligament damage to his left knee was worse than first thought. The early diagnosis was that he would be out of the game for at least six months. In financial terms, Weir was cruelly denied the chance to earn money from the rest of the tour, but, although his pocket was hurt, it was his heart that was really aching.

Weir was to leave the squad on the Saturday evening and, on learning of the news from the specialist, he had retired to his room too distraught to comment. We were asked to respect his privacy and give him twenty-four hours to come to terms with it all. The news from Mpumalanga was that they were probably going to take some action, but, in a rather pathetic 'tit for tat' response, they claimed that a tackle from the Lions' Nick Beal deserved investigation. This was dismissed by the Lions straightaway.

The man chosen to replace Weir was the experienced international Nigel Redman of Bath, who had already got a surprise call-up to the England squad for their trip to Argentina. Redman left Buenos Aires just like his club colleague Mike Catt and arrived in a state of some shock. The England coach Jack Rowell had wanted to keep hold of Redman for the second Test, which was due to take place at the weekend. But as with Catt, the Lions management pressed the go button and called Redman straight over. There were a number of locks who had not been considered because of injury, such as Ireland's Paddy Johns and England's Gareth Archer and Martin Bayfield, who had both missed out on the Argentina trip. The possibility of moving Tim Rodber up into the second-row and calling for a back-row replacement was considered, but this was rejected because of the adverse effect it might have had on Rodber's confidence. So it was Redman, who had played his first international for England back in 1984, who arrived in South Africa on the day before the Lions match with Northern Transvaal at Loftus Versfeld on Saturday, 7 June.

According to Ian McGeechan, this match would herald the start of the toughest-ever month of rugby for the squad. The Lions had chosen another strong side for the match against their first opponents from the four current Super Twelve sides in South Africa. The team was – Stimpson, Bentley, Tait, Guscott, Underwood, Townsend, Howley, Rowntree, Regan, Leonard, Johnson (captain), Shaw, Dallaglio, Miller and Quinnell. The England front five would have to show a marked improvement in scrummaging following their poor display against Western Province. The excellent ball-carrying by the pack in Witbank had also laid down a challenge to the England forwards. Robert Howley, Gregor Townsend and Tim Stimpson were again awarded the key positions at nine, ten and fifteen. Jeremy Guscott's partner was Alan Tait, although Allan Bateman had originally been chosen alongside Tait, until a leg injury forced him to pull out of the game. But the most significant selection of the tour to date was the choice of Eric Miller at openside flanker. Fran Cotton confirmed this when we chatted at length after the training session on the day before the match. It was clear to me that the management could envisage Miller playing at number seven in the Tests, but this was very much dependent on his performance against Northern Transvaal. So, perhaps the Test back-row was starting to crystallise, with Dallaglio and Quinnell as the favourites to play alongside one of three number sevens. Richard Hill and Neil Back had put down the marker, but if the Lions were to play Quinnell at number eight, then they needed a ball winner at the end of the line-out. The versatile Miller had the right credentials.

I was once again impressed with Fran Cotton's directness and uncomplicated way of talking. He was proving to be an engaging and honest manager who had the total respect of his players, and he was winning over the media with his refusal to dodge any question or issue. He agreed that the Lions were about ten per cent further up the mountain than they had expected to be at this stage, but the manager was well aware that the tour had only just left base camp. The next three games would tell him a lot more about this ever-improving set of players.

Loftus Versfeld is a stadium full of history and, on entering the reception area at the ground, I was immediately struck by the imposing images of the past which adorn the walls. The stands rather lavishly fan out from the pitch to give the ground an airy feel. This contrasted to Newlands, where I had felt the sides of the ground almost seemed to be closing in on the pitch. If Newlands is the spiritual home of South African rugby, then Loftus Versfeld is the heartland of the nation's favourite sport. I could almost feel South African rugby's pulse as I wandered around the dark atmospheric corridors behind the stands.

I had watched the Northern Transvaal team train during the week and had spoken with their coach, Dr John Williams, who wallowed in the memories of Lions matches at Loftus Versfeld in days gone by. The big doctor, who represented South Africa at lock in 1974 against the Lions, impressed upon me that it was a tradition that the tourists were always given a tough match by Northern Transvaal. The statistics bore this out, with the margin of victory by the Lions having never been more than eight points. There had also been some controversial matches between the two sides and Williams confidently predicted another game full of incident on the Saturday. Disallowed tries, narrowly missed goals and the odd punch thrown in for good measure – that was Northern Transvaal versus the Lions. John Williams, Jr would also be watching our coverage to see how his father's team fared against the Lions. Another lock forward in the family, he was playing in Kelso and would be picking up our coverage.

The Northern Transvaal side, otherwise known as the 'Blue Bulls', had finished eighth in the Super Twelve series. They had only lost one match at home and had pushed the mighty Auckland Blues to a thrilling forty–all draw. However, they were stripped of their Springbok squad members for the match against the Lions and the absence of the likes of Joost van der Westhuizen and Ruben Kruger would obviously affect their chances; but there is no such thing as a weak Northern Transvaal side and the machismo which surrounds rugby in this part of the world would demand maximum effort from the team chosen to take on the Lions. The anticipation surrounding the build up to this match signalled a change in pace on the Lions tour. The first lap had been a gentle jog in comparison to the gruelling terrain which lay ahead. They were in good shape, but the first big test was about to come.

The thought of the rugby match was a lot more exciting than Pretoria itself, which frankly, I found bland. It is the administrative and financial centre of the country, and the world of civil servants and computerised high finance does little for the average tourist. The numerous attractive gardens are manicured and neatly set out in a prim and proper way. Pretoria lacked sparkle, and the grid system of roads, while easy to use, summed up the orderly and regimented feel to the city.

If you ever find yourself in the area, the one trip I recommend is to the Voortrekker monument, which commemorates the Boers who, in the mid nineteenth century, pushed northward into what was then unknown territory. A big square granite structure, the monument stands at forty metres high on a hill just out of the city. In many ways it is a symbol of the old South Africa and I got the impression that Pretoria had taken time to adjust to the change after years of isolation. The affluence was still very much in the hands of the white population in this part of the country. I felt that for some time the golfers were going to be white and the caddies were going to stay black.

The key rugby question was whether genuine integration was taking place in South Africa. SARFU was seemingly trying to fast-track the development of the black population. But where were these players in the provincial first teams? I did the taxi driver test with a friendly and genial cabby named Keith on the way to Loftus Versfeld. He positively enthused about rugby and clearly did not consider it to be the white man's preserve. In fact, his brother was in one of the junior teams at Northern Transvaal. There was no doubt that Keith had taken his inspiration from the likes of Chester Williams and had detected enough necessary change to feel happy with the general direction rugby was taking in the new South Africa. But he, like the rest of us, longed for the day when a real mix of races would take part at the highest level.

On Saturday morning I read the newspapers and relished the reports on England's start in the first Test match against Australia at Edgbaston. The day before I had overheard Fran Cotton telephoning his best wishes and those of the squad to Mike Atherton and the England team. Now could the Lions increase the feel-good factor with victory against Northern Transvaal to make it five wins out of five?

The atmosphere in the stadium, although it wasn't full, was intimidating and the passion from the rugby-mad locals was there for all to see. For the first time on the tour the Lions did not come out all guns blazing and therefore they failed to quell the crowd's fervour. Subsequently, they went to their first defeat on the tour by thirty-five points to thirty.

Full-back Tim Stimpson, so reliable the week before against Western Province, made a poor start and the home side soon realised he was looking vulnerable underneath the high ball. His Test claims must have been damaged accordingly. John Bentley, who had won the war against James Small in Cape Town, was also exposed defensively when Northern Transvaal scored their opening try. The fears about Bentley's lack of searing pace were realised and he looked a dejected man when he was pulled off in the second half and replaced by Gibbs, a centre, and not a winger. Elsewhere in the backs, Guscott, Tait, Townsend and to a lesser extent Underwood all did their claims no harm at all. Guscott scored two tries, both of which were world class. The first, when he saw that the opposition full-back, the excellent Graeme Bouwer, was for once not at home. Guscott's chip ahead and control of the awkward bouncing ball was sublime. The second try was after a brilliant break from Townsend, when the Lions proved again that behind the scrum they had the firepower to really hurt South Africa.

Townsend, despite giving away an interception try on his own twenty-two, otherwise convinced me again that he, along with Guscott, was the key to a Lions Test series win. The midfield play was on a different level to anything else we had seen. Talking to a few locals in the bar after the match, the feeling was that the Lions were setting the

standards in this department. They would create vital try-scoring opportunities against South Africa as long as they solved the problems up
front.

Just like at Newlands, the England front five failed to come up with
a convincing performance in the scrummage. Immediately after the
game, Jim Telfer honestly identified this as the root cause of the defeat.
Time and time again the Blue Bulls had put pressure on the scrum and
managed to wheel it around to create space on the blindside. Dr John
Williams made the point in the post-match news conference that the
scrum was not merely a means of restarting a game. It was music to the
ears of traditionalists as it was Williams' view that a powerful scrum
sapped the energy and wore down the opposition. The home side had
succeeded in this department and once again the Lions had failed. On
this evidence, the two England props, Rowntree and Leonard, looked a
long way from Test selection. Smith, Wallace and Young would
definitely be given their chance in the tough games ahead.

The poor scrummaging made life difficult for the back-row and
Dallaglio, Miller and Quinnell found themselves tested like never before
on the tour. The opposition were stronger and faster than anything they
had encountered. I felt that all three played adequately in adversity, yet,
Miller had not done enough to demand inclusion in the Test team as an
openside flanker. The jury was still out on whether this was the right
blend in the back-row. The others in the party could see openings.

The euphoria of mid-week had passed away and the stark reality
that the Lions still had a lot of hard work to do started to dawn on us
all. At twenty-five points to seven down, the Lions had been on the rack
at Loftus Versfeld. Although the second half comeback gave us all hope,
they could have lost by a more significant margin because one perfectly
good home try was disallowed and two other clear scoring opportunities
were missed due to marginal forward passes.

The referee, André Watson, could certainly never be accused of
being a 'homer', but he did miss one incident, however, only for the
television cameras to step in for the second time on the tour. Scott Gibbs
had come onto the field like a coiled spring and his tackle on the
Northern Transvaal replacement, Grant Esterhuizen, was in the first
instance quite devastating and perfectly legal. But as the tackled man fell
to the floor, Gibbs produced a short arm jab to make his mark on the
opponent. There were numerous replays and close ups of Gibbs in the
minutes that followed the incident. I knew that there were going to be
some repercussions and Dr John Williams' arrival at the post-match
news conference was delayed by a Northern Transvaal summit meeting
to discuss the possible course of action. The South African reaction was
eagerly awaited in view of the events in Witbank earlier in the week.

On the Sunday morning it was announced that Gibbs was to attend a disciplinary hearing because Northern Transvaal had cited him. This is the transcript of the minutes of that hearing at the Northern Transvaal Rugby Academy.

Present were: the members of the Judicial Committee – Judge Daniels and Messrs De Meyer and Van Vuuren, Mr Cotton representing the British Isles touring side, the player, Scott Gibbs and Mr Rob Hutchinson, the Northern Transvaal Liaison Officer with the touring side and Messrs Piet Butler, Secretary of the Home Union and Piet Olivier, the Manager of the Northern Transvaal rugby team.

1 The parties are agreed that the committee is properly constituted.

2 The charge to the effect that he was cited for having committed an act of foul play, namely by throwing a punch at Grant Esterhuizen in the match between Northern Transvaal and the British Lions on 8 June 1997.

3 Mr Gibbs indicated that he pleaded not guilty to the charge put and explained that he was 'attempting to dislodge the ball where it was held by Esterhuizen under his arm'. We were invited to have regard to a tackle some minutes later where a similar tactic was employed when a Northern Transvaal player was tackled.

4 Those present viewed a taped recording of the incident.

5 No further evidence was presented. The parties were agreed that this was the only evidence available. It is simply a question of interpreting in an objective manner the physical evidence.

It was our unanimous decision that:

'Mr Gibbs threw a deliberate punch. The explanation offered by Mr Gibbs appears to us to be rather fanciful, regard being had to the position of the ball in the opposing player's possession at the time and the fact furthermore that the clear impression is that he deliberately cocked his right arm before delivering the punch.'

Mr Cotton and Mr Gibbs were given the opportunity of addressing us on the punishment to be imposed and the following finding was then made:

'Mr Gibbs has been found guilty of the offence of foul play, i.e. of throwing a punch at a player. We have taken into account the fact that no injury resulted to the receiving player, since the blow was eventually nothing more than a glancing blow. We understand that Mr Gibbs is a former rugby league player and that he is accustomed to playing the game maybe more aggressively. That may be so, but he should adapt his game so as to comply with the rules adopted by the International Board. We considered the guidelines proposed in the tour agreement. Obviously we are not bound by those proposals but retain an inherent discretion to impose such sentence. It should be recorded that had the incident been noticed by the match referee, it would probably have led to a penalty being awarded and nothing more, save the possibility of a stern reprimand.

'Mr Gibbs is a first offender and upon the assurance given by Mr Cotton (to whom we are indebted for the most cordial and gentleman-like manner in which he approached this matter) that this is an isolated incident and that Gibbs is not given to foul play.'

The penalty imposed is the following:

'Mr Gibbs is suspended for one match, i.e. he will not be eligible for the match scheduled for Wednesday, 11 June 1997 – British Lions vs Gauteng Lions.

'Mr Cotton indicated that they accept the ruling and that the decision and sentence imposed will not be appealed against.'

H. Daniels
Chairman, Judicial Committee

Scott Gibbs had rightly been punished for throwing the punch. I have seen a lot worse. The fact that the player wasn't badly hurt and that the Committee concluded that it was only a penalty offence must have helped Gibbs' case. But the timing of the episode was bad for the Lions. It was insensitive in that it came just three days after the events in Mpumalanga and, having quite rightly taken the high moral ground earlier in the week, the Lions had been embarrassed by this rather senseless act from an experienced player who should have known better. The initial tackle had been a real beauty, there was no need for the follow up and it was hoped that the excellent discipline shown prior to that indiscretion would return immediately. What the week had shown was that the whole system of being able to cite a player only if the referee had missed the incident is totally wrong. There should be a right of appeal and central direction from the governing bodies on this contentious point. To rely solely on the referee's judgement in the video age is too fallible. Bosman should have been subjected to a hearing just like Gibbs.

Fran Cotton issued a statement which sought to put an end to the affair. It read, 'We had a fair hearing and we accept the decision – there will be no further action from the Lions management. All we want to do now is get on with the rugby and continue our planning for the match on Wednesday against the Gauteng Lions.' And so said all of us. There was no way that anybody wanted to see the tour dominated by acts of foul play. The Bosman ruling and, to a much lesser extent, the Gibbs incident had threatened to overshadow the rugby. The fact that they had failed to do so was testimony to the attractiveness of the Lions' play.

KINGS OF THE JUNGLE, KINGS OF THE SEA

'Tonight's win could prove to be the defining moment of the tour.'
– Manager Fran Cotton on the morale-boosting victory against the
Gauteng Lions

There are times in life when a reverse is not necessarily a bad thing – taking a step back to see the way forward. Had the Lions sneaked a win in the manic end to the match against Northern Transvaal, when they scampered around the field like red ants looking for safety, it could have masked over their deficiencies. But when the post-match talk is of defeat, then there is no hiding place. The pack had been taken apart again and changes had to be made.

For the Sky Sports team, however, the week could not have started on a better note as, courtesy of Scottish Provident, we were graduated from the crazy golf course and spent the day playing the real thing. The Arcadia course is on the outskirts of Pretoria. It was another beautiful sunny day and the sun block was an absolute necessity, as we were totally exposed on the high ground. My rather sub-standard golf was also uncovered, but luckily we decided to play 'Texas Scramble', which enables players of all abilities to play side by side.

The bulk of our team's good golf came from Alan Wilkins, the former Glamorgan and Gloucestershire cricketer, who now earns a living as a sports broadcaster in both the United Kingdom and South Africa. Sky Sports 'plus one' finished one over par for the round, but it wasn't enough to win; that honour went to the team that included the Lions kicking guru, Dave Alred, who hit a sweet spot of a different kind. The best-placed journalistic team was the all-Welsh combination of John Taylor, Stephen and Chris Jones and Huw Llewellyn Davies.

Once their morning training session had concluded, a few of the Lions joined us. Gregor Townsend, who is a fine golfer, and Mike Catt, who is also a bit of a sharp shooter on the course, enjoyed the chance to take their minds off the rugby. Catt had slotted into the Lions set-up as if he had been there all the time. He was right in the swing of things both on and off the golf course. Will Greenwood won the prize for the longest drive of the day and made a gesture which went down well with our hosts at the golf club: he donated his winnings, a smart golf bag, to his caddy and in return was given the skin of a springbok which had been produced from nowhere. It did seem a strange thing to be carrying around and I had visions of the Lions centre struggling to explain that one at the customs desk at Heathrow.

For a few days I lived off spurious stories of the odd Nicklaus-like three iron or Watson-style putt before the real story got out. But the day had provided some excellent light relief for all concerned. On arriving back at the hotel, I sat down to watch the cricket highlights, having had no idea of the events of the fourth day at Edgbaston. When Alec Stewart hit the winning runs, I went on a lap of honour around my bedroom and enjoyed that rare feeling of England going one–nil up in an Ashes series. I wondered whether the Lions would be in a similar position after their first Test in Cape Town which was now less than a fortnight away.

Before then the Lions had to get back on the rails following the defeat at Loftus Versfeld. The selection of the team for Wednesday's match against the Gauteng Lions was going to be even more fascinating than usual. What would be the selectors' strategy now? After this game at Ellis Park there would be only two more matches to get it right – Natal on Saturday, 14 June and the Emerging Springboks on Tuesday, 17 June. For their part, Gauteng were keeping their cards close to the chest. Nonetheless, I made a call to their coach, the former Springbok winger Ray Mordt, to see if I could get any advance information – a legitimate request, I assure you, as I needed to prepare for the commentary, but it is also one of the perks of the job. No joy. The side would not be finalised until late on the Tuesday evening. This would make my preparation very last minute. But fate was on my side in one respect: the children in the background were distracting Daddy, and he kindly agreed to let me ring him on Monday evening – I suspect I could even have got a 'Yes' to a request for a one hundred thousand rand loan.

The Monday morning didn't start too well, though. I got stuck in a lift in the hotel and was just about to press the panic button when my mobile phone started to ring. I hate the contraptions and I am always being told off for not leaving the phone on. But on this occasion I was glad to take a call from my producer, Piers Croton, who was the perfect man to have on the other end of the line. He had been trapped in the same lift just a matter of hours before and instructed me to try and prise the doors open, as this would trigger the lift into action. It worked and I went straight to the porter's desk to warn him of the potential danger of caging a few Lions later in the day.

But my elevator problems paled into insignificance as the news filtered through that, after a morning medical examination, Scott Quinnell was to leave the tour immediately and return home for treatment. He had aggravated a long-standing groin problem in the match against Northern Transvaal. In the space of a week then, the Lions had lost three men – Grayson, Weir and now Quinnell. Furthermore, Gibbs had been suspended for one game. Whilst Quinnell had not been at his best on the tour, continuing to lose the ball far too frequently in the tackle, he had in each of his appearances shown an ability to hit men hard. I felt he was being earmarked for the Test team because of his immense physical presence and big match temperament. He would be sorely missed.

Ian McGeechan was putting a brave face on it all saying that history shows that on average six players leave a Lions tour through injury. As we were at the half-way point, then the loss of three was not altogether a great surprise. But the Lions, who had been on such a high during the victory over Mpumalanga, had now gone through their first wretched period of the tour. It was important to reboost morale, and the arrival of the cheerful Nigel Redman did just that.

Redman had never expected to get the call and described the experience as the icing on the cake to a long career. When he was told by Jack Rowell that the Lions had been on the telephone enquiring about a second-row, Redman had thought his advice was being sought as to who to choose from the England squad. Rowell said, 'It's you,' and Redman's response was, 'I don't believe it,' to which Rowell answered, 'Nor do I!' After just a couple of days in South Africa, Redman's face was already showing the signs of some bruising contact in the scrummaging sessions. There were big purple patches around his cheekbones and he looked as if he had been assaulted on the street. Redman's shaven head and rubbery features give him one of the most recognisably pugnacious faces in the sport. He has been reselected ten times during his long and disrupted England career (this is Redman's way of avoiding the use of the word 'dropped'). It was plain to see that he was determined to put everything into this bonus tour.

Redman was thrown straight into the side. His name was one of those on the team sheet for match number six, against the Gauteng Lions at Ellis Park. The team selected was – Beal, Bentley, Bateman, Greenwood, Underwood, Catt, Healey, Smith, Williams, Wallace, Redman, Davidson, Wainwright, Back and Rodber (captain).

It was a big match for the team, as, in view of the previous Saturday's performance, they all had chances to push for Test spots. The other new arrival, Mike Catt, would also get his first game. Given Townsend's form, Catt's best chance of a Test place was at full-back, and I was disappointed not to see him in that role. If it was the ultimate intention to play Catt at number fifteen, then the management had reduced the time available to try him in this position. It was also good to see Austin Healey, the forgotten man of the tour, getting a turn. This would only be Healey's second start. His previous game was way back in the rain and mud of East London. During this period of inaction he had managed to maintain his humour, but nonetheless, he was visibly becoming frustrated at the prospect of watching permanently from the bench. One morning we had seen Healey practise kicking long after the others had gone. He looked around, seeking admiration for his successful shots. We gave it, but he would have preferred the management as his audience. Time was slipping away for a player in danger of being left out. Dai Young would again start as a replacement and time was also against the Welsh prop. He didn't offer as much around the field as Smith and Wallace, but Young would have relished a chance at propping up a creaking scrum.

We were all so wrapped up in the tour that it was easy to lose a sense of perspective. For a seven-week period it seemed as if the most important thing in the world was the Lions' journey around South Africa. Of course it was not, and a trip to Soweto to see a coaching clinic for youngsters at the Orlando East Rugby Stadium emphasised this perfectly. It was a trip that was to make a big impression on me.

A group of Lions players and management travelled in one coach and the media in another. The Sky Sports team joined the convoy in one of the trusty old Kombis which had been faithfully lugging us around the country and we set off for the infamous township. I mention the travel arrangements because on this particular journey they were worthy of note. At the head of the entourage was a police vehicle and another one brought up the rear. Both cars were manned by armed officers and it was clear that ensuring our safety was uppermost in their minds. It is a sad fact of life that crime in South Africa is a major burden on a society which is trying to change for the better. The most disadvantaged regions are obviously severely hit by crime, and although I would never condone such actions, it is more understandable in areas where people have been treated in a sub-human way. Give a person a fair chance and they will invariably take it in a positive manner, but deny them the opportunity and you are asking for trouble.

Soweto is, of course, a predominantly black area, but crime in South Africa is not a black or white issue. It affects all colours and all regions. The most affluent parts of Johannesburg are just as vulnerable as some of the most underprivileged sections of society. Indeed, that very evening on my return from Soweto I watched a fascinating television discussion programme about crime in South Africa. The statistics were frightening and the enormity of the issue must be of major concern to the whole of the country. Despite the statistics, I should say that during my visits in South Africa I have never encountered lawlessness and I would recommend a holiday in what is a beautiful country. Like anywhere these days, crime remains a constant threat, but if you take sensible precautions there is no need to live a life of fear.

However, the police authorities clearly were taking no risks on that day and, to be fair to them, I later learnt that there had been seven hijackings of vehicles in Soweto over the previous weekend. But the police presence proved to be totally unnecessary and they had been nothing more than outriders, creating a smooth passage through the traffic. As we drove through the edge of the township it was hard to understand how people tolerated living in such abject poverty. The houses were tightly packed together and, although there was obvious pride in the ownership of those properties, the scene was a sobering one. The visit was sanitised in that we didn't go through the really poor areas, but we saw enough to be thankful of the hand that we had been dealt in life.

To dwell on the negative, though, is in many ways counterproductive, and the people of Soweto who stood and watched the Lions' coach pass them by waved and smiled with great affection. The beaming faces and favourable looks confirmed that they were happy to see us.

As the coach pulled up at the rugby club, we took in a scene which would not have been possible only a few years ago. What we found was a small rugby club doing its best to improve the lives of youngsters in the township through sport. The official figures say that over two thousand people now play rugby in Soweto, with eleven primary school youth clubs being set up to help establish the sport in the area. Clubs such as Eldorado Park, Ennerdale, Jabulani and Eden Park all have three teams and the future looks a lot brighter. SARFU and the Gauteng Lions have helped financially with the provision of equipment and they are to be applauded for this, but the general feeling at Orlando East was that more could be done. A glance around the barren field and the sparse facilities, which merely included two sets of posts and a new changing room block, contrasted with the magnificent Loftus Versfeld where we had been at the weekend. Since 1994, the Gauteng Lions have spent over three million rand on rugby development in Soweto, but this only serves to prove how little had been achieved over the previous one hundred years.

This wasn't a day, though, for what might have been – it was time to reflect in the joy that the kids were experiencing in playing the sport they loved. They also made the most of the chance to be coached by some of the Lions and the players all slotted expertly into the teacher's role. A welcoming address to the Lions was well received, as were the T-shirts and badges handed out at the end of the one-hour session. The level of skill achieved by some of the boys was quite outstanding. Indeed, had I been a scout for a league club back home, I would have had a very close look at a young fly-half with the ability to pass with ease off either side. His balance was that of a star in the making. Thank goodness he now had the chance to show us all what he could do.

We stood talking with Amos, a schools sports co-ordinator and he spoke with passion about the need to spread the sporting gospel. He felt that it was essential for black children to have the opportunity to play the previously white man's sports of rugby and cricket. This would go a long way to breaking down other more threatening political barriers. Like all in Soweto, Amos was frustrated by the slow rate of change in the country, feeling that administrative wrangling at the top was holding back the development of South Africa. But he had a great respect and love for his President and had faith in Mandela's leadership. He talked depressingly about the crime in Soweto, the bulk of which seemed to stem from the taxi wars, the fight for the routes around the township and into Johannesburg. The backdrop to our conversation was a market where merchandise was spread unevenly over the ground as the people tried to scrape a living from their rather shabby goods. But overall Amos was confident that Soweto would prosper because the people had a belief in the future and at last had some control over their own destiny.

As we left Soweto, our route took us past Nelson Mandela's house before he went to Robben Island. We also saw Archbishop Desmond Tutu's residence and Winnie Mandela's home. Hers was a house apart from the rest but was still insignificant at the side of the millionaire mansions in the Sandton district of Johannesburg. Here in the space of a quarter of a mile was a generation of history. We saw the Orlando West High School where the uprising of 1976 had begun and we looked on in sadness at a mural of the young children who lost their lives in the struggle for good against evil. As we drove away from Soweto, the locals continued to wave at the convoy. Behind three children, who gestured so enthusiastically I thought their arms were going to fall off, were two small pigs scavenging in the rubbish on some wasteland. It struck me again that this was a hard way of life and to have this coach-load of people looking in on their world could easily have seemed antagonistic. I self-consciously waved in return, but, as ever, the people were friendly and welcoming. On the outskirts of the town the police cars sounded their horns as they branched off and left us to follow the motorway back to Pretoria.

The emotions of the Lions tour were once again highlighted on the following day, when we were told of Tony Diprose's reaction to the news that he had been called into the party to replace Scott Quinnell, who had now returned home. Diprose, who like Catt and Redman had been on the England tour of Argentina, was preparing to go on holiday to the Caribbean but was more than happy to delay those plans. He is a gifted footballer who had impressed during his first two England appearances against Argentina days before his call to South Africa. The Richmond captain, Ben Clarke, commonly recognised as the outstanding Lion in New Zealand in 1993, had come close to selection, but after a meeting of the senior players and management it was decided that Diprose's handling skills were more suited to the kind of game that the Lions were wanting to play. Surprisingly, Fran Cotton said that he had not consulted Jack Rowell about the player's form in Argentina but had been satisfied with the favourable reports from Catt and Redman. Cotton added that, 'Now England have returned home, the process [of prising a player away from Rowell's clutches] has been a lot easier.'

But if Diprose was feeling elated, Doddie Weir was surely gnashing his teeth back home when he heard news of the paltry fine handed out to the Mpumalanga duo of Van den Bergh and Bosman. The latter received a ten thousand rand fine for his attack on Weir, while Van den Bergh was given a five thousand rand penalty, three thousand of which was suspended. The local union issued a statement which said that both players had been charged with 'acting in a manner inconsistent with the integrity of the game during the course of the match'. True, but the contemptible actions, especially those of Bosman which we thought threatened Weir's career, deserved stiffer punishment. Fran Cotton did not want to get dragged into another row on the subject, but pointedly remarked that the fine wouldn't even cover Weir's consultation fees with the medical experts. Moreover, the reaction of Mpumalanga conflicted with the one-match ban imposed on Scott Gibbs for a much less serious offence. The Lions, and in particular Weir, had a right to feel that justice had not been done.

Later that evening the attention turned to the international at Newlands between the Springboks and Tonga. It was a chance for us all to get a look at the home nation and examine their strengths and possible weaknesses just over a week before the first Test match against the Lions on the same ground. It was almost a full-strength South African side and it became immediately apparent that they were far too strong for the inferior opposition. Almost embarrassingly, the Springboks led by thirty-three points to three with only twenty minutes gone. But it wasn't all good news for South Africa, as their captain, Gary Teichmann, pulled a hamstring muscle and was forced to leave the field. Worse was to come for the Springboks when winger James Small clutched his hamstring after a run on the wing in the second half. If anything this looked a more troublesome injury. South Africa went on to win by a massive seventy-four points to ten, but they would surely have given away some of those points if it had meant these two significant players avoiding damage.

Analysing the performance was a difficult exercise because of the total ineptitude of the Tongans, but one or two issues were confirmed. André Joubert, on his way back from injury, could still do things which other rugby players can only dream about. The same could be said of Joost van der Westhuizen, whose running in broken play was typically world class. One important observation was the predictable way in which fly-half Henry Honiball constantly sought to turn the ball back inside. I suppose when you have a back-row which includes the immense Ruben Kruger and André Venter, the temptation to use them all the time must be a powerful one. But this appeared to be a one-dimensional tactic and one which the Lions would certainly try to counter. The prop forwards, Os du Randt and Adrian Garvey, both carried the ball with pace, and this compared favourably with the sluggish performances of the Lions' England men Graham Rowntree and Jason Leonard, both of whom had struggled to contribute around the field. The one possible weakness was the kicking at goal of the new cap, Edrich Lubbe. He landed seven conversions but missed others which were well within range and it was clear that Lubbe's kicking style needed some attention.

After the match I saw Fran Cotton and Ian McGeechan in the hotel bar and both said they had not seen anything in that South African performance to unduly worry the Lions. Whilst they thought that the home back-row would be a major threat, McGeechan was already working on ways to counteract Honiball's telegraphed intention, when he did decide to move the ball wide. There was a feeling in the Lions camp that come the Test matches they would have learnt enough and adjusted to the Southern Hemisphere style of playing to such an extent that victory was more than possible. Cotton enthused about the back play on the tour saying that he had not seen better work from British backs since the days of the great Lions and Welsh teams of the early 1970s. The key now was to maintain the confidence level to keep the team moving forward. The defeat on Saturday at Loftus Versfeld had hurt, and another reverse, this time at the hands of the other lions from Gauteng, would undoubtedly rock the tourists. The Test series would perhaps be decided at Ellis Park in July, but the match on the same ground on Wednesday, 11 June would go a long way to dictating the state of mind for the Test encounters.

The local newspapers had the same idea, describing the match as a make or break game for the Lions. Gauteng had picked a strong side which included the Springboks Hennie Le Roux and Kobus Wiese, who both had points to prove after their rejection by the national team coach, Carel du Plessis. Other familiar names in the team were internationals Chris Rossouw, Roberto Grau, Pieter Hendriks and Johan Roux. This was going to be just as tough as the defeat on Saturday and the intense atmosphere would be compounded by the fact that the game was the first one on the tour to be played under floodlights.

The men in red had been accused of timidity in the defeat to Northern Transvaal and the mid-week pack knew that they could not afford to be muzzled in the way that the Saturday team had been. Tim Rodber, captain for the match, was verbally table thumping again with bold words such as 'pride' and 'honesty'. He claimed that the pack were 'mentally up for the challenge' like never before. For the Lions' sake, I hoped that they were.

Ellis Park is a magnificent rugby stadium, especially under lights. The scene of the 1995 World Cup final has an aura which has been intensified by the events of two years ago. This is where a nation came together on a day when sport proved again that it can be the ultimate unifying force. I'm not sure whether you talk yourself into these things, but as I walked into the ground there was a strong sense of importance and historical significance. (On entering Johannesburg, you can also convince yourself that there is a potential mugger around every corner. There is a feeling of electricity about the place, and part of this charge is created by the tensions which result from the fact that the city lives on an emotional and political knife edge.) But although the area around Ellis Park has seen better times, I enjoyed the experience of visiting one of the world's most famous sporting grounds. As darkness fell and the crowds started to mill around outside the stadium, it felt like being around Wembley on a match night. The busy hum of a big city crowd was in stark contrast to the social chatter of the mid-afternoon games earlier in the tour.

The Lions had been forced into making a late change. Jeremy Guscott was asked to play again because Allan Bateman's tour was becoming increasingly in jeopardy. The tour doctor, James Robson, had given Bateman a run-out and his hamstring strain had not fully disappeared. Robson told me that it was an unusual injury in that the problem was confined to a very small area. Bateman would now need to be part of Saturday's game against Natal to prove that he was fit enough to be available for the first Test.

The Lions came up against a physical Gauteng side determined to make an impact early in the game. Gauteng led by nine points to three at the interval and there was the distinct prospect of another defeat for the Lions. From our commentary position behind thick glass we felt rather removed from the events of the evening, but at half-time, during a spectacular fireworks display, the realisation that the tour could be on the rocks started to hit home. In the interval Ian McGeechan told his team to stop being over-elaborate in their approach play and to let themselves go in the second half. This is exactly what they did and, despite a late try from Gauteng, the Lions triumphed by twenty points to fourteen and saved the tour from possible disaster.

During that second half, Austin Healey celebrated his inclusion with a fine try, but this was eclipsed by John Bentley's amazing run from the half-way line. It had to be the try of the tour and that was saying something in view of the quality scores that had been made up to that point. Bentley, who had been taunted by his colleagues all week that his tour was over after he had been left floundering on the wing during the defeat at Northern Transvaal, knew that he had to make an impact in this match. The players knew that Bentley could take the ribbing – after all, he was the most visibly upbeat man on tour – but he had been unusually quiet in the build-up to the Gauteng game. As Bentley said, 'It was time to put up and shut up.' Although a Test place had seemed remote after the weekend, he went flying back into contention, taking two men on the outside, coming off his wing to beat two more and then harnessing still more strength to drive another couple of defenders over the line. It was a try that lifted the tour to another level. As he walked away to be greeted by ecstatic team-mates, Bentley's smiling face said it all. He knew he had created a piece of rugby history and that his video collection now had a tape to sit at the top of the pile.

After the match, Fran Cotton said that the squad had gone into the game fully aware that the outcome was key to the rest of the tour. The team had responded in the best possible manner and many of those on show had propelled themselves towards the Test team. I thought the front-row were again magnificent, and Tom Smith and Paul Wallace, who had done all they could against the inferior opposition of Mpumalanga, passed the test against the much stronger Gauteng with flying colours. This match was in a different league and so were the props. Barry Williams proved himself once again to have the roar of a lion on the pitch and seemed to delight in getting involved in the aggro. There were still reservations about his throwing-in, but the same could be said of Keith Wood. The other hooker, Mark Regan, had been part of the suffering scrum in Pretoria. Williams was moving up from number three in the hooker charts towards number one. Admittedly, Nigel Redman made little impact against Kobus Wiese in the line-out, but Jeremy Davidson put in another exemplary performance and was becoming one of the stars of the tour. The back-row were also hot and, although Rob Wainwright was gamely fighting what I thought was a losing battle to oust Lawrence Dallaglio at number six, both Neil Back and Tim Rodber were right in contention for the positions at seven and eight.

In the backs, aside from Bentley's try, it was Will Greenwood who stood out. The injuries to Allan Bateman and Alan Tait plus Scott Gibbs' lack of match practice meant that Greenwood was still in the hunt for a Test place. He had hardly put a foot wrong all tour. Mike Catt grew in confidence at fly-half but his first game on the tour was marred by a shaky kicking display. Obviously he had too much to do to displace Townsend. At full-back, Nick Beal put in another certain performance, but when Neil Jenkins came on to replace the injured Tony Underwood, Beal moved to the wing. Jenkins, who had played far better in his match as fly-half against Mpumalanga, reminded us all that his place-kicking is a major asset. Having written Jenkins off at full-back after the opening match of the tour, I was prepared to revise that opinion based on the fact that Jenkins kicks goals. The defensive frailties of Stimpson and his 'blind-alley' running, the inexperience of Beal and the initial unwillingness to try Catt as a full-back, all meant that Jenkins was still reasonably placed to get the vote.

We drove away from Ellis Park with the heavens having opened and the lightning crashing to the floor. It was a spectacular thunderstorm, and we were thankful that the rain had stayed away until just after the final whistle. This dramatic turn in the weather had not been predicted that morning by South Africa's version of Michael Fish. Having said that, of course, in 1987 Fish did infamously tell that lady not to worry about reports of an impending hurricane . . . who would be a weatherman?

The same question could be applied to a rugby selector. The management team were in for some head scratching over the next twenty-four hours. They had wanted the side to play Natal in Durban to resemble the Test line-up, as the clash at King's Park was only seven days away from that first Test at Newlands. Time was running out and decisions had to be made. But at least we left Johannesburg airport for Durban with the Lions tour back on the road – and with try-scorers by the names of Austin Healey and Bentley, that is probably a good way of putting it!

The bad weather continued and we were told to expect a bumpy ride on the short flight to Durban. I didn't care about the turbulence, though, for one very good reason. Helen had arrived on the overnight flight from London and was to spend the next ten days with me in South Africa. It was her first trip to Africa and she was thrilled about seeing the country and, hopefully, me as well! Three and a half weeks away from home had seemed like an age and it was reassuring to know that we still recognised each other at the airport.

On arrival in Durban, the crew went to the Natal Shark Board to film some footage for the preview to the Lions match against the Natal Sharks. It was fascinating to see one of the beasts face to face, albeit dead. We were treated, if that's the right phrase, to a dissection of a shark. Rest assured the shark had died of natural causes and the research centre was only intent on doing good for 'Jaws' and his friends who roam the shore around Durban. (By the way, here is a health warning. If you have just eaten then don't read these next few sentences. On the day, we hadn't had time for lunch, but despite a rumbling tummy, I was particularly glad to have missed out on a midday meal when the shark's small heart was held aloft like a trophy. The demonstration team were keen to illustrate the position of the heart, which is somewhere around the throat. The theory being that, if it were to be in the middle of the shark's 'chest', then the shark would be decidedly more vulnerable to attack. Dale, the man with the scalpel, then turned his attention to the gut contents. It was quite enthralling, I think not, to see the surface area of a shark's intestine. The young children in the audience seemed to soak up this information with glee. Personally, I thought it was time to get a little air.) As we left, we were told to avoid swimming at night and not to allow blood to seep from the smallest of cuts when in the water because of the shark's ability to detect this from miles away. Frankly, there was no need to worry on my part. The closest I would be getting to the creatures was the view of the Natal Sharks from my commentary position on Saturday.

Apparently, the Great White shark, from which the Natal Sharks get their name, is likened to a lion in the way that it is the king of the sea and fears no other species. This seemed to me to be a promotional gift for those wanting to push ticket sales for the match against the kings of the jungle in Durban. Intrepidly, I went to investigate the opposition and, although I could hardly have claimed to be Jacques Cousteau, I did feel like an adventurer as I braved the strong winds and the torrential rain to stand pitch-side with the Natal coach, Ian McIntosh. I wished I had been wearing mine. The one I had been ridiculed for carrying around with me in the heat for the entire tour had at last come into its own. But like a fool I had left it in the hotel. The genial McIntosh pointed out the players during a warm-up underneath the stand and out of the rain. Once we got out on the training pitch and into the elements, I decided to take back all those jibes about, 'South African winter, what winter?' What a contrast that wet and windy night was with the gorgeous sunny weather when the Lions had made their first visit to Durban at the start of the tour.

There had been a lot of water under the bridge since then, though, and players had moved in and out of contention for Test places. But because of the unexpectedly even distribution of form, the final fifteen for the first match against South Africa was in many ways still no clearer. The team to play Natal gave some major clues, but all the men selected, with the exception of Townsend, Howley, Evans and Dallaglio, knew that big performances were required. Even the captain Martin Johnson had to prove to us all that he was fit enough to play his part. The team for the game against Natal read as follows – Jenkins, Evans, Bateman, Gibbs, Tait, Townsend, Howley, Smith, Wood, Young, Johnson (captain), Shaw, Dallaglio, Hill and Miller.

Sure enough, Neil Jenkins had been restored to full-back. He would start a game in that position for the first time since the win over Eastern Province in the opening match of the tour. Jenkins could certainly provide the answer with the boot, but his defensive positioning would once again be scrutinised in the match versus Natal. The Welshman was, however, well placed to win a Lions cap.

Two other Welshmen, Allan Bateman and Scott Gibbs, who was returning from suspension, would in effect fight head-to-head to play alongside Jeremy Guscott. The England centre had been told that he wasn't going to play again before the Cape Town Test. Bateman was just hoping to get through the match and avoid aggravating his hamstring problem. But his style of play was similar to Guscott's and Gibbs' extra physical presence might win the day. Alan Tait was on the wing after impressing in that role in the latter stages at Loftus Versfeld, but he would have to play exceptionally well to displace John Bentley, who was back in the frame after scoring that try which the whole of South Africa was still talking about. If Tait could defend better than Bentley, he would play in the Test.

In the pack, the issues were even more undecided. I sensed that Tom Smith had done enough to persuade the management that he should be the loose head prop. Thankfully, Dai Young got his first start since the washed-out game against Border and conceivably he could have been about to make a late bid, but Paul Wallace had proved a lot of doubters wrong. Jason Leonard could only sit on the bench against Natal and hope. Johnson and Shaw both needed to shine in the second-row. Without Doddie Weir the management might have been even more intent on playing the England locks but Jeremy Davidson's fine form had upset the apple cart. Davidson wasn't fully fit, though, and this could prove to be the saving grace for Shaw.

The back-row was as competitive as the race for the Conservative party leadership. Lawrence Dallaglio was safely into the second ballot, but Richard Hill against Neil Back, and Eric Miller versus Tim Rodber were fascinating confrontations. Both Hill and Miller again needed to turn it on. The experiment of playing Miller at number seven had been ditched.

*

After the team announcement on the Thursday evening, Helen and I decided to go to a fish restaurant – a brave move, considering our encounter with Mr Shark earlier in the day. This was meant to be a romantic meal for two people who had not seen each other for a while and had lots of news to catch up on. Yours truly, though, managed to reduce the atmosphere to a 'chimps' tea party' by ordering crab curry. I knew I was in for some trouble when the waitress tied a bib around my neck and delivered some metal crackers to prise open the crab claws. The finger bowl soon looked like the muddied waters of Durban harbour on which the restaurant was situated. An hour later, I conceded defeat to the crab and left needing a visit to the dry cleaners.

It had been nice, though, to talk about life back home and find out about the British summer. At this stage of the tour, the half-way point, we had all reached the stage of fantasising about a more normal lifestyle. The food and wine in South Africa are quite exceptional. Portions satisfy even the most voracious of appetites, and even Stuart Barnes finds it difficult to finish his meal on some rare occasions. But the thought of rustling up such culinary delights as beans on toast was appealing. We had all started off the tour eating the cooked breakfasts in the hotels, but by now, for most of us, the cereal was perfectly adequate and we were actually hoping that our next hotel would have a gymnasium. Wonders will never cease.

On that note I had been very impressed with the media's physical activities. The serious approach to health and fitness seemed to be breaking out all over the journalistic ranks, so much so that Stuart had bemoaned the possibility of the media employing their own doctor, masseur and dietician on future tours. He wanted to hark back to the halcyon days when the approach to eating was a little less serious. His plan was to introduce a code of practice for the media which included an eve-of-match curry which would be compulsory for all the 'squad' and a minimum intake of alcoholic beverage to create the right atmosphere. The 'Barrel' knew what he wanted from life and it was usually on a plate or in a glass.

Match day in Durban is a unique experience. To think that they frown upon barbecues at Twickenham in the interest of safety – such an attitude at King's Park would be tantamount to treason. The braais, as I'm sure you've already gathered, are a common feature at all South African rugby grounds, but in Durban the surrounding pitches are covered with thousands of people cooking away. The smoke-filled air creates a haze which covers the fields and the smell of the steak and sausages sizzling away is enough to make you want to forget about the match and concentrate on some serious eating, Stuart Barnes style.

Regardless of the result, the Natalians party the night away and stay at the ground until the last burger has been devoured and the cases of lager have been drunk dry.

The people of Natal were certainly full of anticipation, aware that their team had won the Currie Cup for the last two years and had reached the semi-final of the Super Twelve series. They had never beaten the Lions, though; the closest encounter was as far back as 1924, when the match finished as a draw. John Allan, the Natal hooker, who was playing his final game for the province before taking up a coaching post with London Scottish, further fired up the support by sprinting onto the field alone to receive the plaudits from the crowd. They recognised one of the loyal servants of Natal rugby over the past decade – but Allan was to have a far from enjoyable end to his career at King's Park.

The first half was littered with mistakes, but luckily they were predominantly coming from the home side as the Lions' forwards took control. It all proved how quickly this Lions squad were learning and how hard they had worked on weak areas. Seven days earlier they had struggled to come to terms with Northern Transvaal's forward power but the pack had responded well against Gauteng and built on that performance by keeping Natal on the back foot. A first-half try from Gregor Townsend, following a clever chip ahead by the hooker Keith Wood, helped the Lions to a half-time lead of sixteen points to nine. They never looked in trouble in the second period, and excellent scores from Mike Catt, on as a replacement, and Lawrence Dallaglio rounded off a thoroughly competent display. Neil Jenkins weighed in with twenty-four points and Jenkins 'The Boot' was in the groove. His team totalled forty-two points to Natal's twelve.

The day was pretty well near perfect apart from one aspect. During the first half, the star of the tour so far, scrum-half Robert Howley, was caught at the bottom of a ruck. He fell awkwardly on his shoulder and the alarm bell started to ring. Howley was led away from the field looking like a wounded soldier. As he reached the bench, we got a message that the doctor, James Robson, was being guarded about his initial diagnosis. James later told me that he had not wanted to be alarmist, as he was fully aware that Robert's parents were watching and they would only get worried at the thought of their son being hurt. In the heat of the moment it was a sensitive piece of medical work, but minutes after the end of the match, our hopes that this would not be a serious injury were dashed when the official news came from the dressing room that Howley had dislocated his shoulder and was on the first plane out of the country. It was a crushing blow for both player and squad, and a man who was on the point of achieving greatness had seen his dream snatched away. Fran Cotton's wretched face at the after-match news conference said it all, he had lost a key member of the Test team. It was a time to adopt a stiff upper lip approach and Cotton was the perfect man to rally the troops, but everybody in the party knew that the Lions would go into the first Test without one of their major weapons.

My worst pre-tour fears had come true: we were going to be denied that epic contest between Howley and Joost van der Westhuizen. It was now important to focus on the performance of Howley's replacement, Matt Dawson. He had played well and the battle between Dawson and Austin Healey would be a keenly contested one. Neither of these men would let the Lions down, but we all thought that they were not in the same class as Howley.

All other players involved against Natal that day did their Test claims no harm at all, in particular, Neil Jenkins, who kicked his way into the Test team. He knew it as well. It was heartening to see his beaming face when he spoke on his mobile telephone at the end of the match. Allan Bateman and Scott Gibbs both had fine games in the centre. But Bateman had left the field and there remained a doubt over his fitness. Gibbs was a man on a mission and his powerful bulldozing runs made a strong case to join Jeremy Guscott in the Tests. The pack all scored ten out of ten and the choices between Smith, Wallace, Leonard and Young at prop, Wood and Williams at hooker and Shaw and Davidson in the second-row would all concentrate the minds of the selectors. But if that was difficult enough, then the back-row was a minefield. Dallaglio, Wainwright, Hill, Back, Rodber and Miller had all done enough during the course of the four weeks' action to merit inclusion.

The overriding memory of that day in Durban, though, will be the sight of Howley being escorted down the tunnel and into the darkness of tour oblivion. But I will recall with fondness the party atmosphere generated around the ground: the razzmatazz provided by the supporters club, the glamour girls wearing bathing costumes spelling out 'Natal', the Shark tattoos appearing in some unlikely places and the remote-controlled Shark fin which sped around the field sniffing out the opposition, all added to the event (although, on this occasion, the post-match atmosphere was more muted than usual, as the Natal supporters were forced to reflect on the most impressive performance by the Lions on the tour to date). I was looking forward to returning to Durban for the second Test, but now it was back to Cape Town for the build-up to the crucial first match in the series. My stomach fluttered at the prospect of a momentous week.

WEEK 5

BEATING THE BOKS AND THE RAIN

'There are some things that never change: goalkickers win Test matches.'
– Ian McGeechan prior to the selection of Neil Jenkins for the first Test.

There was a growing feeling that the Lions could take setbacks in their stride and that the Springboks were starting to rue the decision to let their top players miss out on the provincial games. From a home team's perspective, the Lions should have been kicked when they were down – metaphorically, of course – after the defeat to Northern Transvaal. The counter argument was that the tourists would still be taking a step into the unknown when they played in the first Test and they would be shocked by the power of South Africa. In a week's time we would know the answer.

Our passage into Cape Town was again blessed with clear weather, but this time we encountered an aviation rarity – a pilot who radioed down to air traffic control and requested permission to take an excursion around the city for ten minutes of free sightseeing. The cost of airline fuel is not cheap these days and it was a real bonus to be escorted around the Cape, thanks to South African Airways. (This is an unashamed plug, but fair play to them for taking the time out to give us all the experience of a lifetime.) We circled around Table Mountain, journeyed out to Robben Island and even passed over the rugby ground. I imagined the stadium below being a seething mass of bodies just six days later and it was a poignant moment. Mind you, there is no satisfying some people: when we were on the ground waiting for our baggage to come along the carousel, a disgruntled passenger complained that he could have been killed as the plane needlessly took a route through the mountains. Moreover, he could have been on the ground a full ten minutes earlier. I presumed he was a nervous flyer, but regardless of that he was not an individual to put on your party invitation list.

We loaded up another Kombi and trundled into Cape Town feeling a little tired but buoyed by the fact that we were back in the Cape and the knowledge that the homeward stretch had now begun. The first port of call was a Lions news conference at their hotel in Newlands. Robert Howley's replacement was named by Fran Cotton and it came as no surprise that Kyran Bracken was on his way to South Africa, but it did smash his holiday plans to pieces. Bracken had been in Tobago for just one day when he got the call that all rugby players want – unless they've got a cocktail in their hand and the sun is setting on the Caribbean sea. Bracken would not complain, though, and we were told that he had won the vote over Bryan Redpath of Scotland and Paul John of Wales.

If Bracken's personal plans had been thrown out of kilter, then Jeremy Guscott was able to more than match that with news of the birth of another baby girl. He was now going for a netball team and not a rugby side, according to Ian McGeechan. This neglected the rise of women's rugby, but, not wishing to be too politically incorrect, I could see what McGeechan meant. The little Guscott would have to wait to see Daddy because he still had some unfinished business a long way from home. That was hard for a new father to take, but more difficult for the squad to come to terms with was the sight of Robert Howley being left behind at Durban airport. He was departing the tour but was defiantly predicting a series win despite his absence. There was a visible sadness in the squad, as they contemplated life without the talented and likeable Welshman. His parents had been forced to change their travel plans because they had been planning to come out to cheer on their son in the first Test. Sport can be momentous but also cruel.

Our thoughts were now turning to the Test match itself and the clash at Newlands, which had once seemed way in the distance. The games had started to fly by and the day of reckoning was no longer far on the horizon. The team that would play in the match was not going to be announced until the morning of the game. This was a deliberate tactic that was in part designed to maintain team morale for those who still had to play in the Tuesday fixture against the Emerging Springboks in Wellington. It was also part of the mind games starting up between the Lions camp and their hosts. The veil of secrecy was further pulled down as the training sessions in the week ahead were to be closed, apart from the Monday morning run-out and a fifteen-minute period on Thursday. Fran Cotton said that he wanted to get an edge over the opposition in whatever way possible and if this meant playing the cards close to the chest then so be it. The media joked about the inquisitive nature of some journalists and their desire to uncover the team before Saturday, but Cotton looked determined to stand firm on the issue. Even when Ian McGeechan seemed to hint strongly that Neil Jenkins would be in the team by saying, 'There are some things that never change: goalkickers win Test matches,' Cotton stepped in. He realised that, following

Jenkins' kicking display against Natal, this comment could have been construed as cementing the player's position in the team. His response was to point out the fine kicking of Tim Stimpson in the matches when he was selected to go for goal. The underlying feeling to all of this was that the tempo of the tour had suddenly increased. You could almost touch the anticipation.

Later on the Sunday evening we had the pleasure of once again dining with the whole squad. The meal was at a restaurant called Blues in Camps Bay which is a picturesque and rather chic area of the Cape. The Sky Sports team arrived and waited for the Lions to turn up. After a short while, the Media Liaison Officer, Bob Burrows, came in looking a little flustered. He informed us that the Lions coach had broken down. No, Ian McGeechan had not thrown in the towel and burst into tears at the pressure of the job, but instead the Lions bus had straddled itself across one of the main routes out of Sea Point. This was about two miles away and the good old Sky Kombi came into its own again. We discovered a new joke – how many Lions players can you get into a van? The answer, of course, depends on whether they are backs or forwards. You also have to leave room for the backs' handbags! The Kombi was used to ferry the Lions to their food until a reinforcement coach arrived. Everybody saw the funny side of this, but had it happened on match day then it would have severely affected the players' preparations. We thanked our lucky stars that the problem had been identified at this stage.

Talking of stars, the clear night and the view out to the Atlantic from the broad windows which circle the dining area at Blues made for the perfect setting. The food was good and the players were given their weekly free reign to select what they liked from the menu. This meant that the man in charge of keeping an eye on the team's diet, David McLean, was unable to hang over the players' shoulders insisting that the skin was stripped off the chicken and that the cream should not be poured onto the sweet. My abiding memory of that evening, though, was the sight of the burly Fran Cotton dwarfing Helen, who sat on his right-hand shoulder. That is probably the best way of putting it: I could have been crueller and said that she would have fitted into his pocket.

One of the dishes on offer was ostrich steak. If you have never had this form of meat and you get the chance to try it, please do. It is important not to overcook it because the steak becomes quite tough if anything more than medium-to-well done. I suppose it tastes like beef but it has virtually no fat content. Although it is expensive back home, in South Africa ostrich is commonly eaten and therefore cheaper and well worth giving a go.

The dinners with the squad were one of the highlights of the tour and it was a privilege to be able to sit down in a relaxed atmosphere to discuss not only rugby but the other things of life, too. However, the tour was inevitably still a major topic of conversation. The disappointment of losing Robert Howley was plain to see and both Cotton and McGeechan agreed that this would have an effect on the series. But the management also stood by Matt Dawson and Austin Healey, and they emphasised that the aim had always been to create a squad which had individuals who would replace injured players and play in their style. What was of the most concern, though, to the squad members at this particular point was the run on puddings, which had already taken three of the options off the menu. When the Lions eat as a pride they devour their prey.

Monday, 16 June was all set to be the busiest day of the tour so far. I had to see three teams train and the logistics of making all the appointments plus two news conferences kept me on the go. First, it was to the Hamiltons Rugby Club where the Emerging Springboks were due to run out later in the morning. Hamiltons is the oldest club in South Africa, having been founded in 1875. When I arrived, the mist had come down from the mountains and off the sea. It was like a summer's day in Scarborough with a fret in the air and the seagulls flying all around. I waited for the sun to do its best to burn off the low cloud and for the first time on tour I felt genuinely cold. When I arrived at the club there was a distinct 'morning after the night before' atmosphere. It was a national holiday – 'Youth Day' – and I wondered if I had misunderstood the message and had gone to the wrong place. But, I needn't have worried, as the man in charge of the administration of the club, former player Kevin Tucker, opened up the doors and provided a welcome which is unique to rugby at this level. Before I could sit down, the coffee had been poured and the guided tour of the clubhouse had begun. Pictures and plaques adorned the walls and the pride in the history of the club was evident. As the tour proceeded, Kevin's dog played with a bone which had been left over from what seemed to have been a rather raucous party the day before. Apparently, the clubhouse had been used by a local political party for their annual bash. Judging by the waste left over, they obviously didn't have an environmental health policy and poor old Kevin had a job on his hands to clear up the mess. But the dog didn't complain.

Before work could commence, however, the dog's help was required in an effort to try and capture some thieves. This all sounds very dramatic, but in fact it was highly comical. As I was talking with Kevin, his wife spotted two men making across the rugby field carrying a trellis table. They were walking slowly and had not bargained for the quick reaction of Kevin, his staff and his dog, all of whom leapt to their feet and ran down the clubhouse stairs to give chase. Well, all but one. The dog initially showed interest, but then decided that the bone was more appealing, and fearing the burglars coming back for the left-over food, he decided to keep watch over the tasty morsels. Meanwhile, Kevin and his troops were sprinting into the distance and, away in the mist, the two men with the trellis table suddenly found a bit of pace themselves. But the thieves were in a losing battle and were struggling to keep hold of the prized piece of wood. When they were apprehended, their story beggared belief: one man said that he was there merely to help his friend carry the table and the other claimed that it was rightfully his property and that he was off to sell it at the local flea market. What he didn't know was that the table did not belong to Hamiltons but instead was owned by the police sports club and on this occasion there was going to be no need for fingerprints to be taken.

After all this excitement, I calmed down and watched the Emerging Springbok players train. They had only assembled on the Sunday evening and this was one of just two sessions before the Lions match. Their coach, the highly rated Boland coach Nick Mallett, put them through various drills. I thought they looked a big side up front and had a number of talented young backs who were already well known to us from the earlier matches on tour. But I felt that the mere fact that the scratch team had very little preparation time worked massively in the Lions' favour. I saw nothing to suggest that the Lions would lose the psychologically important final game before the first Test.

After about an hour of observation and note taking, I jumped into a cab and headed for the Cape Sun Hotel, the base for the full Springbok squad. At the news conference, the South African coach, Carel du Plessis, responded to the decision by the Lions to delay naming their team. He said that if the Lions were still searching for the right combinations then it could only help South Africa. Du Plessis had already shown his hand and had announced an almost unchanged side following the game against Tonga. The one exception was in the second-row, where Mark Andrews, who had been expected to return anyway, replaced the injured Fritz van Heerden. The team was – Joubert, Small, Mulder, Lubbe, Snyman, Honiball, Van der Westhuizen, Du Randt, Drotské, Garvey, Andrews, Strydom, Kruger, Venter and Teichmann (captain).

Doubts remained, however, over the fitness of Gary Teichmann and James Small. Remember, they had suffered hamstring pulls during that victory over the Tongans. The coach wanted an answer by the end of Tuesday and the Springbok run-out later on the Monday afternoon at Newlands would be a fascinating session to attend. If they did play, there was a severe doubt as to whether they would be singing their national anthems. Obviously the Lions, because of their diversity, do not have one national song which they can call their own. In 1974, the squad had adopted 'Flower of Scotland' as the team song on the bus to games, but this had not been officially sung on the field prior to kick-off because it was clearly too close to one of the four home nations. The 1997 squad had chosen 'Wonderwall' by Oasis as their theme tune. This, although frequently heard on the public address systems at grounds, would have made interesting listening alongside the more conventional South African anthems – Noel and Liam Gallagher really would have made 'royalties' had their famous ditty been elevated to anthem status.

The host nation had specially requested that they could be allowed to sing their songs regardless of the fact that the Lions had nothing to offer in return. They were waiting for a response from the Lions and the rumour was that the Lions were about to say no, citing an International Board ruling. After all, why should the host nation be allowed to whip their supporters into a state of frenzy and not the Lions? The South African captain, Gary Teichmann, insisted that the team would still sing the country's two anthems – the old and the new – either in the dressing room or on the field amongst themselves, as a means of allowing their preparation to reach a crescendo. There was no doubt that the intensely partisan South African public would react badly, and I hoped that the problem would not mushroom.

We waited for the Springbok squad to arrive at Newlands and were relieved when the coach pulled up outside the ground. The wind was biting and it was now jumper and fleece weather, with the clouds gathering menacingly. The news was that a cold front was on its way and that a lot of rain was to be expected over the next twenty-four hours. The clouds certainly deposited their contents that evening but luckily the rain held off to allow the South African squad to train in relative comfort. As they filed past me in the tunnel to go out on the field, I was struck by the size of the players. The likes of Os du Randt, André Venter and even the centre, Japie Mulder, are big men and would pose a strong physical threat. The two injury victims gingerly stretched their hamstrings and Small, who had got off the bus as if he was treading on eggshells, looked the worse of the two. The man tipped to take Small's place should he have to pull out, Justin Swart, looked perky and had the air of a player who felt that the cards might be about to fall his way.

It is at these training sessions when you start to build the thoughts and feelings which are necessary to create the right tone for the commentary on match day. Snippets of information are stored away and are vital ingredients to the overall mixture. The lines of running and back moves are obvious things to look out for, but it is the informal chats with coaches, media advisers and local journalists which, when put together, provide a comprehensive picture of the facts and emotions surrounding the event. For instance, I learnt that the South African team's rooming arrangements for their month-long spell together as a squad were very different to the Lions'. The Springboks were given the chance to take up permanent residence with their best friend. André Joubert and Henry Honiball are apparently virtually inseparable. Although they are very different in character with the gregarious Joubert contrasting with the shy Honiball, they have forged a friendship over the past few years which has a special quality. They both play for Natal and others were also keen to share with provincial team-mates. This was interesting when you considered the definite policy from the Lions to try and split up national and club colleagues. A further tit-bit of infor-mation acquired on that day came from Mark Andrews, the world-class lock. He made the point that, because of the camber to the pitch, the hooker, Naka Drotské, would have to throw at least a foot higher than he would normally expect. I looked closely at the lie of the ground and saw the crown rise to the centre as if the pitch had been transported from behind the Waterloo Hotel in Blackpool. There the crown green bowlers seek to get the bias right as they go in hunt of the jack. But in Cape Town the hookers would have to adjust their game accordingly to make sure they hit the jumper at the line-out.

There were two other younger men running around on the Newlands pitch that day. After further enquiries, I was told by the team manager, Arthob Petersen, that Donovan van Wyk and Johannes Comradie were part of the Rising Stars scheme set up by SARFU. They were to spend the whole week with the South African squad and experience life in the run-up to a Test match. They were eating and sleeping international rugby and were clearly enjoying the chance to develop their skills in such esteemed company. It seemed an excellent idea that the talented players from the disadvantaged communities were being given this motivation. I am not generally in favour of positive discrimination because I believe that in the end this fast-tracking can be counterproductive. I prefer selections to be made on merit because then the opportunities for criticism are non-existent. For example, take the brilliant winger Chester Williams: few would argue that this great role model is not worth his place in the international team and because of that he is the perfect man to emulate. But here the youngsters were being encouraged in the right manner and the Rising Stars scheme appeared to be an excellent way to say that rugby was available to all South Africans. At least something was being done.

I left the ground feeling that in their training session that day the South Africans had solidified the view that they were going to be a major force. It was their power which most impressed me, and memories of the defeat to the dynamic Northern Transvaal team came flooding back. But this was no time to start thinking negatively, especially as it was our wedding anniversary. Helen had been waiting patiently in the hotel enjoying the view of Table Mountain. As night fell, it was a chance to put on the glad rags and go out for a nice meal. We did so on the Waterfront, which is a part of the city that has been renovated with the tourist in mind. It is not the real Cape Town, but if you are in the area then it is a must if only for the twinkling night-time view of the harbour and the excellent restaurants which are in the vicinity. The favourable exchange rate allows you to really push the boat out and after another lovely bottle of South African red and some spicy local cuisine we thought that all seemed well with the world.

All had gone pretty well to plan for the Lions, too, and despite that one defeat at Loftus Versfeld, they were approaching the first Test match in a good frame of mind. The side to play the Emerging Springboks on the Tuesday before the first Test knew that this was their last chance for selection. The team – Stimpson, Bentley, Bateman, Greenwood, Beal, Catt, Healey, Rowntree, Regan, Leonard (captain), Redman, Davidson, Wainwright, Back and Diprose – were all aware that the management had made it clear that there were still places up for grabs. This team told us which players were currently the prime candidates and were being rested and protected from injury. But Bateman, Bentley, Leonard, Davidson and Back were all, in effect, being told to go out and demand that Test jersey. They did their utmost and with the help of the rest of their team-mates they produced another great day for the Lions.

The scene of the match, the Boland Stadium in Wellington, was about an hour's drive from Cape Town. As we left the city the rain started to fall again, and what normally is one of the most beautiful routes to a rugby ground anywhere in the world was blanked out by a wall of grey cloud. Wellington is in the heart of the region's wine country and in days gone by the pretty little town was the wagon-building centre for the Kimberley gold rush. Rugby has been played on the ground since 1882, but this was only the Lions' fifth visit, and the locals were looking forward to their arrival with great anticipation. The ground itself is surrounded by mountains. Sadly, when we arrived they were smothered in cloud. The rain kept coming down and the prospects for the match conditions and scenic view were diminishing by the minute.

We wandered around the ground to try and soak in the flavour of the day and to find some of our own, that is food! Normally on the tour we had been treated to the eats supplied to the M-Net television crew. You tend to find that the food laid on for an outside broadcast team is hearty fare because the workers have been humping cables and carrying boxes all morning. Other employees doing less strenuous jobs cash in on the ample provisions. But for some reason this catering was not available, so we were left to our own devices. I quite liked that, though, because there is no better way to get a taste for an occasion than to mix with the crowd and to listen to the word on the ground. On my way to obtain such culinary delights as a chip bun and coffee, I passed by a couple of Englishmen who had made the trip for the first Test match. They had been watching the tour on television back home, for which I was eternally grateful, and were adamant that Jeremy Davidson of Ireland had done enough to displace England's Simon Shaw. They were out in South Africa to support the men in red regardless of their nationality. They were not little Englanders but instead were part of an ever-growing band of British and Irish supporters who gave my heart a lift with their singing and chanting before kick off. The flags and banners of red, white and blue with more than a hint of green waved and proclaimed the arrival of such notable institutions as Stockport Rugby Club. They had come for a party and were determined to go through the whole repertoire of rugby songs, some of which were cleaner than others. The ones that related to James Small should really have been sung after the nine o'clock watershed!

As we approached the start of the match, and after I had climbed to the top of the ladder which led to the commentary position high over the main stand, the weather took a significant turn for the better. Indeed, I swear that we had all four seasons inside fifteen minutes. Luckily, the majority of the rain cloud was politely taking a circular route around the ground. Eventually the sun came out and the duvet of cloud over the mountains rolled back. What a sight and what a setting for a rugby match. This bowl of excitement sat beneath a heavenly vista as the picture went from a pencil sketch to a vivid pastiche.

The Lions once again proved too strong for the opposition, but the Emerging Springboks did provide something of a scare coming back to trail by just one point at half-time. The Springboks played like a side who had been thrown together at the last moment. Ironically, it was injury to the two half-backs, Van Rensburg and Adlam, which improved the South African fortunes. M. J. Smith, not to be confused with the former Middlesex opener, moved forward from full-back to fly-half. On came Marius Goosen, who at twenty-three is one of the most exciting backs in the country, and his running from full-back transformed the game. The Lions had been coasting until then and quickly realised that they had to find another gear. Ian McGeechan described this sleepy period as 'bloody awful', but the Lions came round and ended up with six more tries.

Nick Beal, restored to the wing, got three of them and he rocketed into Test match contention. One of those tries was made by another meandering run from John Bentley. After the score, Bentley ran over to the crowd and waved his arms à la Stuart Pearce in Euro '96 and he really got them going. But I still had some doubts over Bentley's defence and these worries were compounded when he failed to clear a ball just short of his own line and allowed the winger Paul Treu to score. Nonetheless, he was a great man to have in attack and was a strong influence on the rest of the players out there in the middle. He was also told after the match by our reporter, Phil Edwards, that he had been added to the England squad for the international against Australia in Sydney in the week after the Lions tour was over. This was one of those great moments for a broadcaster, when they are able to pass on good news and the audience can see the facial reaction of the recipient. It makes you glad that you chose a life as a sports journalist and therefore avoided the darker side of news reporting that personally I would find very difficult to cope with. Apart from some very obvious tragedies, sport is usually about the mere fact of winning and losing and nothing more important than that. Bentley was happy for himself, his family and for all those watching his progress back home in Cleckheaton in West Yorkshire.

At number eight, Tony Diprose was a revelation in his first match since his arrival from Argentina. I wondered what he could have achieved had he been on the tour from the start, though that was not a criticism of Miller and Rodber, or indeed Quinnell, who had gone home. Davidson, Back and Bateman were again outstanding. After the game, our studio guest, the England captain, Phil de Glanville, was asked by the presenter David Bobin who should wear the number seven shirt in the Test? De Glanville agonised before making his decision. He would go for Back but felt the selectors would pick Hill. 'How do you choose between those two?' De Glanville pleaded. This was just one example of the soul-searching that the Lions management would have to go through that evening in the selection meeting. They could never have believed that so many players would be vying for the Test places. It is the headache that all managers want – but that presumes they go on and find the right cure.

In the post-match news conference Fran Cotton said that the reaction of the players to rejection would be key to the rest of the tour, but that he felt sure they would respond in the best possible way and would look forward to pulling on the Lions jersey at the first available opportunity to prove they had been wrongly omitted. Anybody who saw the team in Wellington, victorious by fifty-one points to twenty-two, cheered off the field by the non-playing members of the party, knew that the spirit was right. At the end of the match, the squad had lined the tunnel in a show of togetherness and celebration.

Just before we left the ground we bumped into two former England coaches. Geoff Cooke was there in his role as team leader with a tour company and Dick Greenwood had arrived to see the excellent progress being made by his son, Will. Both men speculated about the possible make-up of the Test team and Greenwood had some kind words to say about the way in which the coverage was being received back home. It was good to get this feedback and it came as a reassuring pat on the back for the whole of the Sky team.

On the journey back from Wellington we stopped off in Franschhoek, a delightful little town also in the Western Cape. It was now time for us to play 'pick the Test team' over another fine meal and bottle of wine in front of a roaring log fire. The temperature had plummeted and for the first time on the tour you could actually see your breath in the night air. We hurried into the restaurant to take our seats for a night of rugby talk. I reflected on how my Test choice was so greatly different to the team I had chosen back in the heat of Durban before a ball had been kicked. The opinions of Cotton, McGeechan, Telfer and Johnson were the only ones that mattered that night but selecting sporting teams is too good a pastime to leave to the ones in the know. My choice was – Jenkins, Evans, Bateman, Guscott, Tait, Townsend, Dawson, Smith, Wood, Wallace, Johnson (captain), Davidson, Dallaglio, Back and Miller. And here are my reasons: at fullback Jenkins because of his reliable boot and Stimpson's exposure when under pressure. Evans because he is Evans. Bateman and Guscott because they were just too good to leave out, although I agonised over whether they were the right blend. Gibbs would be on the bench to offer a different style of attack; Greenwood deserved sympathy. Tait because of his pace on the turn and short-term acceleration. (Bentley had been close because of his ability to do the seemingly impossible and his professional determination.) Townsend because he remained the one man who could make the difference. Dawson because Howley had gone home and because he had the self-confidence to rise to the occasion. (Healey had the same attributes but Dawson had been playing the better of the two.) Smith, Wood and Wallace because they provided the best combination of scrummaging and mobility around the field, though Leonard, Williams and especially Young had all been seriously considered. Johnson because he was the captain and had thankfully played back to his best in the win over Natal. Davidson because he had simply done nothing wrong. Dallaglio because he had matured into a world-class forward. Back because he had proved his point. Miller because his youthful self-belief hinted at a great career ahead and there was no reason why this shouldn't begin in Cape Town. Hill and Rodber both nearly got onto the back of the napkin. But, of course, there can only be fifteen names on a team sheet.

The Wednesday of that week was something of a watershed in that it was the first day off on the tour. This is not to say that we had slogged through eighteen-hour stints, but on each day we had carried out some form of work. But this was one day when I was determined to walk away from rugby and recharge the batteries for the rigours of the weekend. It was high time that Helen and I jumped into a car and set off for the hills. The drive out took us through Muizenberg and along the coast up False Bay. The sky was clear, apart from the odd wispy white cloud which hovered over the mountain tops to make them look as if they were giant cooling towers. There was nothing industrial about this scene, though, and out to sea the blue water was lined with green streaks of colour, which gave the impression of the ocean having been mown in neat rows like the turf at Newlands. Our journey took us first to Stellenbosch, a quaint university town with neatly laid out buildings which all appeared to have been freshly painted with brilliant white. The film set scenery continued back out to Franschhoek as we thought we had better see the place in daylight after our journey there on the previous evening. We were not disappointed and drove around open mouthed, stunned by the majesty of the mountain range. Lunch in a restaurant carved into the mountain side provided a perfect release from the pressures of the job. The final leg of the day was the obligatory wine tasting. We pulled into Paarl, so named because of the Paarl rock, a giant outcrop which glistens like a black pearl after rainfall. There was no need to worry about rain on this day, as the sun had provided the perfect conditions for an excursion around one of the most beautiful parts of the country. Mind you, having sampled six wines, most things were looking pretty good at that point. Alan, our driver, laughed knowingly when we chinked our way back to the car weighed down by some local produce – and I don't mean vegetables.

On the Thursday I took my match preparation outside at the hotel and laid it on a table in the sun. What an office! Table Mountain was in the background and the gardens at the Vineyard blended in with the woods at the foot of the mountain. The beauty stretched as far as the eye could see. I got a call on the mobile from the office and was informed that it was raining at Lord's where they were hoping to start the second Test match between England and Australia. Had this news been relayed to me back home, I would have been distraught at the thought of the loss of a whole day's Test cricket. But I admit to having a sadistic chortle that I wasn't missing out on the Ashes action and I compared my South

African winter to the British summer. (At this point you have my full permission to throw the book down in disgust at my smugness.)

The Lions had made a U-turn and decided to reveal their side before Saturday morning. The original plan to delay the news had been scrapped because it was likely to leak out anyway. This was good news for me and made the preparation of my commentary chart a much easier exercise. This is the sheet of paper which acts as a backbone to the eighty minutes of verbal acrobatics. I have two large sheets which are filled with the most relevant information for the day in question. Colouring pens are used to grade the importance of the detail. On the left-hand side, I have notes on the management teams, the history of contests between the two sides, team and individual records and themes for the game, which are always discussed on the day before the match with my commentary partner Stuart Barnes. On the right-hand side are the names of all forty-two players involved in the match plus the officials. Beside their names I try and cram in as much data as possible, such as their caps, points scored in internationals, age, height and weight. It is here that I also try and make more general observations about the players' potential roles in the specific match. For instance, I highlighted the threat of Joost van der Westhuizen in broken play and his chip out of hand on the run, which is simply the best in the world. It was an area of play which at some stage I would be looking to point up to the viewer. Well, at least that was the plan. So often the course of events during a game take over and then it is quite right to ditch the notes and let the emotion of the day drive the commentary. But a commentator would feel naked without his or her preparation – forewarned is forearmed. I have a library of all these commentary sheets and they provide not only an invaluable reference tool but also bring back some great memories of matches which I have been fortunate enough to cover. I know this sounds silly, but I can often remember more about a game and how I felt at the time by looking at the commentary chart and my scribblings during a game than from watching a video of the match. This was undoubtedly the most important commentary chart that I had ever prepared. During my career I had commentated on other rugby internationals and cup finals, plus Wimbledon tennis finals and big football and cricket occasions. But I had never felt so much antici- pation forty-eight hours before the event. I joked with Stuart that, although I would not have been much good to the cause, I had levels of adrenaline which almost made me feel as if I wanted to go out and play in the match myself. Stuart peered over his glass and like a scornful professor gave me an indulgent look. Even so, we both knew that we were in for an emotional broadcasting experience.

*

The players had been informed of their participation in the game or otherwise by a letter slipped underneath their hotel room door. It was hard for those in the squad who had missed out on selection, but equally it was a thrilling moment for those who had been successful. It must have been like opening an envelope that contained your A-level results. In most cases, the difference between success and failure had been minimal. I was reminded of a story from before the tour started when Austin Healey, Will Greenwood's house-mate, hid Greenwood's selection letter, only to flaunt his own while pretending to commiserate with his Leicester colleague. I wondered if Healey had now suffered the same treatment?

Fran Cotton arrived at our hotel to carry out an interview with Sky Sports and he revealed the team to us an hour before the lunch-time news conference on an embargoed basis. This is a fairly common occurrence and allows the interviewee to get promptly away after the more general media questioning to avoid taking too large a slice out of an important day. Cotton confirmed that it had been a protracted and wide ranging debate. But eventually the Lions had settled on this team for the first Test match – Jenkins, Evans, Guscott, Gibbs, Tait, Townsend, Dawson, Smith, Wood, Wallace, Johnson (captain), Davidson, Dallaglio, Hill and Rodber. Eric Miller had been chosen, but because of the onset of flu he had been forced to withdraw from consideration and Tim Rodber had got the number eight jersey. Cotton said that they had wanted to get the balance right and it was clear that there was a genuine effort to combine guile with power. The bench is also a vital part of an international these days and the names of the men in reserve were – Bentley, Catt, Healey, Leonard, Williams and Wainwright. I felt sorry for all the players who had missed out, but in particular for Allan Bateman and Neil Back who were both desperately close to selection. Cotton had told the squad that it was a series and other chances would probably come. The dilemma for the players who were forced to sit out the Cape Town Test was that they would cheer on their colleagues, but if those on the field secured victory, then an unchanged team was always the most likely option for the second Test. But there was a long way to go before the Lions went one–nil up.

Who would have thought that the England tight five would have been reduced to just one for the opening Test? What money would you have got on three Irishmen being in the pack following their country's performance in the Five Nations Championship? (It would have been four had Miller not had flu.) Name one person who put money on Matt Dawson being the Lions scrum-half after he dropped down to number four in the England ranks following injury during the previous winter. Now, he would play alongside his club partner Gregor Townsend.

Thoughts also went out to the man who should have been wearing that number nine jersey, Robert Howley, and to Scott Quinnell and Doddie Weir, who all could have been in the Test side but for terrible misfortune. There was, however, no point harping on about what might have been. We now knew that we had initially been denied a rematch of the John Bentley–James Small confrontation, yet we had been offered so much more. I only hoped that the Lions would not get to within spitting distance of South Africa and then regret the fact that the artful Bateman and Back had been left out. I felt that if they were going to win it was by stretching the South Africans out wide, but if I had been in the selection meeting, could I have taken that risk and left out the likes of Scott Gibbs and Richard Hill, whose power would combat the home team's intention to out-muscle the Lions? It's all very different to scribbling the names on a serviette in a restaurant.

Probably the nicest story of the day was the awarding of a Lions cap to the Irish hooker Keith Wood. His late father Gordon had been a Lion in New Zealand in 1959 and when I asked Keith about the feelings that he had, he said that he had never set out to emulate his father but now that the moment had come it was tugging at the heartstrings. Wood had spoken to his mother, the proudest lady in Ireland. She was going to be following her son's progress with an extra special interest.

Just after speaking to Wood, I saw the great South African back-row forward, Morné du Plessis, about to leave the players' hotel. I went over and asked one of the politest men in the sport for a quick interview. Du Plessis was about to jump in his car to drive to a meeting, but typically he delayed his plans to accommodate others. He talked with great passion and gave us the perfect preview of the Test from a home player who had experienced the emotion surrounding these matches at first hand. He went misty eyed at the mention of his last appearance against the Lions and over the prospect of seeing the green shirts take on the red after a seventeen-year gap. Du Plessis added that he had not felt such a tingle of anticipation for a rugby match in Cape Town since the World Cup – and remember, the All Blacks had been there less than a year ago. The Lions were big news and nobody could wait for the kick-off.

The Friday morning before the match was spent at Newlands. The workmen were applying the final licks of paint to the tunnel surrounds and the sign writers were spraying the grass to make sure that we were left in no doubt as to who was sponsoring the game. A big crane hovered over one end of the stadium as work continued on the removal of a section of the roof. The plan was to increase the size of the end stand in order to bring it into line with the higher constructions on either side of the pitch, but for some spectators that meant there was the prospect of a wet evening. The sun shone brightly just thirty-six hours before kick-off, but we had been warned of a cold front which was scheduled to arrive the next morning.

Our commentary position was magnificently situated over the half-way line. Again we had been given the best seat in the house. The decision as to where we would commentate from had been made on the Thursday morning prior to the game, as the riggers had wanted to know where to route the lines of communication. At the half-way line, should the rain come, we and our equipment were liable to get a soaking, but the alternative was an inferior commentary site, tucked away behind a concrete pillar. We took the gamble to hang out in the elements. The team invested in some plastic sheeting to cover the electronics in the event of a storm, but there was little that one could do to protect us commentators, aside from recommending a coat and a hat.

Another person preparing for the day of reckoning was the Lions full-back, Neil Jenkins, as he went through a tough kicking session with Dave Alred. We stood watching and willed every kick over, but I have to report that Jenkins missed a lot more than he got that morning. What would have normally been easy attempts for him sailed wide and we left hoping that he had purged the bad ones out of his system.

The next stop was the last Lions news conference before the Test, and there was an air of tension as the panellists took their seats for the final round of questions. Jim Telfer talked boldly about the strengths of his men and when asked to draw a war analogy the tough Scot said that he would be delighted to have the forwards alongside him in the trenches. He made the telling point that the players would have to draw on reserves that had never previously been tapped and, as they did that, they would also have to maintain a high level of concentration when their fitness was being stretched to new limits. This, according to Telfer, was the main challenge of the day – how to keep it going when they were 'knackered'.

I was feeling the tension as well and having done as much preparation as was possible before match day, I decided to let off a bit of steam by watching the sunset at Chapman's Peak. The drive up to one of the most popular viewpoints in Cape Town is via a winding passage along the side of the cliffs which is considered to be one of the most beautiful but dangerous rides in the area. Each year somebody takes their vehicle over the edge and down into the sea. The road took seven years to build in the early part of this century and a few men perished during its construction. But the modern accidents happen during the bad weather and when people ignore the advice to take an alternative route. On this day the drive was a pleasure, there were no rocks falling or tyres slipping. The view when Helen and I got there was idyllic as the evening sun melted away into the Atlantic Ocean.

As we and a party of Lions supporters waited for the sun to drop, a familiar face turned up to join us. The South African World Cup captain, François Pienaar, is one of the most recognisable men in sport and the word soon spread that he was getting out of his car. It was a real bonus for the fans to have not only a photograph of the sun going down but also one with a rugby hero. Pienaar was with his new boss at Saracens, Nigel Wray, and as ever he conducted himself with great poise. No picture or autograph caused him a problem and he left wishing the British and Irish supporters all the best for a great day out at Newlands.

The day ended with the none too onerous task of taking out the wives and girlfriends of the Lions players. Quite a few had made the trip, but on the eve of the match they were lying low to allow their loved ones to prepare in isolation. It was a thoroughly enjoyable night and a fascinating one as well. Martin Johnson's other half, Kay, who had just arrived, said that she would only be seeing him on three occasions during the tour. It was hard for her to keep a distance, but she was only too well aware of how important it was to allow him to carry out his duties as Lions captain to the full. Natalie, the lady behind Matt Dawson, sneaked out half-way through the meal to give him one last good luck message. He had been straight on the telephone as soon as he had heard of his selection and she was as excited as the man himself over the prospect of seeing Matt in action on a momentous day. I hoped that they would both have fond memories of the match. Nigel Redman's wife, Lorinda, had had her world turned upside down with the news of his addition to the squad. A hastily arranged spell of unpaid leave courtesy of the school governors allowed the physical education teacher to bundle up the children and whisk them away to see Daddy in South Africa. This was not without alarm, though, because her luggage was also nearly turned upside down. It had been inspected at the airport and there had been a flurry of activity when the x-ray machine revealed a layer of small containers hidden away in one suitcase. But there was no threat posed to security – it was just a mother making sure that the favourite baby food was on hand to satisfy the needs of the little Redmans. Finally, after the realisation from April Young, wife of David, that I was the voice behind the Sky Sports coverage, there was a piece of invaluable information passed on to yours truly. Although widely known as Dai, I shall never call the Welsh prop anything other than David from here on in. This is on the strict orders of his mother, who apparently bemoans the fact that nobody gives her son his proper name!

Saturday, 21 June and the day had finally arrived when the Lions would play their first Test match in South Africa for seventeen years. To say I was in a state of frenzy would be a gross understatement. The players and commentators wanted dry weather, so I nervously looked out of the hotel window and saw the cloud bubbling up over the mountain. It was as if somebody was puffing smoke from behind the ridge with a pair of bellows. The predicted storms seemed to be on their way and it was just a matter of whether they would hold off until after the game – but with the late kick-off at a quarter past five in the afternoon the chances were slim. I made sure that my coat was packed in the bag and extracted those thermals from the bottom of the suitcase.

Killing time and focusing on the game was my main priority for the next few hours. I watched the live coverage of Australia versus France in Sydney as a means of relaxation, but I am not sure that analysing another rugby game was the best solution. It only worked to a certain degree, and the adrenaline levels kept increasing. This was the biggest game of my broadcasting life so far and it was imperative to try and get everything right. In particular, I knew it was important to maintain a balance between on the one hand feeling keyed up, but on the other staying calm and collected. At lunch-time, when I missed my mouth with a spoonful of minestrone soup, I knew that I had failed!

The short walk to the ground was accompanied by ever-increasing amounts of cloud. The wind refused to die down and there was no doubt that rain, and lots of it, was in the air. Despite the grey skies, the vivid colours sported by the spectators lit up the stroll through the crowds and as we got to the stadium there were all the signs of a big match day. Faces were being painted with the national colours. Flags were waved out of car windows and a vehicle proclaimed its support by having one flag from each of the home unions adorning its four corners. The travelling support from home was immense and they had arrived early to guarantee a sufficient level of alcoholic intake. There is a disused railway carriage adjacent to Newlands station which acts as a convenient resting place before a match. It is now a bar and the hoards of fans who had arrived long before kick-off were spilling over into the street outside. The strong smell of beer was compounded by the presence of a brewery on the other side of the road. It was rugby heaven for many a supporter.

Having struggled through the lively but well-mannered crowd, it was time to check in with the crew and make sure all was well with the start of the game just a couple of hours away. I chatted with the South African commentator Hugh Blaydon – we were both pessimistic about our side's chances. I suppose this was quite natural, and I for one always find it is better to be pleasantly surprised than brought down to earth at the end of a big game. But although my heart desired a Lions victory, I

Kicking guru Dave Alred shows Jenkins the way to win a Test match.

Match day – hard at work (for once!)

Testing each other out – as the battle for the series begins.

André Joubert sees the first Test slip through his hands.

The worst moment of the tour – Greenwood is stretchered from the field.

Back in training – 'can-can' they win the second Test?

Guscott finds the key to success. (Or in the professional era should that be the swipe card?)

Monty misfires.

His dad would have been proud of him – Keith Wood emulates his late father by becoming a Lion.

'Two–nil to the Li-eons, two–nil to the Li-eons. . .'

'Bentos' celebrates.

Honiball, moving out.

The 'Ox', looking a little sheepish.

Dallaglio, my man of the tour.

Davidson reaches new heights.

The captain's smile says it all.

genuinely believed that it was going to be the Springboks' day.

On my way up to the commentary position, I stopped on the stairway and looked down on the mayhem below. The South African team bus had just arrived and it was struggling to break through the crowd. Everybody was straining to glimpse, or even touch, their heroes, and the expression on the faces of the players as they disembarked from the coach confirmed that they were focused on the task. The people that lined the pavements also looked tense, emphasising the importance of the match by their body language. This is a country which takes its sport seriously and the thought of defeat was too much to contemplate.

I had to turn my mind to the commentary. After an inspection of the position and a few adjustments to the angle of the monitor and the level of sound from the different sources in the headphones, I sat down to survey the scene. At this point I felt a little detached from the event, almost as if I was the viewer at home watching it all happening on my television set. But as the crowds came filing in and the volume increased, the enormity of the situation dawned on me. This was for real and it was every commentator's dream to be involved on such an important day.

The former Scotland and Lions captain, Gavin Hastings, had joined our team out in South Africa having been a regular guest in the studio during the earlier games. Of us all, Gavin was the most optimistic about the Lions' chances and his upbeat mood gave reason for hope. I don't want to sound as if I had written the Lions off – believe me, every bone in my body wanted them to win – but South Africa had proved time and time again that they could grind down the opposition into submission. It was going to take a Herculean effort from the Lions to overcome this obstacle.

Rugby's version of cricket's 'barmy army' had descended on Cape Town and they were making their presence felt. I peered over the commentary box balcony and down below was a mass of red jerseys worn by the partisan spectators. Their spirits were high and there was no telling this mob that their team were not about to make history. The singing echoed around the ground as we approached kick-off and if you shut your eyes you could imagine being in Cardiff, Dublin, Edinburgh or London. They had their own brand of musical entertainment, but with minutes to go before the teams ran out, the South African singer Jennifer Jones more conventionally treated the crowd to a song from her repertoire, as she had done before some of the World Cup games in 1995. It was also time for the Webb Ellis trophy to be handed to the chairman of Rugby World Cup, Leo Williams. To a great cheer from the home crowd, it was paraded one last time on South African soil before going to Wales in preparation for the 1999 competition. This seemed to whip up the crowd fervour to an even greater extent and it now just remained for the teams to come out onto the field.

I heard the studio back in London go to a commercial break and knew that on the return they would hand straight to me. I am not ashamed to say that my heart was beating a merry tune and my mouth was dry. I took one more sip of water, a deep breath and waited for the cue. There it was, 'It is now time to cross to our commentary team in the stadium, Stuart Barnes and first, Miles Harrison.' After a brief pause, I launched into the words that I had already written for the first ten seconds of commentary. I don't always do this, but on the big occasions I feel it is necessary to momentarily adhere to a script just so that the early phrases are delivered at the right pace. There is nothing worse than a nervous gabble to begin proceedings of such importance. It is up to the commentator to set off in a measured fashion which allows the event to build and the emotion to grow.

Down in the tunnel we had shots of Martin Johnson preparing to lead his team onto the Newlands turf. He also knew that weeks of preparation would now culminate in eighty minutes of rugby. The vital first Test match would shape the rest of the series. It is a long way back from one–nil down in a three-match contest. Johnson ran out, determinedly followed by fourteen other pumped-up Lions. The roar was deafening. Out came the South Africans, racing past the chorus girls. The Lions management had magnanimously allowed the Springboks to give vent to their feelings by singing their two anthems; but, when the home crowd stood to their feet and sang with such gusto that the whole of Cape Town must have been able to hear, they may have rued that decision. The hairs on my body were literally standing on their ends as we waited for the start of the series which we had been thirsting for.

Ominously, the South Africans set off well, but they were helped by a poor kick-off from Neil Jenkins which immediately put the Lions on the back foot. The home scrum looked as powerful as we had feared and the signs were bad when the Lions front-row buckled under the pressure. After an exchange of penalties between Edrich Lubbe and Jenkins, the first try was scored. Following a comfortable win by Mark Andrews at the line-out, prop forward Os du Randt rumbled round to drive over. The 'Ox' hadn't needed much support. He was a potent weapon and had been used effectively.

The Lions, though, continued to show great character and came back with ferocity. They started to find their feet up front and the forwards were making an impact. Amazingly, at the interval, the Lions actually led by nine points to eight, courtesy of Neil Jenkins' boot. We went to the break knowing that the game was perfectly poised. Excitedly, I chatted away with Stuart during half-time feeling that something special might be just around the corner.

Those hopes seemed destined to be dashed early in the second half. After another Jenkins penalty, the South Africans scored their second try. For the first time their backs looked the part, and the replacement, Russell Bennett, who had come on for the injured Lubbe, scored with his first touch of the ball. A young man winning only his second cap delighted in going around the Lions cover to finish in the corner.

I was none too pleased, though this had little to do with the fact that the Lions had conceded a try. The 'talk-back' system from our men down on the pitch had temporarily broken down. Martin Knight was frantically trying to contact me on the radio link to tell me that South Africa had made a change at half-time. The first I knew of Bennett's presence on the field was when he was receiving the scoring pass. 'Oh !!?,' I thought, or words to that effect! Going to those training sessions earlier in the week to spot the players had saved my bacon.

Following the try, I swear the few remaining sections of roof at the end of the ground where the reconstruction was taking place almost came off. The Springbok supporters were already celebrating the thought of victory and fully expected their team to pull away. The lead increased as they went sixteen points to twelve in front when Henry Honiball landed a penalty. I must admit, at this stage I felt that South Africa were going to live out my pre-match prediction. I was preparing for the worst, trying to find those words which would sum up a brave but losing start to the Test campaign.

Surprisingly, the Springboks began to commit basic errors in the face of some colossal Lions tackling and what happened over the final ten minutes will live long in the memory of any British or Irish rugby supporter. With time ticking away, Matt Dawson made a score which he and the rest of us would never forget. He outrageously dummied at the base of an attacking scrum, put his head down and went. He left the South African cover for dead and could hardly believe it when he reached the try line unopposed. Having totally fooled the defence, Dawson put the ball down and carried on running towards the crowd in a football-style celebration. That was the lead and there was no stopping the Lions from there. The Springboks looked flummoxed and their desperate attempts to get the ball away from their own line failed time and time again. Their standard of play spiralled down in the face of the Lions onslaught. The tourists' fitness was supreme. They were rewarded for their continued bravery by running in a try which involved all facets of the team. The only way the Springboks were going to score was from a breakaway from their own line. Tim Rodber ignored such possibilities and floated a pass out to Alan Tait, who was the lucky man to be on the end of a classy move. All he had to do was put the ball down. The Lions had conquered, and once again the tourists had finished the stronger of the two teams.

I don't remember much about that second half apart from the fact that, like all home supporters, I was living on the emotion of the event. Time seemed to stand still after Dawson had edged the Lions in front. All I could think of was what everybody was going through as they watched back home. In commentary, I also admitted to having 'officially come off the fence'. When the final whistle went there were scenes of delirium all around as the players embraced each other and were joined on the pitch by the rest of the bench plus the other members of the squad. The image that I will always cherish was the sight of Matt Dawson hugging his club and Lions coach, Ian McGeechan. As McGeechan said in the flash interview after the match, some young men had been to places that they had never visited before and the whole of the squad could afford a night of rejoicing. It was a terrific feeling for everybody connected with the team: players, officials, supporters and even commentators.

I found it very difficult to conceal my excitement and in the after-match news conference there was a lot of unprofessional punching of the air by the British and Irish media. We all knew that we had witnessed one of the great victories. But, South Africa had played badly and Carel du Plessis admitted to having underestimated the strength of the Lions. Some world-class players had a shocking day. André Joubert, the Rolls Royce, had failed to get out of the garage and had gone through a harrowing evening looking a long way from his best. The much-vaunted pack had failed to make the predicted inroads and the backs had looked unrehearsed. Du Plessis certainly couldn't claim that he had not had the necessary time to work with the squad. But to dwell on the South African inadequacies, of which there were many, would be to neglect what was a sensational effort from the Lions. At the start of the match it was felt that at least five Lions would have to put in the greatest game of their lives for victory to be possible. But in the event it was much nearer fifteen. Neil Jenkins had a set of five all to himself, as his accurate penalty attempts helped settle the team when they were under severe pressure. Scott Gibbs tackled as if he was dumping the rubbish out in the backyard. The Welshman had no respect for his opponents. Dawson and Townsend combined coolly at half-back. But for me, it was the pack who deserved the major plaudits. They had thought their muscles were going to burst after that first scrummage when South Africa had turned the screw. But they had recovered from a shaky beginning to stamp their authority on the game. Who would have thought that a Lions eight would put in such a display after the earlier nightmare scrummaging on the tour? The names of Smith, Wood, Wallace, Johnson, Davidson, Dallaglio, Hill and Rodber deserve to take their place in Lions history alongside the best. I smiled as Tom Smith, who had to leave the field injured towards the end of the match, hobbled back out of the tunnel long after the final whistle had gone. The crowd had stayed on, singing all four home anthems and Smith held his arms aloft to take their acclaim. The shy man of the tour really came out of his shell and beamed with delight as he posed for the photographs which would fill the morning newspapers. Smith had propped up the scrum along with the fast-talking Irishmen, Keith Wood and Paul Wallace. They had all come of rugby age.

Minutes later, the rain started to come down. We scurried under cover and called in at a braai which had been kindly provided by our broadcast hosts, M-Net. The sausages in mustard sauce and local beer tasted magnificent as the sheets of rain drifted through the beam of the floodlights. Had the clouds burst an hour earlier, we would have been drenched on the commentary gantry; but the weather had smiled on us and, although the walk to the hotel would be a soggy one, we simply didn't care. It was time for singing in the rain.

RED ARMY GOES BARMY

'I have preached all tour the importance of getting the right man in the right place.' – Jeremy Guscott with a smile after his series-winning drop goal.

It was quite incredible. The Lions had timed their run for the final lap of the tour to perfection. By way of contrast, South Africa seemed boxed in. The Lions needed another big effort from the mid-week side in the next game against Free State to keep their momentum. A win, preferably in style, would make the thought of a series victory in Durban irresistible.

The atmosphere in the hotel on the morning after the victory was understandably upbeat. The taste of victory had been made all the more sweet because it had been so unexpected at the start of the tour. It was time to leave Cape Town and head across the country back to Natal. Sadly, it was also the point when Helen had to return home to London. Her presence had given me a real lift and having my wife on tour had got rid of any feelings of homesickness. The sad goodbye was tempered by the fact that she had seen a Lions win on foreign soil and that the end of the trip was now in sight. But what a last two weeks it promised to be.

On arrival in Durban we met Andy Irvine at the airport. He had flown out to take part in one of those very popular 'golden oldie' tours which are now springing up around the big internationals. Having said that, Irvine still looks young enough to take part in more conventional matches. He is the Cliff Richard of rugby, although he would probably question that description! Irvine had been thrilled by the Lions win and just like his fellow countryman, Gavin Hastings, had seen his optimism rewarded. What with Ian McGeechan and Jim Telfer having master-minded the victory, I was left thinking that they must teach the power of positive thinking north of the Border.

Of course, the whole post-match atmosphere could have been so different had referee Colin Hawke not decided to award a scrum for a forward pass, thus denying the Springboks another second-half score. It was a crucial decision and one which in effect determined the result.

There would have been no way back for the Lions had another try been conceded. The former England captain, Will Carling, agreed. He had arrived on a flying visit to Durban on business for his club, Harlequins, and he said to me that had that try stood, the Lions would have been playing catch up. There were no signs of bleating, though, in the South African press. Their sole concern was with the way in which the side had played. There was universal condemnation of the performance and the headlines said it all. 'Boks blow it' and 'Woeful Boks fall prey to the Lions' were just two examples. Already there was pressure building on Carel du Plessis and, although he was putting on a brave face, there was a growing feeling that another defeat in Durban would spell trouble for the coach. The South African rugby public is impatient and demands immediate success.

Not a word was uttered in the Kombi on the way to the hotel. It was late on the Sunday evening and we were all feeling the effects of a hard working day and a long night of celebration on the Saturday. Graham Simmons, our regular rugby union reporter, had now replaced Phil Edwards on the tour. Just before the start of the tour, Graham's wife, Maria, had given birth to their first child, Hanna, so Graham's departure had been delayed. We were all glad to see him and producer David Tippett, who, along with his wife Sarah, had also just welcomed a first-born into the world: their son, James. But the team was sad to lose Phil, who had become a good friend during the course of the trip. He had also been the character of the tour and his impressions of the cast of the television comedy *Blackadder* would be sorely missed.

To wake up again in Durban was a strange experience. It was our third visit to the city and, although I have nothing against the place, you wouldn't even choose to go to your favourite holiday destination three times inside six weeks. I was not surprised to see that the hotel décor hadn't changed since our previous stay. What was different, though, was that we now had a realistic belief that the Lions could take the Test series. The happiest people in the hotel were wearing the team tracksuits – but they also knew that the hard work was only half done. Ian McGeechan said that the squad had celebrated to the full on Saturday night but then had immediately centred their attention on the second Test. These were the right words, of course, but with his team they were also entirely true. At no time had the players given the impression that they were not in South Africa to carry out a very specific task. This wasn't about to change. It was inevitable that during a long haul some players would spend more time with those that they already knew – for instance, the Healey and Greenwood double act – but the squad unison had undoubtedly been further enhanced following the weekend victory. Nigel Redman remarked, 'It doesn't get better than this. People have reacted outstandingly on this trip, better than I have ever seen before.'

Redman was the main focus of that day because, having only recently been plucked out of the international wilderness, he was to receive yet another honour – that of captaining the Lions. Redman would take charge for the mid-week game in Bloemfontein against Free State. This was an unexpected privilege. He recalled that he had once led the England under-twenty-three team against Spain many years ago and looked forward to this latest honour. The rest of the team announced for the game was predictable – Stimpson, Bentley, Bateman, Greenwood, Underwood, Catt, Healey, Rowntree, Williams, Young, Redman (captain), Shaw, Wainwright, Back and Miller. So, none of Saturday's Test side had been included, but the bench for the Test, bar Jason Leonard who had got into action at Newlands, were all given an outing to keep them sharp. Eric Miller had recovered from flu, but now had to work hard to replace Tim Rodber.

There was a telling moment during the news conference when John Bentley made the case for the mid-week team. He said that 'if Fran Cotton was true to his word', then the selection for the Test team would be made on the Wednesday morning after the match against Free State. Bentley desperately wanted to be part of the second Test match and he wanted all around him to know this. Afterwards, he joked that if the Lions went two–nil up, then they would perhaps consider not turning up in Johannesburg for the third game. It was, of course, tongue-in-cheek, but it again showed Bentley's bubbling enthusiasm for the common cause.

That afternoon I retired to my room to begin the preparation work for the match in Bloemfontein. As an accompaniment I had the television on and watched the rain interfere with the first day's play at Wimbledon. I felt a tinge of sadness, as this was my first year away from commentating on the Championships for some time. I had always enjoyed my time as part of one of the fun programmes on the radio. The show is brilliantly hosted by John Inverdale, who has to be one of the best radio broadcasters in the country, and along with the likes of Richard Evans, Christine Janes, Tony Adamson, Frew McMillan and Barbara Potter, I used to have a ball.

Ironically, I had bumped into John Inverdale at Cape Town airport on the Sunday evening as he was returning home after the first Test match. I asked him to pass on my best wishes to the rest of the team, but, although I would miss them, this was one year when I really didn't regret not being able to be in two places at once. The Lions tour was on such an upswing that I felt that I was in the right place and was one of the luckiest broadcasters around.

The television coverage soon switched over to the second Test match at Lord's. Although it was a relief to see that England had managed to save the game on the final day, the vagaries of the British weather were illustrated by the fact that the cricketers were playing in bright sunshine as, just across London, the tennis players sat and waited for the showers to stop. We would arrive home during the third Ashes Test. How well would England be placed then? But a more vexing question was, what would be the outcome of our series which would have just ended in Johannesburg?

The Springboks' preparations for the second Test in Durban were being severely affected by injuries to a number of players. James Small, Japie Mulder and Edrich Lubbe were all struggling to be fit in time. Carel du Plessis said that he wanted to stay with the team that he had chosen for the series and that changing the side was not necessarily the answer. But it appeared that his hand was going to be forced. As the coach pondered the selection, the criticism continued to rain down. A couple of the South African journalists had contacted the out of favour Hennie Le Roux, who was possibly in line for a recall. Du Plessis claimed that he had talked to Le Roux and, because of injury, had ruled out his inclusion. The journalists said that they too had spoken to Le Roux and they were adamant that the coach had not been in contact. Du Plessis was questioned on the matter. He said he could not understand the confusion and had appreciated the 'honesty and openness' of Le Roux in labelling himself as unfit for the Test. But conflicting stories were not what the South African camp wanted during their preparation for a match that they could not afford to lose.

We arrived in Bloemfontein on Tuesday, 24 June, just as news of the emerging row over Hennie Le Roux was coming to light. The decision to fly into the Free State on the morning of the game was taken because we had wanted to coincide our travel arrangements with those of the Lions. They would touch down a lot later than us, however, and there were a few members of our party who regretted having to get up so early for the first flight of the day. As I have mentioned before, I, for one, am not at my best at a quarter to five in the morning. Our journey to Durban airport was delayed by a certain member of the Sky team who had forgotten his airline ticket. He shall remain nameless, but suffice to say that he has played for the Lions and England at fly-half. We turned back to get the ticket and the culprit kept a low profile as our driver muttered about having to pick up some more people from a different hotel. He was not a happy man and it was a case of letting him slam the doors and get the early morning blues out of his system.

Once at the airport, having checked in our baggage and still peering through half-open eyes, we boarded the bus to take us to our plane. The coach took us out past a couple of jumbo jets; then onwards we went, leaving the middle range of aircraft in our wake before we finally arrived at a line of propeller-operated planes. Sitting shyly at the end of the row was a tiny machine which didn't look capable of cutting the grass, let alone leaving the ground and taking us across the hills to Bloemfontein. As we hunched our shoulders and squeezed down into the aircraft, we were informed that this Jetstream 41 was one of the newest additions to the South African Airways fleet. I wondered what had happened to Jetstream 40 and if they had finished building number 42 . . . The journey was perfectly comfortable, though, and as we passed over the mountains we could clearly see snow on top. We were heading back to high altitude and the day was breaking, both crisp and clear.

Bloemfontein is the kind of place which even South Africans poke fun at. I suppose the British equivalent is Bognor Regis. There is little to do in 'Bloem' and the negative publicity stems from this basic fault. The land all around is barren and dry and the days are monotonous in their meteorological regularity. The skies are perpetually cloudless and the nights are cold. You tend to find that those travelling to the city never actually admit to living there. Our impressions were not enhanced by the amount of time it took to check in at the hotel and, as we waited to be let into our rooms, I decided to sit down and wait outside in the fresh air. This was going swimmingly until the garden sprinklers were triggered. We had no warning of the attack, and before we could react, the firing squad of spray jets had soaked us. Each time we moved around the garden a new battalion of sprinklers sprang into action. When they started approaching from the concealed raised flowerbed over our heads then we knew it was time to surrender and retreat inside.

A breakaway party from the Sky team had decided to use the free morning to investigate the local game reserve. It is not one of the best in South Africa, to say the least. In fact, a sighting of two giraffes represented such a meagre return that, their safari instincts frustrated, they decided to go to the local zoo instead. It was more Whipsnade than Kruger National Park. Back in the hotel, we waited for the Lions to arrive, but they had been delayed and their military-like operation was severely affected. They had chartered a plane to take them in and out of Bloemfontein in the day, but were running out of time as we approached kick-off.

The Lions eventually set foot in the hotel just as Stuart and I were approached by a genial group of Irish supporters who had managed to get through their day courtesy of the local brew. They asked us if we wanted to become honorary Irishmen for the day and we willingly accepted the offer of their touring badge. We also promised to wear this token of their affection on screen that evening when we presented our chat from the touch line shortly before the game started. The idea was to use the Irish badge as a way into talking about the excellent performances of the three men of green in the first Test match. We also wanted to highlight the possibility of another Irishman, Eric Miller, making a bid for inclusion in the second Test in Durban. If Miller had a big game against Free State, he had a chance of replacing Tim Rodber despite the Northampton captain's brilliant defensive display in Cape Town. Miller was offering more dynamism when running off the base of the scrum and more all-round ability with the ball in hand. It promised to be the main selection problem.

Free State were without some key players. Du Randt, Drotské, Venter and Swanepoel were all with the national team, but Johan Erasmus had been released from that squad to be allowed to play versus the Lions. He joined the rest of what was, despite absences, still a strong side drawn from only eight local clubs. It is a fiercely proud area which has spawned many talents over the years, and now, because of lucrative sponsorship, they had a much better chance of hanging on to their stars. Free State had finished seventh in the Super Twelve table and their five wins had included a victory over Northern Transvaal at Loftus Versfeld, an achievement which had eluded the Lions.

The Free State Stadium holds nearly forty thousand people and it is a state of the art ground. The rugby venue towers over the adjacent cricket ground: it is like the big brother looking after the little brother in a show of local sporting excellence. The team also benefit from an intensely partisan support, but at times their following can become over-zealous. On the final stretch of the walk to the ground we started to see signs of the old South African flag being waved by young men listening to Afrikaner music while standing cooking at their braais. There is a boisterous element to the crowd in these parts. Others rather forcibly encouraged us to try the biltong which was hanging down from the roof of their makeshift side stall. The dried-meat sausages are a local delicacy, but the sales technique was far from subtle. The presence of the old national flag remains an embarrassment to many both inside and outside the region. I remember being at the ground in 1996 for the Tri-Nations international between South Africa and Australia. It was the first Test involving the Springboks since the ground's redevelopment and the day was marred by the constant echoes of the past. A year on, little had changed.

But once again, the Lions silenced the vociferous home support with a display which further enhanced their already growing reputation in South Africa. A recurrent theme throughout the tour had been the lack of a dirt-trackers side. As I have said previously, many believed that, despite the rhetoric, a second string would have to emerge by the end of the trip. In many ways it had as soon as the side had been announced for the first Test. But most importantly, the Lions players who had been left out in Cape Town had refused to accept that their tour was over. The constant reminders that places were still up for grabs and the intense desire to maintain a healthy team spirit both on and off the pitch had combined to act as an incentive to the whole squad. Perhaps it was a case of the players trying to prove to themselves that, despite their lack of Test recognition, they were still every bit as good as the 'first fifteen'. Whatever the psychology, it had worked and this mid-week Lions side produced the performance of the tour, even taking into account the first Test match. At the start of the tour we would have been stunned by the quality of the performance, but not any more. This was the way that Ian McGeechan's Lions had learnt to play and they were relishing the opportunity to show how far they had progressed. Seven more tries were scored and the victory margin of fifty-two points to thirty flattered the home team and flattened the opposition.

In their by now established style, the Lions dominated the opening exchanges and they scored tries of unbelievable excellence. John Bentley argued his point with fine deeds on the field which were just as powerful as his words off it. Three more tries took Bentley to seven for the tour. He finished with his usual power and carved his way around the field with real purpose. His verbal encouragement from the wing was rarely repeatable, but it came as a shot in the arm for those who wanted to see total commitment from all quarters. One of the other tries went to Tim Stimpson, who also kicked at goal like a dream. Dave Alred's painstaking work was still paying off. The brilliant Allan Bateman also got on the scoresheet. He was in danger of being one of the best-ever touring Lions to miss out on Test selection. Tony Underwood was rewarded for his roving sharpness and the replacement Neil Jenkins came on to get a try from the position of centre.

The arrival of Jenkins in the game, however, was a legacy of the night's one dark moment. It happened just before half-time and it was one of the most testing incidents of my broadcasting career. Will Greenwood, who had been having such a marvellous tour, went on another of his energetic runs. He half broke the first line of defence before taking a crushing tackle from the Free State powerhouse number eight, Jaco Coetzee. Greenwood went down and appeared to lose consciousness immediately. The medical team, led by Dr James Robson, rushed onto the field. It initially looked awful and the replays made it look worse. Greenwood lay motionless on the floor and we heard the referee, Jonathan Caplan, instruct the worried players who had gathered around to 'get away lads, because it's a bad one'. The referee's microphone link to the commentators was also being broadcast to the audience. This is now often the case both at home and abroad on Sky Sports. Normally it is a useful aid and is designed to keep the viewer in touch with the decisions being made on the field. But these were chilling words that none of us wanted to hear. Greenwood is a likeable and intelligent young man who had been a star personality on the tour. Yet here he was being lifted onto a stretcher with his neck protected to prevent any movement. Imagine what his parents must have been going through as they watched from the stands. Will's mother, Sue, had leapt from her position and frantically run down to the touch line. She was shouting out, pleading for more information and her husband, Dick, bravely tried to act as the calming influence. They both knew that their son was in the best medical hands, but as the young Greenwood was carried off the field, we all feared that it was a major injury.

In these situations it is difficult to find the right words. It is important to report the events objectively as they are unfolding. The viewer has a right to know and share in the concern, but the impact of every word must be carefully considered. It is also time for the production team to spring into action. The commentator becomes totally reliant on their ability to gather the information on the player's latest condition. The emphasis is also on speed, because the longer it goes without any news, the more worried the viewer will become. The problem here is: how does the reporter or producer approach the medical staff involved without intruding? This is where the relationships established over a period of time come in so useful. If the television team is trusted, then the individuals who are working hard at their own job to help the injured player can also consider the wider implications of what is happening.

Wrongly, in my opinion, the referee decided to restart the game for the short time that was left before the interval. It was virtually impossible for the remaining players on the field to concentrate on the task of playing with their minds fixed on the state of their injured colleague. Rather sombrely, I went to the commercial break and it was all hands to the pump as we tried to establish the latest news. James Robson kindly told us that Greenwood was going straight to hospital for tests, having suffered concussion, and our hearts were gladdened when, to his immense credit, Dick Greenwood made his way to our reporter Graham Simmons and informed him that the injury was not as bad as previously thought. Dick wanted Graham to broadcast this information because Will's grandmother was watching at home and would be beside herself with worry. As soon as we returned for the second half, I handed down to Graham and he articulated the thoughts of the Greenwood parents. Thankfully, we could once again concentrate on the rugby knowing that

Will was already on the mend. On our return to the hotel, James Robson informed us that the concussion had been serious and that, although all the brain scans had showed nothing to worry about, Will was going to be kept in hospital overnight for observation. James would then fly back with Will on the following day, as it would be unwise to let him travel in the air without a doctor on hand. As serious as the outcome might still be, there was an overriding feeling of all's well that ends well.

Safe in the knowledge that Greenwood was feeling better, the Lions were left to bask in the glory of another stupendous win. The Free State captain, Helgard Muller, had even gone as far as saying, 'We will never see tries like that again.' Praise indeed from a proud South African wounded by the Lions. John Bentley had quite rightly been named as the M-Net most-valuable player. He held the Lions badge on his jersey up to the camera and reiterated that nothing would make him prouder than to pull on the Test version in Durban. I wondered whether he had done enough to make the selectors change a winning team, but he certainly would get mightily close.

The big story of the Wednesday was the announcement of the South African team, but in order to be in a position to receive that at first hand, we had to leave Bloemfontein. It was another early morning flight and the eyes needed to be prised open by matchsticks, 'Tom and Jerry' style. This time it was Martin's turn to leave the obligatory article back in the hotel. The offending item was one of our mobile phones, and he was grateful to the person who answered it and told him of the phone's whereabouts. Graham also got into a frenzy that morning when he claimed to have seen a zebra in a field. Nobody else spotted the creature and he was goaded by the team. The theory that it was a horse wearing a Newcastle United strip did not go down too well. Graham's annoyance at our disbelieving attitude increased by the minute and his will finally cracked when it was pointed out that the so-called zebra had a number nine and the name Shearer on its back. A cardboard breakfast and one hour later, we had landed again in Durban and on the drive back to the seafront hotel Stuart promised to take a dip in the sea at some point during the day. We desperately tried to pin him down on the time of his bathe because we thought it would make for good sport to witness this piece of athleticism. Rather cruelly, Graham enquired if we had a team harpoon? It was good to know the ridicule factory was still in good working order.

The Springbok team was given out to the media at a lunch-time news conference in Umhlanga. Carel du Plessis looked relaxed as he came down the spiral staircase and into the sun room which faced out onto the rocks and the ocean down below. The team manager, Arthob Petersen, read out the names – Joubert, Snyman, Montgomery, Van Schalkwyk, Rossouw, Honiball, Van der Westhuizen, Du Randt, Drotské, Garvey, Strydom, Andrews, Kruger, Venter, Teichmann (captain).

The three men who had been struggling with injury – Small, Mulder and Lubbe – were, as expected, ruled out. Their places went to Pieter Rossouw and Percy Montgomery, both of Western Province, and the Northern Transvaal centre Danie van Schalkwyk. He had been the best centre that the Lions had come up against on their travels and was recalled to the team having got two tries in Northern's win at Loftus Versfeld. But the news that he would win his fifth cap had been received in unusual circumstances. When we asked about his whereabouts at the time Van Schalkwyk owned up to being on the toilet! His honesty demanded respect. The other centre, Montgomery, and the winger, Rossouw, would both make their international début, although Montgomery would be meeting the Lions for the third time, having played for Western Province and the Emerging Springboks. Rossouw had missed out in the Western Province game, as he had only just recovered from a hamstring injury. André Snyman was moved over from the left to the right wing and had not been considered at centre despite the fact that he could have teamed up with his provincial partner, Van Schalkwyk. The pack had stayed intact but Du Plessis called for a better performance from them, knowing that they had to improve on the first Test. Five men of Natal would be playing in front of their home crowd, including the skipper Gary Teichmann and André Joubert.

Joubert was disappointed with his performance in the first Test, which I thought was the worst of his international career which has spanned eight years. He could only improve and, if he returned to his best, then the Lions would have problems containing him. Gary Teichmann must have been having flashbacks to a year ago when his team were struggling against the All Blacks. South Africa were defeated in the first meeting versus New Zealand in Cape Town and then went to Durban with a team severely weakened by the loss of injured players. The captain did feel that his team were better equipped to cope with the pressure this time around and would not 'freeze on the day'. But he did admit to having watched the video of the first Test against the Lions and was shocked by just how badly South Africa had played. Sky Sports asked the lock Mark Andrews if his team were about to try and step up a gear. His response was that they were going to change the whole gear box; the terminology seemed appropriate, as earlier in the day I had seen Andrews roar away from the team's hotel in his sports car. The Lions would be facing a motivated side in Durban and it was promising to be an enthralling Test match.

*

Two men who no longer would be involved in the tour were Will Greenwood, who, having been concussed, had also suffered a dislocated shoulder, and Ieuan Evans, who had pulled a muscle during training on the Wednesday afternoon. We caught up with both players at the final public session before the Test on the Thursday morning. In the warm sunshine Evans cut a sad figure as he watched his team-mates train for what promised to be a historic occasion. The winger said that as soon as he had felt the pull he knew that it was serious and that, although there was never a good time to get injured, this was a particularly bad time. His family had just arrived to see him in action in the second Test and he had to explain that his Lions days were over. Will Greenwood was looking sprightly and passed on his thanks to the Sky team for keeping his grandmother informed as to his state of health during those harrowing few minutes on Tuesday night. He was also angry at some newspaper reports which he felt had sensationalised his injury. Greenwood agreed to join our team on the touch line on Saturday, and he is the kind of articulate individual who could well go on to make a career in broadcasting. Before that, though, he has a lot to achieve on the rugby field. As far as this tour was concerned, he would fly back on the Sunday after the second Test and prepare for a long season back home.

After watching the team warm up and train for a short time, we were asked to leave while they went through their rehearsed moves behind closed doors. Obviously the bulk of the media obliged, but we stayed on because there was some general filming to be done inside the main stadium, away from the practice pitch. I also wanted to check the commentary position with the producer, Piers Croton. When we emerged from the stadium, we drove away from the ground and interestingly passed a batch of onlookers who had got out of their cars and were peering through some railings to watch the Lions train. The concept of a closed session is good in theory, but if teams are worried about the opposition getting a sneak preview, they would be wise to police the extremities of the field. It all sounds very cloak and dagger, but modern Test matches can be won and lost on such small margins. Prior knowledge of a special move can often make a vital difference.

Back at the hotel it was time to sit and wait for the team announcement. This came at two o'clock in the afternoon and the media interest was phenomenal. To cater for the increased number of journalists who had flown in for this match, the hotel had moved the news conference to a room large enough to house what I estimated to be over one hundred working media. The press seating allocation at the ground on match day had been oversubscribed by two to one. SARFU lamented the fact that only sixty-nine seats had been given out to the press and they therefore had to purchase seats in the stand from the Natal province so that the journalists could gain entry. It all seemed very amateur for an otherwise professionally run union.

There was no doubt: this match was big news. The team to play in it was as follows – Jenkins, Bentley, Gibbs, Guscott, Tait, Townsend, Dawson, Smith, Wood, Wallace, Johnson (captain), Davidson, Dallaglio, Hill and Rodber. The bench – Back, Catt, Healey, Williams, Leonard and Miller. Few could argue with the decision to give John Bentley the right wing spot in the absence of Ieuan Evans. Ian McGeechan heaped praise on his winger saying that Bentley had come to the tour with the attitude of a youngster because it had all represented such an unexpected challenge at this late stage of his career. He had become something of a cult figure both with the travelling supporters and the South African public. He was the team's Midas, and there was a feeling that everything he touched was turning to gold.

As many as five positions had been seriously under consideration according to the management. At the forefront of these discussions was the back-row, but it had been decided to retain the services of Hill and Rodber, who had both done so much to ensure victory in Cape Town. However, by putting Back and Miller on the bench, McGeechan had given himself the chance of totally changing the angle of attack if required. I saw Neil Back in the hotel lift just shortly after the selection announcement. He was pleased to have been included and was confident that at some stage he would be involved in the action. Miller must have been exceptionally close to starting the game, but clearly the plan was to use Rodber's defensive qualities to weather the storm that would no doubt rage for the opening twenty minutes of the match. Martin Johnson said that he expected the home team to throw the kitchen sink at the Lions. Having read the newspapers that week, the South African nation was demanding a ferociously aggressive response to the previous week's defeat.

Later that evening we had another one of our meals with the Lions party. This time we had chosen Langoustines as the venue and, again, it didn't disappoint. As I talked with Ian McGeechan it became even clearer why the players had so enjoyed working with their coach. He talked passionately about the style of play that he had always wanted to bring to the Lions. The players who he had picked were assembled because of their ability to adapt to his requests. The most pleasing aspect for McGeechan was that, regardless of the victories, the face of the game in Britain and Ireland had been changed for ever. He believed that the Lions would go back to their countries and clubs and would be unable to accept anything less than a total commitment to the modern style of game being developed by the Lions and the countries of the Southern

Hemisphere. McGeechan was also well aware of the history of the Lions but had never set out to impose those heavy traditions on the shoulders of his players. They were there to make history of their own and he was visibly excited about the possibility of a momentous series win. He had realised after the victory against Western Province that something special could be around the corner. The loss to Northern Transvaal had come at just the right time to give the squad a jolt and the mid-week win over Free State had been the most complete performance that he had ever seen from a British or Irish rugby side. The fact that it had come on the back of the Test win spoke volumes about the squad's attitude.

The only time that McGeechan had been forced to hand out a severe ticking off to the players had come during the morning training session on the Monday after the first Test. He had sensed a rare lack of concentration but had moved in quickly to stamp out the negativity. Now he waited nervously for the job to be completed. Amazed that he could have quite happily gone into the Test match playing the mid-week team, we joked that his choice of players had been better than his wine selection. This was unfair, though, because the smiling Scot clearly knows his grapes as well as his onions. We sipped the excellent wine and only wished that we could have been toasting success instead of hoping for it. One phrase uttered by the coach that evening will always stay in my mind. He said that his side must fight fire with fire in what would be the most demanding of physical confrontations, but that somehow his players had to keep 'their brains in the fridge'. If the players had the icy coolness that their thoughtful coach desired, then they would be leaving South Africa victorious. Fran Cotton had no doubts that his boys would win. He left the dinner table and bade farewell with the words, 'We are going two–nil up.' We all hoped that his dream would come true.

The Friday morning before the match was spent at King's Park. I had to record a piece to camera setting the scene from the ground for our preview programme to be broadcast later that night. It was decided to shoot the film from the very top of the stadium and once up there we got a marvellous panoramic view of the city. It was another beautiful sunny day with a steamy haze covering the tips of Durban's skyscrapers. The awesome stand, which had been upgraded as part of the redevelopment of the ground before the 1995 World Cup, was frighteningly steep. The seats climbed into the distance and the gradient was such that the railings in front of you were most definitely required to overcome the feeling of toppling down onto the pitch below. It would be a nightmare for a spectator with vertigo, but the view of the game and the surrounding city must be amongst the best in the world.

I left the ground with my nerves starting to build, as all thoughts had now officially turned to the match. As in Cape Town, I wondered what would be going through the minds of the players. They had nothing planned for the rest of the day apart from afternoon tea and an early evening team talk. It was a matter of getting the mind and body in tune with the assignment. I returned to the hotel and, with even more rain ruining the hopes of tennis, South African television showed the 1995 World Cup final in full. It was fascinating to see the change of personnel in Springbok rugby inside just two years. I was also reminded of the sheer guts displayed by South Africa on that day, and concluded that the recent criticism levelled at the current squad would only serve to inspire a rearguard action in the second Test.

During the coverage of the final, the director cut away frequently to show Nelson Mandela sitting in the stand and living every moment of that famous day. It had been a time when South African rugby had been identified as a major integrating force for blacks and whites, but there were now newspaper reports that Archbishop Desmond Tutu had spoken out about what he considered to be the 'mean-spirited' attitude of the current rugby powerbrokers in South Africa. Tutu had considered telephoning Carel du Plessis to register his displeasure over the omission of the talented Hennie Le Roux. More pointedly, however, the Archbishop wondered why no black players had been given the chance at full international level. 'I would have rooted even more loudly if he [Du Plessis] had said, "Let's take Breyton Paulse and see what he can do." ' Paulse, who had scored thirteen tries in just eight games for Western Province, is one of a number of black players knocking on the door of higher honours. These words echoed other conversations that I had been involved in during my stay in South Africa. As the Archbishop put it, there was a growing concern over the 'lily white' look of the South African side. I have said earlier in this book that I do not believe in discriminating positively and I stand by that statement. Talent alone should always be the deciding factor in selection; but if there are two players with similar ability, and it is almost impossible to draw a playing distinction between the two, then surely it would be a positive step to select the black player. The greater good must be considered and the move for change would be hastened. It is an area that I hope SARFU will address in the near future. The talented black players, in the A team and at Emerging Springbok level, must start to come through soon to make sure that we all keep the faith.

Saturday morning eventually arrived and so had even more Lions fans. They had been flying in all week as part of the specially designed supporter tours and it seemed that Durban had been taken over by a British and Irish army. Our hotel had undergone a metamorphosis overnight and I came out of the ground floor lift to be greeted by the sounds of a Scottish piper and two specially erected stalls selling Boddington's bitter. Next it was Paul McCartney and the 'Frog Song' blasting out over the sound system. It was surreal, the beer was flowing and it was only a quarter to eight. I went to breakfast thinking that once in the dining area I might have been able to find some peace. All was going well until two men with banjos, looking as if they had just stepped off the streets of New Orleans, wended their way in and out of the tables serenading the guests. It was a colourful if a little noisy start to the day, and I decided to take my newspaper up to my room and let the revellers enjoy their pre-match build-up. When I looked out of the window I noticed Gregor Townsend down on the sun deck reading his newspaper. He appeared to be totally relaxed, and if he was feeling the anxiety of the day, he certainly wasn't showing it. Townsend told me that he likes to focus on the technicalities of his game on the day of the match. The approach of the fly-half contrasts with the ways of the burly centre Scott Gibbs. He lies in bed until midday when a game has a late afternoon kick-off. On the Friday before, Gibbs had assured us that, once up, he would be offering words of encouragement whether they were 'blasphemous or not'. Gibbs the motivator was sure to be play a major part in the Lions effort.

Having watched the second Test match between Australia and France over lunch, and what a pleasing game of rugby it was too, we jumped into a taxi and headed off to the game. Australia had won again, could the Lions do likewise? Unlike the previous week, my heart had not been in my mouth all morning – I was a little calmer, but as the ground came into vision, I felt a surge of anticipation. Looking at the crowds of people present, it again confirmed what a momentous occasion was lying in wait. The party had already begun and just like in our hotel lobby the music blared out from the loudspeakers as the fans inter-mingled to share their food and drink. Arms were linked and the Lions supporters were enjoying the chance to sample the South African way before a big rugby game. There was no telling those Lions fans that they were not going to witness history being made. The ground was littered with bodies lying back in the sun and drinking a toast to the prospect of British and Irish success. If it was down to sheer willpower, then the Lions were going to win and I began to sense that there was something very special in the air – and it wasn't the smell of sausages.

Into the stadium we went and the big match feeling hit me straightaway. I don't know whether this is just an irrational sense which is created in the mind, but there are certain times in sport when arriving at a venue you instantly know that the event is of monumental signifi-cance. I think it may have something to do with the amount of chatter which ripples around the stadium. But that alone would not explain the electrical sensation which passes down the spine. It is almost spiritual and I for one would be a believer if anybody was to start the Church of the Sporting Spirit. King's Park Durban on that day seemed a good place to worship.

I walked out of the tunnel and passed a number of Lions players who looked tense. There was a warm-up game taking place on the pitch and I decided to watch it for a while and to use the numbers on the shirts of the unknown players to act out my commentary to the main event. I went over to the chairs which are bracketed onto a side wall at the pitch edge. I pulled down the seat to reveal a small piece of paper stuck to the surface. It read: 'Lions bench'. This was the designated area where those waiting to play their part would sit and agonise for the afternoon. What a passionate place this would become over the next three hours. Jim Telfer came and sat down on one of those seats, but he didn't stay long. Seconds later he had moved over to the touch line and then back to the tunnel. He was on the prowl and you could sense torrents of suspense racing through his veins. Gavin Hastings came over, having just spoken to Telfer. 'I've just had a word with Jim,' he said. 'This is what it's all about for him – he won't rest until we've won.' Meanwhile, Lawrence Dallaglio, his face like a rock, stared impassively at the stands, which were now rapidly filling up. 'Not since the World Cup final have we felt like this,' said Stuart. I was inclined to agree.

Next, it was to the media room for a reflective read of my notes. It is always best to have a few words or phrases in mind for those broad-casting moments which may be replayed for years to come. I had to be prepared for that eventuality on this day. The most memorable words, though, are always the spontaneous ones and they suit the moment. Why have the set menu when you should be picking the best dish from the à la carte? The most famous commentary words of all time, spoken by Kenneth Wolstenholme in 1966 – 'Some people are on the pitch', 'They think it's all over', etc. – were perfect because they responded to what was happening and not what he thought should have happened. I know some commentators actually write down a pre-cooked statement to be used on the final whistle and they stick rigidly to it come what may. This is misguided and I was determined to go with the flow of the day. It is bad to have a preconceived idea of how a match is going to progress. After all, the series could have stood at one game all at full-time.

The atmosphere was getting better and better by the minute. The Lions supporters played their part, moving from 'Bread of Heaven' to 'Swing Low', and from 'Flower of Scotland' to 'Molly Malone'. It was wonderful, and the arrival of the local dancers from KwaZulu-Natal made for great entertainment in the minutes before kick-off. They swarmed over the pitch, spears held high and their eyes opened wide. It reminded me of the film *Zulu*, and I had a vision of the South African team coming out of the tunnel with similar intent and metaphorically charging over the top of the hill to attack the British. In their red uniform the Lions would perhaps be ordered to fire at will, not by Michael Caine, but by Martin Johnson.

As Johnson gathered his players in a huddle, just before the kick-off, it was Scott Gibbs, as he had promised us, who pushed himself to the front to issue the battle cry. Gesturing with his hand, he seemed to indicate just where the Lions 'army' had reached in their campaign. He then thrust his arm way above his head to show the level of commitment required to win the 'war'.

Referee Didier Méné blew the whistle and it signalled the most ferocious start to a game that I have ever seen. How the Lions survived the first quarter of an hour I will never know. I remember saying in the commentary that the Lions defence was like a red rash all over South Africa, who could not find the antidote. After surviving with great fortitude, the Lions amazingly went up field and Neil Jenkins slotted a penalty goal to give them the lead. But it was inevitable that South Africa would score at some point and, although they were denied a try in the corner by another close refereeing decision, they did cross the try line in the shape of the lethal Joost van der Westhuizen. Even so, it was the Lions who went to half-time ahead, thanks to another Jenkins penalty: the parallels with the previous week were uncanny. It was South Africa with the forward-inspired try in the first half, but the Lions leading by one point thanks to the exemplary kicking of their full-back, driven on by the constant singing of 'Bread of Heaven'. The Welshman must have thought he was at Sardis Road in Pontypridd. His team were forty minutes away from their goal – but what a forty minutes lay ahead.

Six points to five was a slender advantage and it was whittled away right at the start of the second period – again just as had been the case in Cape Town. This time Jenkins the defender got in a muddle underneath the high ball. Tait didn't look convincing either, and as the ball bounced around, the result was a try for the débutante, Percy Montgomery. The weakness that had always been present was at last being exploited by South Africa. It had taken them one and a half Tests to work this out, but now they started to pepper Jenkins with bomb after bomb. Another anticipated problem was the lack of speed from John Bentley when on the turn in defence. He was exposed by André Joubert who elegantly went on the outside and sped into the corner. South Africa had scored three tries and the Lions had never even looked like crossing their opponents' line. But we still had hope based on one fact alone: the kicking at goal from South Africa had plummeted to new depths. They had surprisingly started the match with Henry Honiball taking aim, he had then passed the baton on to Montgomery and then Joubert had his turn. Not one kick threatened the uprights and this sheer wastefulness had enabled the Lions to maintain heart. Added to this was the fact that South Africa conceded twice as many penalties as the Lions throughout the match. The home team were committing rugby suicide – but they were helped in taking the overdose by some heroic Lions defence. The pack stood their ground like never before and behind the scrum Scott Gibbs roamed the field looking for victims. On one memorable occasion in the second half he identified the giant prop, Os du Randt, as the recipient of his attention. Gibbs took aim and made for the 'Ox', and laid him out flat on the floor with a rampaging charge which reverberated around the stadium. (Later, Gibbs said that he had been too lazy to run around him. If only we could all be that workshy!)

Gibbs was off the leash, but it was his fellow countryman, Neil Jenkins, who continued to really hurt South Africa. Five penalties were scored by the metronome from Wales, the last of which levelled the scores, although this penalty award was not without controversy. The Springboks had been penalised for playing the ball on the floor in a ruck, but that had been far from clear on the replay. In fact, it looked as if the home side should have been given the put in to the scrum after a knock-on from Keith Wood. Jenkins didn't complain and stepped up with nerves of steel to make it fifteen points all. A draw would have meant that the Lions had assured themselves of at least a share of the series. But they had gone to South Africa to win. Bravely, they trusted their superior fitness and boldly made for the opposition try line. When they were within range, I turned to Stuart and said, 'Surely, the drop goal.' Jeremy Guscott, after an evening of defensive tackling and precious little attacking, sized up the possibilities and let fly. I'll leave the rest of the description to the man himself: 'Daws had the ball and he looked up to see where Gregor was, and when he saw me he had panic written all over his face. But he sent a sweet pass to me and it was straight over, three points, Test series wrapped up.' The cocksure Guscott grinned like a naughty schoolboy when he delivered these words at the post-match news conference. In the minutes that remained after Guscott's triumphant strike, the Lions tackled everything that moved, as South Africa threw wave after wave of attacks at the Lions. As the high ball went up again and the full-back tried to get under it, I cried, 'Go on, Neil!' All that talk earlier in the tour about maintaining a certain degree of detachment when at the microphone had gone flying out of the window. I might as well have been wearing a Lions jersey.

After what seemed like an eternity, the whistle went and the arms were held aloft. The Lions had won.

They had clung on to a slender three-point lead, but this didn't make their victory any less sweet. The Springboks knew that they had thrown it away and, rather ironically, had been beaten by a drop goal. Guscott's effort would sit alongside Joel Stransky's historic World Cup final kick.

Ecstasy washed over the ground and the celebrations began. The whole party rushed out to greet their victorious colleagues and they embraced each other as the flashes from the cameras illuminated the Durban night. The first professional Lions team could say it was a job well done.

The Lions, who had refused to talk about 1974 during their time in South Africa, would now be mentioned in the same breath as the most famous rugby team to leave the shores of Britain and Ireland. They had entered into the realms of greatness. Never had I witnessed a side win an international, having played for such long periods in their own half. It had been a smash and grab victory, but nobody who had made the trip from home cared for such sentiment.

It was by far and away the most emotional sporting experience that I have ever had the pleasure to witness. As I handed back to the studio, Stuart and I put down our microphones and I am not ashamed to say that we both had to wipe away a tear. The smiles soon returned, though, as we watched the interviewees file in one by one to be greeted by Graham Simmons in the dressing-room area. Jeremy Guscott said, 'If it had to be, I'm glad it was me.' Fran Cotton proclaimed, 'We didn't play well, but we got our rewards for the commitment.' John Bentley, who memorably ran straight over to acknowledge the crowd when the referee blew for full-time, said that he had been overwhelmed by the number of things that he wanted to do all at once. They included hugging his wife, commiserating with the opposition and raising a glass with everybody watching back in Cleckheaton. Good old Bentos was at it again. And an emotional Martin Johnson, the hard man, looked as if he was about to join the crying brigade. He had, of course, taken his place alongside Willie John McBride in the great story of the Lions.

Personally, I just wanted to hang around the ground for as long as the security men would allow. I didn't want the day to end. If I work until I am seventy I will have to go a long way to better that feeling. The players filed out of their after-match reception with their shirt collars open and hair still drying. They had the scars but also the plaudits. They looked like men who had come through a battle and won. Stopping to sign autographs and hug their friends and relatives, their every move was followed by the television cameras, as the curtain came down on some amazing scenes. Our cameraman, Leon Hagen, a South African who had to endure the friendly jibes which were inevitably directed at the losing team, made sure that he got the shot of Dr Louis Luyt as he climbed into his car. These were worrying times for the South Africa supremo: he had seen the World Cup euphoria disintegrate into home Test series defeats to New Zealand and now the Lions.

But the politics was for another day. We made our way over to the practice fields all around the main ground, where masses of spectators had stayed to party the night away. The celebrations had begun long ago and the swaying groups of Lions supporters sang their way into oblivion. The alcohol was flowing, but you could get drunk on the atmosphere alone, as the happiness was overwhelming. Back in the hotel everybody wanted to shake the hand of a Lion. I met Jim Telfer and he said that his wife was currently watching a re-run of the game, half fearing that the result had been wrong. He chuckled and said that it was just before half-time and the score was still the same as it had been at the identical stage during the real match. Telfer, McGeechan and Cotton deserved their moment of glory, as did their players and they all prepared to paint the town red (white, green and blue).

WHITEWASH AVERTED BUT THE PAINT WAS DRY

'We have learned a lot from the Northern Hemisphere.' – South African scrum-half Joost van der Westhuizen's admission after his country had come back but lost 2–1.

Thankfully, there are still some things in sport which matter. There are prizes that will always be cherished and never diminished by the merry-go-round on which sit meaningless internationals, pre-season football friendlies, exhibition tennis tournaments and seven-match one-day cricket series. A Lions victory in South Africa needs no more embellishment.

This was the final stretch, then, and what a voyage of discovery the whole experience had been. The one word that kept coming back to my mind, after the euphoria of the weekend, was destiny. The Lions had taken a winning two–nil lead in the series but could so easily have lost both matches, especially the second Test. The fact that they didn't was down to great professionalism and a team spirit which was second to none. Now it was time to push for what had never been achieved before, a series whitewash on South African soil. Nobody had predicted it seven weeks previously, but our faith in the Lions was now such that it was more probable than possible. The Saturday night party had rocked long into the early hours of the morning. There were some bleary eyes and aching heads in our hotel when the sun came up. The first face that I saw, when emerging from the lift to try and tackle breakfast, was that of Fran Cotton. He beamed with delight, fully aware that what he and his squad had set out to achieve had now become reality.

Our flight from Durban to Johannesburg was later on that morning. The weather had changed from sunshine to cloud and the grey skies matched the mood of the Springbok team as they mounted the steps of our plane. Their demeanour was not improved by their fellow countryman and pilot, who welcomed the rugby team on board his aircraft and congratulated them on their success in taking the series. The pilot was under the impression that he had charge of the Lions party and not the South Africans. This faux pas could have hardly helped the team overcome their after-match blues. Nevertheless, Carel du Plessis looked surprisingly relaxed as he collected his baggage and prepared for a challenging week which would test his coaching credentials. The prospect of changes to the side loomed, especially in the backs, and if the team failed to win in convincing fashion, the chances were that there would also be a change at the top.

Outside the airport the Sky Sports team considered such weighty matters as the colour of our next Kombi. It seemed a great chance for a wager and the uncanny alternation in vehicle shade from red to white, from venue to venue, suggested that red was the favourite for this final leg of the trip. Having studied the form like the true gambler that he is, Stuart Barnes committed himself to red, but Martin Knight led the rush to back white. The relatively new tourist, David Tippett, who had no knowledge of what had gone before, rather outrageously plumped for blue. It was a long shot and David won the support of the neutrals who hoped for the unexpected. As the van came around the corner it became apparent that white had won, and Martin celebrated a cash win lucrative enough to look after his immediate financial concerns, such as a visit to the pick 'n' mix sweet counter. Such triviality had helped to ease us along throughout the long trip and I reflected on just how well it had all gone from the point of view of maintaining harmony in our close-knit team.

Next it was time to find our way from the airport to the Sandton district of Johannesburg to the north of the city. This nearly caused a few ructions and, although I don't like making any excuses, for obvious reasons our brains were not in full working order on that Sunday. The celebrations had taken their toll and it was the humans who needed a 'handle with care' sticker and not our suitcases. Inevitably, wrong turnings were taken and the immortal line was uttered: 'I think we are somewhere near the garage where we got lost last time.' Our navigation had not been one of the strong points of the tour. After an interesting detour around the city we eventually stumbled across our hotel and decided that it was time to sleep off the effects of the night before.

The Monday morning started with a call to Northern Free State, the side which would play the Lions in their penultimate match. I freely admit it was difficult to stoke up the fire for this contest. It was a game which the Lions were expected to win with ease. The series was in the bag and deep down I think that we all felt there was only one remaining match which really mattered and that was the final Test at Ellis Park. These minor games are the ones which test a commentator. The reaction to the coverage of the Test at the weekend had been very positive and I was pleased with the response, but to portray the emotion of such a pulsating event is not too demanding. Inevitably, you are carried along by the atmosphere in the stadium and the importance of the occasion. Furthermore, the identification of the players in a big match does not present a problem. It is the games played in front of a small crowd, when there is a certainty about the score line, the spectators are nowhere near fever pitch and the players are none too recognisable, which are difficult. After big matches, people often say, 'I enjoyed your commentary on that game,' but what they really mean is that they enjoyed the match. The 'two men and a dog' style of commentary is the real examination.

In the telephone call to Northern Free State I made the mistake of using verbal shorthand and calling the team just 'Free State'. This was obviously the ultimate sin and the general manager of the team came down on me like a ton of bricks. It was further evidence that the intense local rivalries in South Africa have to be seen to be believed. Of course, the Lions had played Free State, formerly Orange Free State, in the previous week. To be remotely connected to their neighbours was a fate worse than death for Northern Free State. I had meant no harm, and I was fully aware of the difference between the two sides, but I would not make that mistake again, even in the most informal of circumstances. The conversation also revealed that the Northern Free State team had no star names to boast about, yet they were promising a full throttle performance. My temporary match-weariness, and therefore apathy, had been overcome by one simple telephone call. To make matters even more interesting, the news from the Lions camp was that a number of players had also felt the effects of the Test victory. Alan Tait, Keith Wood, Richard Hill and Eric Miller were injured. This was no time to slack and, after all, it was a game of rugby to look forward to, which is always something to shout about.

Wood had busied himself in other ways, though, and had taken on the mantle of tour barber. Ian McGeechan, whose wife, Judy, was still trying to rediscover her voice after the weekend's excesses, had startled his other half and the rest of us by having his head cropped. The coach had rashly agreed to the forfeit prior to the team leaving home. The players' side of the bargain was to win two Test matches: if they did, their leader would accept a full army cut. Wood delighted in the opportunity to use the clippers and, to the other players' joy, he had not spared the horses. The madness was set to continue with a similar fate awaiting Fran Cotton should the series be won three to nothing. The thought of a 'head to head' between big Fran and 'Vidal' Wood was an intriguing one.

On a more serious note, the Lions management had refreshingly stated their aim to finish the tour in style. 'There was a meeting with the senior players on Sunday night,' said Cotton, 'and they reported back to a players meeting. What we resolved to do was to ensure that the next two games be played to a standard befitting a successful Lions team. We are ready to play some great rugby on the last week of the tour.' The squad were spending the majority of the run-up to the final Test in a place called Vanderbijlpark, which is a good drive out of Johannesburg. That was the only thing that was good about a locality which reeked of the sulphurous smells of the local industry. The site had originally been chosen because the Lions did not expect to have won the series at this point. They had selected a hideaway where they would have been able to recharge their batteries for one final push for victory. The hotel resort alongside the Vaal River lacked sparkle and there was little to do apart from focus on rugby. For a player that is not a bad thing, but for others it is tantamount to disaster. One morning I saw some of the photographers who had been in desperate search of the local nightlife. They claimed to have driven for half an hour in each direction away from the hotel and had discovered absolutely nothing. The conclusion had been to scurry back to their rooms and watch Wimbledon on the box. Thank goodness for the exploits of Tim Henman and Greg Rusedski. The BBC Radio Five reporter, Alastair Hignell, apparently broadcast a piece from his hotel bedroom lamenting the fact that he had looked out of his window at the early morning view and this had left him with nothing to do for the rest of the day. I was glad that we had taken the decision to stay back in Johannesburg and travel to the team hotel to carry out our filming.

Stuart and I took the Monday afternoon 'off tour'. It was a chance to relax over a long lunch and contemplate life with only one week of the trip to go. I considered the appealing thought that in less than seven days I would be eating my midday meal on British soil. The conversation was also tinged with sadness because we had unquestionably enjoyed the seven weeks. Of course, it had been made more pleasurable by the success of the team. To be around a winning squad had made all the difference.

The place where we stayed in Johannesburg was an area called Sandton City. This part of town is known as a 'safe' area and it is dripping with affluence. The shopping centres are as chic as anything you would find in Paris, but the gilt-edged malls conflicted sharply with the downtown districts, which we had been warned to avoid. Johannesburg is a city of contrast and many believe it is sitting on a time bomb. The money has moved away to the outskirts and, therefore, so have the white people. The barricades, high fences and barbed wire with venomous spikes on the top, which surround the big properties, hint at a total insecurity in the way of living. The previously downtrodden black population had been trained to accept this but with emancipation, they now had every right to expect more. Nonetheless, the class and colour distinction was there for all to see. It was perhaps most telling when one considered peoples' occupations: during my spell in South Africa I had never seen a white chambermaid. On the security aspect, I was reminded of a note left on the top of my television set in the hotel room. 'May we suggest you look out for our special tourist ambassadors, who will assist should you wish to walk to any of the shopping centres, restaurants and other attractions in the area. They are on duty from 14h00 to 02h00 and are easily identified by their high visibility waistcoats. They are equipped with maps and radios and will help you to discover South Africa's premier shopping complexes safely.' The country had become the rainbow nation, but its people still needed to share in the pot of gold. It was food for thought and I was left feeling that such an existence was a strange way for both blacks and whites to spend their lives.

Following lunch, we dropped into a local bar in search of a pool table to continue the duel which had rather ground to a halt during the recent weeks. It was there that we stumbled across a group of Welshmen from the Bridgend Sports and Bryncethin Rugby Clubs. They were tremendous company and were naturally delighted with the performances of Scott Gibbs and Neil Jenkins in the second Test. One of the group was Jonathan Griffiths, the former Bridgend back and now a coach in the area, who told a great tale. He had watched the second Test back home and had been thrilled by the Lions' achievement. He had turned to his wife and said that he would love to go out for the final game. She got straight on the phone and arranged the flight and hotel bookings there and then. Jonathan was off for a trip to remember, as such spontaneity is what loving rugby is all about. This band of supporters were determined to share in the Lions' success and have the time of their lives. Some hours later, having no joy, we decided to abandon the search for a pool table and I began negotiations with Stuart to call the final result as a victory for me based on the early encounters. (I am still working on a settlement and it could take some time.)

Recreation time over, it was back on the job as news came through of the South African team for the final Test match. The team read – Joubert, Snyman, Montgomery, Van Schalkwyk, Rossouw, De Beer, Van der Westhuizen, Du Randt, Dalton, Theron, Strydom, Otto, Erasmus, Venter, Teichmann (captain).

Carel du Plessis had made five changes, of which two were forced by injury. Mark Andrews and Ruben Kruger had withdrawn on medical advice so in came the lock Krynauw Otto and Johan Erasmus, for his first cap on the flank. Also in the pack two changes were made in the front-row, with Dawie Theron replacing Adrian Garvey at prop and James Dalton getting the vote over hooker Naka Drotské. It was the backs who had received the bulk of the criticism following the second

Test defeat, so alterations to a pack which had performed well had not been entirely expected. Admittedly, the coach's hand had been forced by the loss of two key injured players but the reaction in the South African media was on the whole one of surprise. Having said that, though, Dalton is the kind of quarrelsome competitor which the Springboks needed in a time of crisis. The inclusion of the giant Theron and the bulky Otto and the rejection of the more mobile Garvey and Van Heerden suggested that South Africa were going for even more power. They still believed that they could blow the Lions away up front. Their main worry, though, was behind the scrum. First South Africa had to find a goalkicker and they had plumped for the Free State fly-half Jannie de Beer. He had kicked well in Free State's defeat at the hands of the Lions, but would be winning his first cap with the weight of expectation firmly placed on his shoulders. The main question was: would De Beer be able to release the backs who had struggled to provide any cutting edge in Durban? The game plan was clear, South Africa were looking to kick it deep and step up the pressure on Neil Jenkins and to keep driving it through the forwards to force the Lions into submission. It was rugby of the past and hardly the brave new world of attacking policy promised by the coach when he took over. But a win was needed, and if the young backs could come up with the necessary innovation as the Lions strength was sapped by the onslaught, then Carel du Plessis was going to have something to show to those who wanted him out of a job.

The decision to once again ignore the claims of Hennie Le Roux mystified and annoyed many South African commentators. Apparently Le Roux was now clearly saying that he thought he had been fit enough for the second Test and had proved this in his appearance in a local club game on the eve of the match in Durban. There were so many claims and counter claims on the whole issue that it was impossible to know what to believe, but the Le Roux affair suggested a backstage row which went right to the top of South African rugby. In my view, the Springboks' loss by not playing Le Roux was the Lions' gain and Du Plessis was surely hoping that the naïve back-line on show in the second Test would produce sufficient quality in Johannesburg to stop the screams for the experienced and talented Le Roux.

Before we found the answer to that riddle, the Lions had to win the penultimate and twelfth match of the tour against Northern Free State. The side chosen to play in Welkom was predictable. It read – Stimpson, Stanger, Bateman, Beal, Underwood, Catt, Bracken, Leonard (captain), Regan, Young, Redman, Shaw, Wainwright, Back and Diprose.

Tony Stanger had joined the party to replace the injured Ieuan Evans. The winger had been on tour with Scotland in South Africa, so he had already become acclimatised to the conditions. Indeed, I had seen him finish off a beautiful try in their game against Northern Transvaal at Loftus Versfeld. Scotland had won the match and ironically succeeded where the Lions had experienced their only failure to date. Stanger was now looking to make an impression in a Lions jersey alongside Kyran Bracken, who after a two-week wait, finally got the chance to make his début. This match was about finishing on the crest of a wave for what had been a highly successful mid-week team. Also it would represent one last opportunity for the likes of Bateman and Back to shout from the rooftops and insist that they must play Test rugby before the end of the tour. I, for one, hoped that the Lions management would make changes for the final Test. The whole trip had been built around the squad ethos and this was the perfect chance to say to those players who had been a part of the success but who had missed out on the ultimate prize of winning Test status that they were good enough. It was also a way of keeping things fresh and making the South Africans think about other attacking threats. But having said this, the growing list of injuries would probably determine selection changes anyway. It was becoming clear that we were going to see two very different sides in action in the third Test.

It was the first day of July and the final day of the provincial leg of the tour. The destination was Welkom, which is about two and a half hours' drive to the south-west of Johannesburg. The journey took us past another example of the poverty being experienced by some people in South Africa. Away to our left, just yards off the road and sitting forlornly on a patch of bare land, was what can only be described as a corrugated jungle of shacks. The inhabitants were no doubt trying to live to the best of their ability in what were appalling conditions. The tatty washing hung limply on the flimsily erected lines and the smoke trickled out of the makeshift chimneys, coughing and spluttering its way into the air. The putrescent smell and dark appearance of the scorched earth did little to dull the senses. One man wearing a tawdry old winter coat trudged along the side of the shanty town carrying a receptacle as he searched for water. The squalid conditions contrasted with our five-star existence and it was amazing to think of the ease with which we could turn on the tap to find fresh clean water for our next cup of tea.

Welkom itself is a mining town and its wealth is built upon the deposits down below, which range from coal to gold, platinum and diamonds. The roads of the town are wide and open plan and this does give the place a surprisingly airy feel. The local people are proud of the series of 'circles' (roundabouts) which limit the need for 'robots' (traffic lights). This is a rather dubious selling point, but I can assure you that the traffic did move smoothly (although it was hardly of rush hour proportions). The rugby ground is away on the edge of the town. We arrived to be greeted by an army of stewards who were regimental in their attitude. There was no getting into the North West Stadium without the right ticket and had we argued about where to put the Kombi, then I was under the impression that our lives would not have been worth living. We touched our caps, showed our passes and sighed with relief when we gained entry. Having crossed the border checkpoint, the view from our commentary position high on the roof of the stand was of flat barren fields with only two landmarks of any note. There was a large slag heap and a reservoir. The slag resembled Table Mountain in shape but that was where the comparison abruptly stopped. I was told that the water is a hot-spot for anglers and the local bird life is worthy of the attention of a keen 'twitcher', but the surrounding countryside was none too pretty – nor was the local food on offer at the one kiosk open behind the main stand. I'm sure it was perfectly acceptable and I know that first impressions are not always right, but a fluorescent pink cold sausage does little for my saliva glands. I resolved to buy a packet of crisps and look forward to the after-match meal.

It will come as no surprise to you that Welkom is Afrikaans for welcome and the locals were certainly looking forward to greeting the Lions for the first time. Their big day was dominated by a match which provided another avalanche of tries, with the Lions getting ten more to take their total on tour to fifty-five. Tony Underwood was scorching the already parched earth and ran in a first-half hat-trick, just as Rob Wainwright had done against Mpumalanga. The stopwatch timed Underwood's as a tad slower, but he didn't care for such statistical considerations and, with Alan Tait's injury, Underwood had shot into the frame for a Test place. Sadly, Allan Bateman had his worst match on tour, dropping a clear scoring pass and I felt sorry for a man who really had nothing to prove. But Neil Back strengthened his almost irrefutable case for a third Test spot. If the Lions really wanted to spin it out wide against South Africa, then they had to play the in-form Back. The extra dimension that he was giving to the play of the mid-week team could no longer be ignored. Back had buried the size issue by making some telling tackles and was clearly thriving on the Lions' continued policy of attack.

The match did, however, have an end of term feel and the Lions lost the defensive sharpness which had been one of the major pluses of the tour. Here were the first signs that the mental discipline which had characterised the tour was on the wane following the victory in the Test series. Northern Free State took advantage of this and scored four tries of their own. In doing so, they managed to compile a total of thirty-nine points in response to the Lions' sixty-seven. The tourists, then, had passed their highest score of the trip, but they had also conceded a record number of points for any match ever played by a Lions team. But this was not the only disappointing aspect of the day.

I walked into the after-match news conference which was taking place in the rather primitive surroundings of a big tent. The facilities at the ground had been basic, but the local union had done their best to provide phone lines for the journalists and I had not heard any voices of dissent. When things go wrong at big Test match grounds where the conditions of work should be first class, then you will hear a journalist complain. When the venue is small but the people are willing and try their best to accommodate the media, then it is very rare to hear grumbles coming from the press corps. I believe it is important to take the sport out to the regions and away from the comfortable environs of Test match grounds, and if this means some minor adjustments to normal work practices, then so be it. Likewise, for the players it surely does no harm to take professionals out of the comfort zone and offer them the challenge of the less glamorous venue. So, I admit to being surprised when I heard that the facilities had been criticised by Fran Cotton. It wasn't the Ritz, but the Lions knew what they were in for when the match schedule had been agreed. Cotton was also unhappy with the hard ground and indeed it was the first time on tour that we had seen a straw-coloured pitch. It was like the olden days of South African rugby when the yellow turf dazzled the eyes in bright sunlight. Certainly the ground should have been more extensively watered, and when Kyran Bracken scored a try, he hurt his shoulder as he hit the floor. But these were not unusual conditions in the more 'rural' areas of South Africa and the officials were mystified by the complaints. Cotton argued that Bracken along with three other players, Jason Leonard, Tony Underwood and Mark Regan, had been taken away from the ground early to go back to the hotel to receive treatment.

Cotton's irritation didn't stop there and the normal cool, calm and collected Lions leader lost his temper. He directed his ire at the Northern Free State players: 'There were two or three stampings, which is totally unacceptable, and there were several other incidents which put our players at risk,' said Cotton. He then moved his attack to the referee, Dan de Villiers, for failing to keep a hold on the match and for not protecting the Lions players. In his after-match interview, Mike Catt said that it was the first time on the tour that the team had questioned the official. Admittedly, the referee was not one of the best that I've ever seen and should not have awarded a try to Northern Free State when the ball was grounded short of the line. But he didn't seem to lose control of the game and didn't penalise anybody for serious foul play. Indeed, sitting alongside Cotton in the post-match news conference was Neil Back, who said that he was not aware of any untoward incidents. He should have known, having spent the majority of his afternoon at the bottom of every ruck. The manager was asked whether he was going to cite any players from the Northern Free State team and he responded by saying that first the Lions would have to look at the video. But I, along with the majority of those present at the news conference, was confused by this outburst. In all the replays that were shown throughout the afternoon's coverage I had seen nothing to cause any great alarm. Maybe time would tell and a citing would follow, but my initial reaction was that there was no comparison between this match and the disgraceful performance by Mpumalanga earlier in the tour.

After Cotton had left, in marched the Northern Free State manager and coach, Pote Human. He said, 'The fact that Cotton is saying he wants to watch the game and look for incidents seems to suggest he has a poor attitude. I cannot believe his comments.' The captain of the side, Jourie Jerling, was equally affronted. These disagreements had soured what had been an otherwise enjoyable day. True, the match had lacked a cutting edge and, despite a strong presence from the 'barmy army', the day had generally failed to take us to the heights to which we were now accustomed. But it had all been pleasant enough and it came as quite a shock when our conversation on the drive home was dominated by talk of the alleged foul play and the possible repercussions.

It was not a drive without incident, either, as was normally the case on the South African roads. Piers Croton had taken on the majority of the driving workload in the Kombi and again he had to be at his most alert, as various people between Welkom and Johannesburg decided that they were immortal. It is the norm for individuals to run or even stroll across the path of a vehicle on the badly lit roads. That night was no exception and after a couple of close shaves we encountered a broken-down vehicle which sat in the inside lane without giving any warning to the oncoming traffic. Two people worked underneath the car, oblivious to the fact that they were on the main highway. We swerved out of the way of that hazard and were not surprised to stumble across yet another accident as we prepared to take the turning for our hotel. Fire engines and police cars were on the scene as they tried to free the injured people from the wreckage. It was an all too familiar sight in a country where a large proportion of the accidents are caused by thousands of drivers who possess fraudulent licences. I read a report in a Johannesburg newspaper which claimed that one thousand and six hundred forged dockets were being investigated in that city alone, and that this was only the tip of the iceberg. The bottom line is: take care if you are about to visit the country and drive on the roads. They simply don't have the same rules and standards as we do. As our cameraman, Leon, would say with a sigh and a shrug of the shoulders, 'This is Africa.'

*

On the Wednesday of the final week we had a very pleasant time hosting a drinks party and braai for the M-Net crew as a way of saying thank you for all their help during the tour. They had been a splendid bunch to work with and their highly professional approach had given us some good pictures and sound quality to send back home. It was also a chance for us to meet and talk in a social and not work environment. As the afternoon wore on, there was the predictable sporting challenge, and it will not come as a bombshell to learn that it was a game of pool which won the vote. Harrison and Barnes were involved in the decision-making process. A three-match series was decided upon with South Africa, in the shape of M-Net, taking on the British and Irish Lions, sponsored by Sky Sports. Dennis, our sound technician for the tour, stood on the table and called on the first two pairs to step forward. Dennis is also a boxing announcer at some of the big title fights in South Africa and consequently he had the perfect voice to grab everybody's attention. We all prepared to 'rumble'. It was Tippett and Knight who went in to bat first for the Lions. Seconds later, South Africa led one–nil. Enter the commentators having to win the next frame to stay in the series. We wondered whether a drop goal was allowed in pool as this seemed to be the 'Lions' best chance of victory. After a re-racking of the balls following a rule dispute in the original frame (if commentators know one thing it is the laws) we saw the eight ball disappear at a ridiculously early stage. It was a foul shot by Sky's diminutive fly-half and it was all over. This was one series that had not gone our way and we watched and snarled as South Africa celebrated.

It was a case of injured pride for us, but for the Lions the injury news was much more serious. Wood, Tait and Miller had all been declared unfit for the third and final Test. Wood, who had been key to the Lions success in the first two Tests, was annoyed that he couldn't finish off the job. Tait's absence was not so much of a body blow because Tony Underwood was pushing hard for selection anyway. Miller had at least got onto the field to experience the elation at the full-time whistle in the second Test, but he had also become the unluckiest man of the tour. Flu had stopped him from appearing in the first Test and now a bizarre injury picked up when he jumped off the bench to come on as a replacement in Durban had ended his tour.

The follow up to the accusations of foul play in the Northern Free State game was, as predicted, far from dramatic. After viewing the tape, the Lions management had decided not to cite any players but still maintained that boots had been used illegally. None of the instances were deemed to be sending-off offences, but the Lions were to contact Northern Free State and ask them to take an appropriate course of action. I sensed that they would meet a stone wall of a response from a local union, which believed that their team had done nothing wrong. The Media Liaison Officer for SARFU, Alex Broun, had been incensed by Cotton's attitude to the venue. In a strong interview with Sky Sports, Broun made his feelings quite clear. But the storm would undoubtedly blow away with the tour nearing a conclusion. If nothing else, the episode had kept the Lions in the news and the column inches were still being feverishly compiled. It was high time, though, to concentrate on the Test match at Ellis Park and to finish on the right note.

The announcement of the side for the final match of the tour was almost as eagerly anticipated as the unveiling of that first Test team in Cape Town. Four changes were made to the fifteen that played in the second Test. The team was – Jenkins, Bentley, Guscott, Gibbs, Underwood, Catt, Dawson, Smith, Regan, Wallace, Johnson (captain), Davidson, Dallaglio, Back and Rodber. In came Tony Underwood, Mike Catt, Mark Regan and Neil Back. The decision to play Back was a tactical move at the expense of Richard Hill. Back, who had been involved in the best attacking performances on the tour, was raring to go. After years of rejection at the highest level, he had finally been given his reward. Mark Regan had seemed destined to miss out on involvement in the Test series, but his barnstorming display at Welkom on the Tuesday had propelled him into the side in front of the unlucky Barry Williams, who would sit on the bench for the third Test in a row. Gregor Townsend's absence through injury paved the way for Mike Catt. Townsend had been struggling in the second Test and during training in the final week had been unable to prove his fitness. So here was Catt, a man about to play against his country of birth and against a fly-half, Jannie de Beer, whom he had met on numerous occasions at schoolboy and under-twenty-one level. Ian McGeechan had told me that he had been greatly impressed with Catt since his arrival from Argentina and the way in which the England fly-half had fitted into the squad's style of playing. But Catt needed a top-class game to dispel the doubts over his ability to control a match at the highest level. It had been decided to stick with the centre combination of Guscott and Gibbs but McGeechan hoped that he would have the opportunity to bring on Allan Bateman before the end of the Test. Nobody could argue with that sentiment.

Injuries had also taken their toll in the Springbok camp and we woke on the Friday morning to the news that André Joubert was the latest casualty. He had aggravated a long-standing groin strain in training and was to be replaced by Russell Bennett. Had we been told at the start of the tour that the South African side for the final Test would not include Joubert, Small, Mulder, Le Roux, Honiball, Andrews and Kruger then we would have never believed it. The changes in the Lions line-up had brought an extra buzz to their training but there was a negative atmosphere surrounding the South African preparations. They would need to dig deep in their reserves if they wanted to avoid a clean sweep by the Lions.

The one consoling factor for the Springboks was that the game was to be played at their favourite ground. Ellis Park has been a fortress for South African rugby in recent times and even the All Blacks have struggled to come to terms with the venue, losing six times and winning just twice in return. I went to the ground later that morning and recorded a piece to camera for the Friday evening preview programme. For the recording, I stood on the spot from where Joel Stransky kicked the most famous goal of all time, but now I was also able to talk about a drop goal which ranked alongside Stransky's effort. Jeremy Guscott's kick meant that the Lions had the chance to become the first team to record a series whitewash over South Africa on home soil. History was tantalisingly close and this would act as one of the main incentives for the Lions. I thought it necessary to stress the fine home record which the Lions had to overcome. They would also be driven on by the need to stay professional in their approach. A year ago, the All Blacks, a team with a professional attitude long before players were paid for playing, had won the series and went to Ellis Park only to suffer a Springbok backlash. The Lions had to be aware that a similar fate could be waiting in store for them.

Some people think that Ellis Park is a disjointed looking ground with various bits seeming as if they have been added on almost as an afterthought. But I like the ground mainly because there is an energy which electrifies the surroundings. The stadium once held ninety thousand spectators – for the Lions' visit in 1955 – and that was a conservative estimate because fences were trodden down in the stampede to get in. There would be a more safety-conscious sixty-two thousand capacity crowd for the third Test, but even so, the arena would rock with noise and passion. The additional feeling that something important had happened on the turf also filled me with excitement. After all, a nation had been united on World Cup final day and sport doesn't get more influential than that. The vast stands which tower over the carefully tended grass seemed to look down at the pitch with an approving nod.

Talking of politics being helped along by sport, back at the hotel we were shown a copy of a letter sent from 10 Downing Street to the Lions team. There had been some disappointment over the lack of an early response from the British Government in the wake of the second Test victory. But the Prime Minister wanted to convey his good wishes prior to the final match. Tony Blair had been otherwise occupied in

Hong Kong, with the colony hand-over to China taking place at the time of the second Test, and he was keen to make that point in his communiqué to the manager:

> On my return from Hong Kong I wanted to send my congratulations to you and the Lions squad on your magnificent triumph at the weekend. It has truly been a team achievement and every one of your squad can feel enormously proud of its success. The team spirit you have so clearly fostered is priceless on the pitch, as you showed on Saturday. Under the greatest pressure the team held its nerve and pulled off another stunning victory to delight us all back home. To the great Lions team of Willie John McBride of 1974 must now be added the team of '97. I shall be holding a sports reception at Downing Street later this summer and would be delighted if you and the Lions squad were able to come. Well done again. Now go and make it three–nil. The whole country is behind you.
>
> Tony Blair

Saturday, 5 July and the final day of the tour. At times I had thought it would never come, but now that it had, there was a sad end of term feel. In many ways the tour had ended the week before, when the Lions had won the series, but, as for the players, it was important for us mentally not to pack our bags. It had also been sunshine all the way in Johannesburg and that lifted the flagging spirits. The shaft of light that burst its way into my room through the curtains acted as a civilised wake-up call. I actually had been sitting up in bed thinking about the match long before the sun had rubbed the sleep from its eyes. The motivation was clear, there must be no slip-ups and no falling at the final hurdle. During the second Test I had called a kick by Neil Jenkins as going wide only to see the ball drift back into the posts and glide over the crossbar. That mistake had added to the drama, but it had also rankled and, although during the course of a live commentary these things can happen, they still annoy. I was determined not to let it happen again. There would be no further chances after this match to get an error out of the system. It was vital to finish well.

The players were thinking the same way, but there was doubt in some people's minds whether the squad was still focused on the job. Surely this most professional of teams would not allow itself to lose sight of the objective, but around the hotel that morning there was an air of relaxation which slightly unnerved me. There were plenty of smiles from a team who had already achieved what they had set out to do. I must confess to momentarily falling into the trap of believing that the concentration had waned and the desire was not as great. But perhaps that reflected my own state of mind and not the players', so I gave myself a severe ticking off for a lack of faith.

Fran Cotton, who all through that final week had continued to stress that his side were not going to fall at their final fence, was in deep conversation with Ian McGeechan and Lawrence Dallaglio. The reason was soon revealed: Tim Rodber had gone down with flu overnight. This meant that the Lions had lost all three of the originally selected number eights on tour and it was decided to move Dallaglio across the back-row and bring in Rob Wainwright on the blindside. It was an interesting change, especially as Wainwright had played quite a bit of rugby at number eight. But Dallaglio was considered to be the more explosive player off the back of the scrum and this had been a tactic well used by the Lions in previous matches.

The decision to have a Thai curry for lunch was perhaps one of my worst moves on tour. My stomach spent the rest of the afternoon doing an impression of a tumble dryer, but that was probably more due to pre-match tension than red chillies. My constant thought was, 'If only we can have a match to remember with plenty of entertaining rugby, what a way to end that would be.' The setting was perfect for a big show. Ellis Park is the one ground in South Africa where the atmosphere can sometimes resemble a rock concert more than a sporting fixture. We had seen the circus jamboree at Newlands, the seaside fun fair in Durban and now we had the big city bash organised by the people of Johannesburg. But standing outside the ground an hour before kick-off you would never have believed that a major international was about to take place. Where were the South African fans? Graham Simmons went in search of some Lions supporters to get their views of the likely outcome. As usual, they were in high spirits and one gentleman was keen to appear in front of the camera because he had to tell his wife of his whereabouts. She thought he had gone to work but he had actually got on a flight to South Africa and wanted to apologise for leaving a pile of dishes to wash. I admired his bravery but hoped that he would take home a present by way of saying sorry. Inside the ground there was a growing army of Lions followers and the bright late afternoon sunshine turned their jerseys to an orange glow. They were everywhere and as the singing started to build there began to be a charged atmosphere in the stadium.

The design of Ellis Park is strange in that you walk in at ground level and the pitch is down below, cut into the earth. It's like stepping into a giant cereal bowl, somewhere around the rim. It is also one of those grounds that looks bigger on television than it does in real life. If you have been to a tennis tournament you will know what I mean. The court looks so small in comparison to the big wide angle shot on the TV screen. But what Ellis Park can do is generate a noise and this is amplified by the loud public address system which blasts out all things South African. This cacophony is described in the event running order as a period of 'fan motivation', but with their team down by two matches to nil, the home crowd hardly needed the help of a tape recorder. South Africa simply could not contemplate a third defeat in a row and I sensed that if it had anything to do with the fans, then they would not suffer such ignominy. As kick-off approached, the sound built to an almost deafening level. I spent more time adjusting the level of my headphones than ever before. I just couldn't get the right balance because of the din. In the end, I settled for a headache and loved every roar. It was fantastic.

As the Lions players got off their coach I had watched their faces on the monitor – at that point their desire to win was totally confirmed. The stern look of Mike Catt said a thousand words and it was clear that the side were determined to make history. Down on the pitch, Fran Cotton told us that motivation was not an issue. 'We must not give them the upper hand early on. If we can avoid that, then I think we will win convincingly.' These were the words of a man who had total confidence in his squad. There was another familiar face at the pitch side and that belonged to Doddie Weir. He had flown back out to South Africa for the final Test match. Somebody had joked that perhaps Marius Bosman, the man who had caused Weir's demise, should have paid the air fare. But the news from Doddie was good. He had seen a number of specialists, all with differing opinions, but had taken the median view and was going to be playing again within two months. Crucially, no operation had been required and the genial Scot was delighted to relay the news to our audience. He also wanted to thank Angus for supplying the pancakes over the last two weekends of watching the big screen back home. (I am as mystified as you are!)

Stuart came into the commentary box about fifteen minutes before kick-off and with one glance we acknowledged the importance of the day. We looked for a means of relaxation and jested about the possibility of stumbling over the pronunciation of Rob Wainwright. What's the problem you may well ask? But you trying saying it quickly ten times and I think you will begin to get my drift. There had been much hilarity earlier in the tour when I uttered 'Wob Wainwhite' before the start of the match against Mpumalanga only to see him score three tries in eighteen minutes. I have nothing against the man and I think he's a super player, but my heart always sinks when I see his name on the team sheet. What was really funny was that Graham had fallen into the same trap during his interview with Fran Cotton and had almost burst into laughter. Stuart and I threatened to fine each other severely if we committed the 'wound the wagged wock' crime during the match. The other device which we used to calm ourselves down was to trade insults over our dress sense. If you watched our coverage of the tour then you will know that Stuart likes to brighten up our lives by wearing all colours of the rainbow. He came in for some unbelievable stick from Gavin Hastings, Phil de Glanville and the rest of the team. His colour combination on that final day was a green jacket, purple shirt and yellow tie. He thinks he is making a fashion statement, I think he is making us all ill. But I have to admit that a splash of colour on the television doesn't go amiss and at least we were in Africa where anything goes. If he wears the same clothes on a cold Saturday in Gloucester in December then I might ask a few more searching questions. Finally, the nerves were all but eradicated when a jug of water was delivered shortly before the start of the match. It had the appearance of the Thames on a bad day and we looked in amazement as the foreign bodies floated around as if they were in some kind of scientific experiment. We thanked our good fortune for having remembered to pack some fruit juice. The mind had been taken off the match and the larynx was going to need the sustenance because as the teams ran out you could hardly hear yourself speak. The South African fans were finally making their presence well and truly felt. Their team had a major problem to solve and they and their supporters were determined to find the solution.

The match began with even more fire and brimstone than the previous two Tests. I had not thought this possible, but again the Lions were hit hard by the awesome power of the Springboks. The difference this time was that they also had a kicker, and Jannie de Beer started his international career with two well-struck penalties. After a spell of concerted pressure, South Africa deservedly crossed the Lions' line. Percy Montgomery was on hand to finish off a move started by a bulldozing run from Os du Randt. Montgomery had scored his second try in as many Tests and the Lions were wobbling, down by thirteen points to nil. The pass from Van der Westhuizen to De Beer to set up the try was forward but the Lions could not complain having been on the right side of refereeing mistakes earlier in the series.

But we didn't doubt the Lions' willpower and they started to play some excellent rugby to haul themselves back into the match. The Springboks lost their discipline and Neil Jenkins passed Gavin Hastings' record of thirty-eight points in a Lions series with three first-half penalty goals. The Lions were back in it and well placed considering their tendency to provide a strong finish.

At times the game was spilling over, with one punch-up on the far side refusing to die down even as play continued on the opposite side of the field. It was the first overtly violent incident of the three Test matches, but during the course of this game numerous players were cautioned, including André Venter for a dangerous stamp. This was a crude piece of play, but it stood out in isolation in what had been a tough but fair series. Mistakes were being made by both teams, but only because of the pressure being put on by the opposition. Yet, amidst all the big tackles, there were some dazzling moments. Memorably, the Lions moved quickly away from their own twenty-two and for a split second it looked as if Tony Underwood was free. But the almost-crazed Springbok cover was such that they swallowed him up and protected their line again. The whistle went after forty minutes and the Lions had gone three halves of Test rugby without a try. They knew that they would have to find something special in the final period of the tour if they were going to prevent a home victory.

After the break, South Africa created a bit of daylight between themselves and the tourists when Joost van der Westhuizen scored another one of his own brand of tries. His opposite number, Matt Dawson, had failed to put in an effective clearance kick, which allowed Pieter Rossouw to run the ball back at the Lions. There was a suspicion of a knock-on, but the referee let it go and South Africa again got the rub of the green. The resultant attack created the opening from short range for Van der Westhuizen and he scurried over as if he was trying to scramble for cover avoiding low flying bullets overhead. When Van der Westhuizen gets down almost on his knees, he is impossible to stop. De Beer kicked the conversion and it was twenty points to nine. The Springboks reached twenty-three points when De Beer landed his third penalty, but the Lions were never going to give up. Matt Dawson, a player who had really come of age on the tour, jinked his way through and dived in for his second try of the series, and Jenkins' conversion reduced the gap to seven points. At this point another incredible comeback seemed possible. At half-time the Lions had lost Guscott with what turned out to be a broken bone in his arm, but this had meant that Allan Bateman had come on, and he almost turned the game the Lions way. A brilliant run from underneath his own posts led to a charge up field. The support was good and after some slick handling Bateman got the ball again. But then he made a crucial error. His refusal to use the overlap and his decision to hold onto the ball for a split second too long could have cost his team a score and maybe the match. Possibly Bateman, having been overlooked for the first two Tests, wanted to do too much by himself in an effort to prove that he should always have been there. But when that chance went perhaps so did the hopes of victory.

The match had taken its toll, as along with Guscott, Tony Underwood had been forced from the field and South Africa were now having to do without De Beer, Teichmann and Du Randt. For once, though, the home side finished the stronger, and after a needless penalty was conceded by Jeremy Davidson when he dived over the top at a ruck, South Africa re-established territorial control. They finished off the game in style with two well-worked tries. One was scored by André Snyman, as John Bentley's tackle came too late, and the other by Pieter Rossouw, winner of the most-valuable player award for his performance on the wing. He rounded Neil Jenkins to seal the victory. The Lions' defensive frailties out wide had been exposed, but it had taken a long time for South Africa to get to that point. The final whistle went and South Africa, just like in 1974 when they drew the final Test match against the Lions, and in 1996 when they beat New Zealand, had avoided the series whitewash.

The score of thirty-five points to sixteen flattered the Springboks, but they deserved victory having again scored the majority of the tries. This time they had also kicked their goals and, more pleasingly for Carel du Plessis, they had much more shape to their game. But his broad grin at the end of the match was ultimately down to the contribution made by his young players. Russell Bennett swerved his way to potential stardom at full-back, and Snyman, Rossouw, Montgomery, Van Schalkwyk and De Beer all made their mark in the backs. The new cap Johan Erasmus, who fitted alongside André Venter and Gary Teichmann in the back-row, looked as if he had been there all his life. James Dalton had more experience but was still young enough to be classified as a prospect and his contribution was a telling one.

For the Lions' part, nobody had a poor game. In many ways it was the best performance of the series in that they moved the ball well and had they taken scoring chances it could have been different. Individually, Jenkins' lack of pace was exposed, just as it had been in the first game of the tour, but he is right up there with the all-time great reliable goalkickers and he played his part. The second-rows, Johnson and Davidson, strangely lost their discipline and at times this cost the Lions dear. There is a difference between having to win and merely having the desire to win, and as bodies and minds tired, the concentration wavered. It was important, however, to emphasise that they had won the series. Typically, John Bentley was the one to remind everybody and gathered the players in one final huddle after the whistle had gone. They linked arms as Bentley shouted, 'We are the winners, we are the winners!' And if there was any remaining doubt, Fran Cotton rushed onto the field and, with a Winston Churchill-style victory 'V', he let it be known that the series had finished two–one to his side.

I watched as the appropriately named Lion lager trophy was handed over to Martin Johnson, the victorious captain, and then sat back contented as the players went on a lap of honour, which they so richly deserved. In the post-match interviews, Johnson admitted to feeling a little strange, having lost but also having won. Ian McGeechan felt that his team didn't get out of the final game what they had deserved, but wondered what might have been possible had this side, especially the young forwards, been able to stay together for another five years. This was not to be, nor would we see another classic confrontation between these two teams for some time to come. But for those wishing it could go on for ever Fran Cotton pointed out that, because of the mounting injury list, he didn't think that the squad would have lasted for another week. He was right and these weary words confirmed the end of a momentous tour. As the management team and captain stood up and left the news conference to walk away down the corridor, a feeling of finality swept over me. That was it – all gone. The preparation, the anticipation, the travel, the thrills, the laughs, the tears, the privilege. Seven weeks, thirteen matches, eleven wins, two losses and a lifetime of memories.

A JOB WELL DONE

'Their attitude is already ten years ahead of 1993 in the way they manage themselves.' – Ian McGeechan on his first professional and favourite tour as Lions coach, having been in charge during 1993 and 1989.

To think that before the tour began there was a doubt over the continued presence of the British and Irish Lions in the professional era of rugby. In the aftermath of the 1997 tour to South Africa, the irony is that the latest Lions team turned out to be the model that all professional rugby squads should now try and emulate. Professionalism is not just about money, it is about attitude; and while for the first time the Lions were offered a financial incentive, they also had the right approach.

The players were given the authority to determine their own destiny. Earlier in the book I described the trip as the first 'orange juice tour' for a domestic rugby team. In many ways the thought behind this statement was true, but it was not to say that the Lions avoided bars like the plague and were all tucked up in bed by nine-thirty. On the contrary, they played hard on the field and made sure they enjoyed themselves off it, in the free time that was available. But none of the extracurricular activities were carried out to excess and they were all done with the players themselves acting as their own guardians. Towards the end of the tour, Fran Cotton told me that on average the squad's fat content ratio had been reduced by two per cent per man during the trip. Needless to say, the Sky team had gone the other way, some more so than others. But the players, aware of their professional responsibilities, had taken control and shown the maturity that was expected of them. The great rugby athletes of the future will be the ones who can cope with a rigid structure to their diet and a set calendar of events. Talent, though, sometimes needs to be given freedom of expression and this was recognised as well. One of the triumphs of the Lions management was their willingness to let the more temperamental individuals run their own lives within the confines of squad pressures.

Another important factor had to be the influence of the ex-rugby league men, who brought to the Lions a way of sporting life which left nothing to chance. Gibbs, Bentley, Tait, Bateman, Young and, before he left, Quinnell, all accepted nothing less than total commitment to the cause. From a media point of view, this was even reflected in their attitude to interviews. They knew the score, were conscious that they had responsibility to a wider public and were also aware that increased exposure was good for their personal profile. Everything they did was out of the top drawer; the rest of the squad knew it and followed their lead.

Even though they were at home in the series, South Africa pulled their squad together with similar hopes and ambitions of fostering a team spirit. In my mind this was their biggest mistake. Not because the players didn't get on, but because it denied them the chance to keep playing rugby. What coach Carel du Plessis had decided to do was, in effect, to remove the opportunity for match practice in the run-up to the Tests. We all saw how the Lions came together during the course of the tour and how this mix 'n' match of players started to feel happy in being around each other on the field. South Africa were never going to benefit from that cohesion which is peculiar to touring teams, but when the Test fifteen was given just one meaningless warm-up international against Tonga, it was asking too much of them to come out and perform against superior opposition such as the Lions. No surprise, then, that South Africa put in their best performance in the third Test when the 'getting to know you' process was nearly over.

Even more significantly, the removal of the Test players from the provincial matches allowed the Lions to build an inner confidence which became the heart of their success. Long before the Lions left, many people thought, yours truly included, that they would not win the series. I believe that, initially, deep down many of the players thought that as well. When they met in Weybridge before departure the psychology team got to work and the first seeds of a positive mood were sown. By the time they got to the first Test match in Cape Town, the team were bubbling after victories against sides which they had genuinely feared. These weakened provinces, minus their top players, had not made the impression that they were capable of doing at full strength. A self-belief had been born in the Lions camp and it carried them through the opening two Tests and nearly the third.

The folly of Du Plessis' policy is perhaps best illustrated in the case of reserve scrum-half Werner Swanepoel. He sat on the international bench for four weeks on the trot and was denied the chance to play for his province Free State against the Lions. Had the first-choice scrum-half, Joost van der Westhuizen, been injured in the opening minute of a Test match, Swanepoel would have had to come on and be expected to play at the highest level while being totally ring rusty. At the root of this decision to hold back the stars from the 'minor' matches was the expectation prevalent in South Africa at the start of the tour: that the Lions were nothing more than an hors d'oeuvres before the bigger fish arrived from New Zealand and Australia. By the time they had realised that the Lions were cooking, South Africa were out of the frying pan and into the fire.

The first two matches against Eastern Province and Border had done little to change the preconceived South African ideas. Then, in match three, Western Province had given the Lions, or should that be the England pack, such a torrid time that the host nation was convinced they could crush the Lions up front. After the defeat at Northern Transvaal this view still seemed plausible. But the manner of that loss convinced the Lions that their increasingly excellent back play would not win them the day unless they addressed the forward problem. They had to get the basics right before adding on the frilly bits. If they could combat the South African forwards in both the scrum and line-out, and stop their back-row from crossing the gain line, they had a chance. Up stepped Tom Smith, Keith Wood, Paul Wallace and Jeremy Davidson. They joined a skipper who was working his way back into form and together they created the platform for victory. Martin Johnson surely never expected to be the only member of the England front-five in the Test team. But in the end, he was the only one who deserved to be there. Leonard, Rowntree and Regan were in danger of being seen as the tour dinosaurs. To their credit they went away and came back having added to their game. If there was one beacon which shone through this tour it was that players were always learning and therefore improving. Mobile and talented forwards who could scrummage and carry the ball comfortably, combined with backs who were prepared to have a wider vision and trust their own wits. Was this really a British and Irish rugby team?

The hard work started to pay off. The match against the Gauteng Lions on the Wednesday following that first defeat was a must-win game. It didn't matter how the victory came just as long as it did. The fact that the win included a try the like of which only comes along very rarely, boosted the Lions' endangered confidence. It also came from the man who was becoming the most visible face on the trip, the cocksure and unafraid John Bentley. Bentley said in the after-match news conference that the Lions were 'back on tour'. He was right. They finished off a week – which had been dubbed as the Bermuda triangle, where the tour could have been lost – with victory over Natal. This gave them the lift which won the series. It also gave them the mind-set which overcame the disappointment of the loss of Robert Howley. Natal fielded an under-strength side, but the Lions didn't care. They could now afford to have anything thrown at them.

The tour peaked with victories over the Emerging Springboks,

South Africa, Free State and South Africa again. These two weeks of gruelling but successful rugby were only possible because of the troughs which had gone before. Selection had remained in doubt as all the players, including the replacements who had flown out to join the tour, were in contention for Test places. Never before had the competition been so open on a Lions tour. It was a free market of opportunity and if you put in the work then the rewards were great. But when it came to the crunch, few would say that the selection for the Test matches was wrong. Credit for this goes to McGeechan, Telfer, Cotton and Johnson. Their differing personalities combined to make a potent force both on and off the field. They were straight-talking, hard-working and thoughtful.

They had moulded a team that they wished could stay together, but that is not the essence of a Lions tour and never should it be. Their beauty is their rarity and, although it would sometimes be nice to see the Lions play at home, and what a unifying force that would be for the four nations who spend the rest of their rugby lives re-living old battles, the Lions must never become commonplace. Too many sports in the modern era are over-egged and the end result is banality. The 1997 Lions will rank alongside the great teams of the past and will be more memorable because they will never be lost in a morass of fixtures.

It may not have been the greatest rugby team to ever leave our shores, but it proved to be a great achievement and put the pride back into Northern Hemisphere rugby. New Zealand are still out in front, but the Lions have pointed out the way to go to catch them. Ian McGeechan preached that the Lions players wore the same coloured jerseys but took the numbers off the back. Everybody was encouraged to feel comfortable with the ball in hand. The challenge now is for this approach to transmit down into all levels of rugby in England, Ireland, Scotland and Wales. It is the only way forward and it promises great things for the future of the sport.

The tour was over, but to illustrate the demands on the modern professional, many of the Lions squad immediately headed off to Sydney, where England were to play Australia. Come to think of it, this was my next assignment. But that is another story.

TOUR AWARDS

Tradition demands that the media provide their nominations for tour awards as a fun exercise at the end of a long trip. For what it is worth, these were my selections, with a few alternative honours thrown in for good measure:

Player of the Tour: Lawrence Dallaglio, for leading with the best possible examples both on and off the field. Tom Smith and Jeremy Davidson were also in my top three.

Best Forward: Tom Smith (Dallaglio was not entered because of his earlier success), for his unerring ability to prop up a once-creaking scrum and for his all-round contribution to the Lions running game. The fact that he hardly batted an eyelid said volumes for the quiet man of the tour, a man who does not actively seek recognition, but has nonetheless become one of the most recognisable faces in rugby.

Best Back: Scott Gibbs, for proving himself to be a big match player and a big player in a match – just ask Os du Randt, who is probably still nursing his bruises. Robert Howley and Allan Bateman, with just one half of Test rugby between them, came close. The Welsh still have a large market share in this particular commodity.

Most Improved Player: Paul Wallace. A man who wasn't even originally selected, he took on one of the best props in the world and won. Matt Dawson and Barry Williams were in with a shout.

Best Match: Lions v Free State. This was the most complete performance against a far from weak side. The first and second Tests were obviously considered as was the victory over Gauteng Lions. But they were better performances than matches.

Worst Match: Lions v Border. This was by far and away the pits.

Unluckiest Player: Eric Miller, for going down with flu shortly before the first Test, then losing his place to the excellent Tim Rodber in the second Test and finally pulling a muscle when running onto the pitch as a substitute in that match and therefore missing the final Test. The only consolation being that, at twenty-one, his time will come again.

Best Hotel: The Vineyard in Cape Town. The view of Table Mountain was...well, for once words fail me.

Best Playing Moment: John Bentley's Rolls Royce impression when he roared away from the cover to score against the Gauteng Lions. Also considered were Jeremy Guscott's drop goal and Scott Gibbs' slaughtering of the 'Ox'.

Worst Playing Moment: Will Greenwood's concussion against Free State.

Best Quote: Ian McGeechan after the second Test win: 'We won it through fifteen-man rugby, it was just that we didn't have the ball.'

And additional Sky Sports team awards are given to the following:

Best Kombi of the Tour: The white one in the first week, which had power steering and central locking. How we were lulled into a false sense of security.

Worst Kombi: The red one in Cape Town, when the accelerator pedal came off.

Best Mechanic: Phil Edwards, for knowing what to do with a detached accelerator pedal.

Best Navigator: Leon Hagen, our cameraman and a resident of Johannesburg, who, via mobile phone, talked us through a difficult period through some of the less fashionable parts of the city.

Best Sky Sports Quote: Leon Hagen again: 'For God sake don't turn left!'

Most Obscure Quote: Leon Hagen, yet again: 'Well, that's another day in Africa that the Queen Mother knows nothing about.' Why? We still don't know.

Most Pitiful Phrase: 'I'm only going to have the fruit this morning.' This was closely followed by: 'I think I'll have an early night'. Or: 'Damn, I've missed the laundry again.'

All members of the Sky team receive honours.

Most Romantic Moment: Production manager Martin Knight proposing to his girlfriend Sue in Cape Town.

Most Surprising Moment: Sue saying yes, also in Cape Town.

Best and Worst Moment: Touching down at Heathrow.

STATISTICAL APPENDIX

MATCH ONE: 24 MAY

Eastern Province Invitational XV
at Telkom Park, Boet Erasmus Stadium, Port Elizabeth
Eastern Province XV 11 British and Irish Lions 39

Eastern Province XV – T: Kayser. Pens: Van Rensburg (2).
Van Rensburg, Kayser, Van Jaarsfeld, Le Roux, Pedro, Ford, Alcock;
Saayman, Kirsten (captain), Enslin, Wiese, Du Preez, Webber, Scott-
Young, Greeff.
Reps: Lessing for Enslin (38 mins), Fourie for Ford (42 mins).

The Lions – T: Guscott (2), Weir, Underwood, Greenwood. Con:
Jenkins (4). Pens: Jenkins (2).
Jenkins, Evans, Guscott, Greenwood, Beal, Townsend, Howley; Smith,
Wood, Leonard (captain), Weir, Shaw, Dallaglio, Hill, Quinnell.
Reps: Underwood for Evans (67 mins), Williams for Wood (67 mins),
Davidson for Shaw (77 mins).

MATCH TWO: 28 MAY

Border Buffaloes
at the Basil Kenyon Stadium, East London
Border 14 British and Irish Lions 18

Border – T: Claassen. Pens: Miller (3)
Bennett, Hilton-Green, Hechter, Malotana, Claassen, Miller,
Bradbrook; Kok, Van Zyl (captain), Du Preez, S. Botha, Gehring,
Swart, A. Botha, Fox.
Reps: Maidza for Malotana (44 mins), Coetzer for A. Botha (80 mins).

The Lions – T: Bentley, Regan, Wainwright. Pen: Stimpson.
Stimpson, Bentley, Gibbs, Bateman, Underwood, Grayson, Healey;

Rowntree, Regan, Young, Weir, Davidson, Wainwright (captain), Back, Miller.
Reps: Tait for Gibbs (44 mins), Dawson for Healey (54 mins), Wallace for Young (68 mins).

MATCH THREE: 31 MAY

Western Province
at Norwich Park, Newlands, Cape Town
Western Province 21 British and Irish Lions 38

Western Province – T: Muir (2), Brink. Cons: Montgomery (3).
Swart, Small, Fleck, Muir (captain), Berridge, Montgomery, Hatley;
Pagel, Paterson, Andrews, Van Heerden, Louw, Brink, Krige, Aitken.
Reps: Van der Linde for Pagel (57 mins), Koen for Muir (57–68 mins), Skinstad for Krige (65 mins).

The Lions – T: Bentley (2), Tait, Evans. Cons: Stimpson (3). Pens: Stimpson (4).
Stimpson, Evans, Tait, Guscott, Bentley, Townsend, Howley;
Rowntree, Williams, Leonard, Johnson (captain), Shaw, Dallaglio, Hill, Rodber.
Reps: Quinnell for Rodber (63 mins), Greenwood for Tait (73 mins).

MATCH FOUR: 4 JUNE

Mpumalanga Pumas
at Johann van Riebeeck Stadium, Witbank
Mpumalanga 14 British and Irish Lions 64

Mpumalanga – T: Joubert (2). Cons: Van As (2).
Von Gericke, Visagie, Potgeiter, Gendall, Nel, Van As, Van Zyl: Swart, Kemp, Botha,

Bosman, Van den Bergh, Rossouw, Joubert, Oosthuizen (captain).
Reps: Buekes for Oosthiuzen (70 mins), Van Rooyen for Nel (77 mins).

The Lions – T: Wainwright (3), Underwood (2), Evans (2), Dawson, Jenkins, Beal. Cons: Jenkins (7).
Beal, Evans, Bateman, Greenwood, Underwood, Jenkins, Dawson;
Smith, Wood, Wallace, Weir, Davidson, Wainwright, Back, Rodber (captain).
Reps: Regan for Wood (52 mins), Shaw for Weir (57 mins), Young for Wallace (74 mins).

MATCH FIVE: 7 JUNE

Northern Transvaal Blue Bulls
at Loftus Versfeld, Pretoria
Northern Transvaal 35 British and Irish Lions 30

Northern Transvaal – T: Van Schalkwyk (2), Richter, Steyn. Cons:
Steyn (3). Pens: Steyn (3).
Bouwer, Lourens, Schutte, Van Schalkwyk, Steyn, De Marigny,
Breytenbach; Campher, Tromp, Boer, Grobbelaar, Badenhorst, Van der
Walt, Bekker, Richter (captain).
Reps: Esterhuizen for Lourens (34 mins), Laufs for Grobbelaar (39
mins), Brooks for Tromp (40 mins), Schroeder for Van der Walt (65
mins), Proudfoot for Boer (71 mins).

The Lions – T: Guscott (2), Townsend. Cons: Stimpson (3). Pens:
Stimpson (3).
Stimpson, Bentley, Guscott, Tait, Underwood, Townsend, Howley;
Rowntree, Regan, Leonard, Johnson (captain), Shaw, Dallaglio, Miller,
Quinnell.
Reps: Gibbs for Bentley (60 mins), Young for Leonard (74 mins).

MATCH SIX: 11 JUNE

Gauteng Lions
at Ellis Park, Johannesburg
Gauteng 14 British and Irish Lions 20

Gauteng – T: Vos. Pens: Du Toit (3).
Du Toit, Gillingham, Van der Walt, Le Roux, Hendriks, Van Rensburg,
Roux; Grau, Rossouw, Van Greuning, Wiese (captain), Thorne, Vos,
Krause, Brosnihan.
Reps: Dalton for Rossouw (53 mins), Swart for Grau (62 mins).

The Lions – T: Healey, Bentley. Cons: Jenkins (2). Pens: Catt, Jenkins.
Beal, Bentley, Guscott, Greenwood, Underwood, Catt, Healey; Smith,
Williams, Wallace, Redman, Davidson, Wainwright, Back, Rodber
(captain).
Reps: Jenkins for Underwood (54 mins).

MATCH SEVEN: 14 JUNE

Natal Sharks
at King's Park, Durban
Natal 12 British and Irish Lions 42

Natal – Pens: Lawless (4).
Lawless, Payne, Thomson, Muller, Joubert, Scriba, Du Preez; Le Roux,

Allan, Kempson, Slade, Wegner, Van Heerden, Fyvie (captain), Kriese.
Reps: Strudwick for Van Heerden (32 mins), Smit for Le Roux (75 mins).

The Lions – T: Townsend, Catt, Dallaglio. C: Jenkins (3). Pens: Jenkins (6). DG: Townsend.
Jenkins, Evans, Bateman, Gibbs, Tait, Townsend, Howley; Smith, Wood, Young, Johnson (captain), Shaw, Dallaglio, Hill, Miller.
Reps: Dawson for Howley (13 mins), Catt for Bateman (65 mins), Leonard for Smith (67 mins), Wainwright for Johnson (25–34 mins).

MATCH EIGHT: 17 JUNE

Emerging Springboks
at Boland Stadium, Wellington
Emerging Springboks 22 British and Irish Lions 51

Emerging Springboks – T: Brosnihan, Goosen, Treu. Cons: Smith, Montgomery. Pen: Smith
Smith, Kayser, Montgomery, Hendricks, Treu, Van Rensburg, Adlam; Kempson, Santon (captain), Du Toit, Opperman, Els, Brosnihan, Smit, Coetzee.
Reps: Myburgh for Adlam (15 mins), Goosen for Van Rensburg (20 mins), Malotana for Smith (61 mins), Campher for Kempson (64 mins), Brooks for Santon (67 mins).

The Lions – T: Beal (3), Rowntree, Stimpson, Catt. Cons: Stimpson (6). Pens: Stimpson (3).
Stimpson, Bentley, Bateman, Greenwood, Beal, Catt, Healey; Rowntree, Regan, Leonard (captain), Redman, Davidson, Wainwright, Back, Diprose.

MATCH NINE – FIRST TEST: 21 JUNE

SOUTH AFRICA
at Norwich Park, Newlands, Cape Town
SOUTH AFRICA 16 BRITISH AND IRISH LIONS 25

South Africa – T: Du Randt, Bennett. Pens: Lubbe, Honiball.
Joubert, Small, Mulder, Lubbe, Snyman, Honiball, Van der Westhuizen; Du Randt, Drotské, Garvey, Strydom, Andrews, Kruger, Venter, Teichmann (captain).
Reps: Bennett for Lubbe (HT).

The Lions – T: Dawson, Tait. Pens: Jenkins (5).
Jenkins, Evans, Gibbs, Guscott, Tait, Townsend, Dawson; Smith, Wood, Wallace, Johnson (captain), Davidson, Dallaglio, Hill, Rodber.
Reps: Leonard for Smith (79 mins).
Referee: C. J. Hawke (New Zealand).

MATCH TEN: 24 JUNE

Free State Cheetah
at Free State Stadium, Bloemfontein
Free State 30 British and Irish Lions 52

Free State – T: Brink (2), De Beer. Cons: De Beer (3). Pens: De Beer (3).
Smith, Van Wyk, Muller (captain), Venter, Brink, De Beer, Fourie; Groenewald, Marais, Meyer, Opperman, Els, Van Rensburg, Erasmus, Coetzee.
Reps: Jacobs for Fourie (26 mins), Heymans for Meyer (60 mins).

The Lions – T: Bentley (3), Stimpson, Bateman, Jenkins, Underwood. Cons: Stimpson (4). Pens: Stimpson (3).
Stimpson, Bentley, Bateman, Greenwood, Underwood, Catt, Healey; Rowntree, Williams, Young, Redman (captain), Shaw, Wainwright, Back, Miller.
Reps: Jenkins for Greenwood (41 mins), Leonard for Young (70 mins).

MATCH ELEVEN – SECOND TEST: 28 JUNE

SOUTH AFRICA
at King's Park, Durban
SOUTH AFRICA 15 BRITISH AND IRISH LIONS 18

South Africa – T: Van der Westhuizen, Montgomery, Joubert.
Joubert, Snyman, Montgomery, Van Schalkwyk, Rossouw, Honiball, Van der Westhuizen; Du Randt, Drotské, Garvey, Strydom, Andrews, Kruger, Venter, Teichmann (captain).
Reps: Van Heerden for Teichmann (3–5 mins) and for Kruger (50 mins), Theron for Garvey (67 mins).

The Lions – Pens: Jenkins (5). DG: Guscott.
Jenkins, Bentley, Gibbs, Guscott, Tait, Townsend, Dawson; Smith, Wood, Wallace, Johnson (captain), Davidson, Dallaglio, Hill, Rodber.
Reps: Back for Hill (57 mins), Healey for Tait (76 mins), Miller for Rodber (76 mins).
Referee: D. Méné (France).

MATCH TWELVE: 1 JULY

Northern Free State
at North West Stadium, Welkom
Northern Free State 39 British and Irish Lions 67

Northern Free State – T: Penalty try, Ehrentraut, Wagener, Van Buuren, Herbert. Cons: Herbert (4). Pens: Herbert (2).

Ehrentraut, Harmse, Van Buuren, De Beer, Nagel, Herbert, Jerling (captain); Applegryn, Wagener, Nel, Heydenrich, Niewenhuyzen, Kershaw, Delport, Venter.
Reps: Burrows for Ehrentraut (68 mins), Fouche for Delport (75 mins).

The Lions – T: Underwood (3), Shaw (2), Stimpson (2), Back, Bracken, Regan. Cons: Stimpson (7). Pen: Stimpson.
Stimpson, Stanger, Bateman, Beal, Underwood, Catt, Bracken; Leonard (captain), Regan, Young, Redman, Shaw, Wainwright, Back, Diprose.
Reps: Rowntree for Leonard (41 mins), Healey for Bracken (55 mins).

MATCH THIRTEEN – THIRD TEST: 6 JULY

SOUTH AFRICA
at Ellis Park, Johannesburg
SOUTH AFRICA 35 BRITISH AND IRISH LIONS 16

South Africa – T: Montgomery, Van der Westhuizen, Snyman, Rossouw. Cons: De Beer (2), Honiball. Pens: De Beer (3).
Bennett, Snyman, Montgomery, Van Schalkwyk, Rossouw, De Beer, Van der Westhuizen; Du Randt, Dalton, Theron, Strydom, Otto, Venter, Erasmus, Teichmann (captain).
Reps: Honiball for Montgomery (53 mins), Garvey for Du Randt (63 mins), Drotské for Dalton (69 mins), Swart for De Beer (71 mins), Van Heerden for Teichmann (73 mins), Swanepoel for Van der Westhuizen (81 mins).

The Lions – T: Dawson. Con: Jenkins. Pens: Jenkins (3).
Jenkins, Bentley, Gibbs, Guscott, Underwood, Catt, Dawson; Smith, Regan, Wallace, Johnson (captain), Davidson, Wainwright, Back, Dallaglio.
Reps: Stimpson for Underwood (30 mins), Bateman for Guscott (HT), Healey for Dawson (81 mins).
Referee: W. J. Erickson (Australia).

Leading Points Scorers:
Tim Stimpson 111.
Neil Jenkins 110.
John Bentley 35.
Tony Underwood 35.
Jeremy Guscott 23.

Leading Try Scorers:
John Bentley 7.
Tony Underwood 7.
Nick Beal 4.
Jeremy Guscott 4.
Tim Stimpson 4.
Rob Wainwright 4.